RIDIN' WITH RICK

THE 21 KEYS OF SUCCESS

RICK ROSS
KOLIE CRUTCHER

Published by Kolie Crutcher
GET MONEY Media

ISBN: 978-0-9814643-4-3
ePub: 978-0-9814643-5-0

Library of Congress Control Number: Available upon request

Book Design by Kolie Crutcher

1. Crutcher, Kolie. 2. Freeway Rick Ross. 3. Success Principles. 4. 21 Keys. 5. Cocaine. 6. Entrepreneurship. 7. Critical Thinking. 8. Achievement. 9. Ridin' With Rick. 10. Self-Help. 11. Money

Direct orders of this book may be placed.

Printed in the United States of America

Dedication

This book is dedicated to everyone striving to overcome life's adversities and live the life you want.

Table of Contents

Author's Note

This book outlines and details the principles of success as interpreted through my up-close and personal experiences with "Freeway" Ricky Ross, arguably the greatest cocaine dealer in American history. Over the course of several months of "ridin' with Rick" daily in Los Angeles (and through knowing him since 2009), this work slowly took form.

It is worth mentioning that neither Rick nor myself began with the intent of "writing a book" on these principles. As opposed to starting off with what I believed to be a principle of his success and attempting to prove it, the process unfolded in a more natural way. As I spent time with Rick, I started having questions about certain things he did or said, or why he was the way he was. For example, I often wondered, "How was the biggest 'crack' dealer in U.S. history able to presently move around so freely without weapons or bodyguards?" Cocaine destroyed the lives of so many people and was associated with so much death and violence. Yet no one ever showed a desire to cause Rick physical harm. As I rode with Rick, the "answer" to this question slowly unfolded in the form of a certain principle that he lived by.

Another question that often popped into my head was "How was this man in his fifties constantly able to move around like a man half his age?" Again, through my first-hand experience of daily ridin' with Rick, the "answer" revealed itself in the form of another principle by which he lived. Another common experience was Rick saying something that shocked people. In a car full of people, I once heard Rick say, "I don't believe in God." And again, something that initially "made absolutely no sense", became logical in light of discovering the hidden principle that was at work in his mind. My curiosity regarding the unconventional (by society's standards) methods of Rick led to questions that simply couldn't be answered by the conventional interview. These questions could only be answered by attempting to understand the deep-rooted (subconscious) nature of Rick—the philosophy and principles which he had internalized. As an electrical engineer, the one thing I knew about principles was this: *Principles are universal, and no respecter of person. If a principle worked for Rick, that principle can work for anyone.* When all was said and done, I felt that Rick's philosophy of success had been built through the internalization of 21 principles—21 keys of success.

Obviously, if you are a drug dealer, the inclined interest you might have in this book is no different than the inclined interest that someone in the field of e-commerce might have towards the principles of success as outlined by Jeff Bezos—the CEO and founder of Amazon.com. It is no different than the inclined interest that someone in the movie business might have towards the principles of success as outlined by Steven Spielberg. And it is no different than a fashion model's inclined interest towards the principles of success as outlined by Tyra Banks. All of us carry within ourselves a natural tendency to seek insight and guidance on the principles of success from those who have already succeeded in our field. One cannot be a success "in a vacuum". In other words, to be a success, you must be a success *at something* or in some particular field. Jeff Bezos is seen as a success *at e-commerce*. Steven Spielberg is seen as a success *at movies*. Tyra Banks is seen as a success *at modeling*.

With that being said, the natural tendency is to automatically interpret a "success" book written by or about Rick Ross as a book on how to become successful *at selling cocaine*. Rick Ross is known first and foremost because he was a success at selling cocaine—as much as one can be successful in that particular field. And in truth, to say that *The 21 Keys* could *not* be interpreted as a sort of guide on "How To Successfully Sell Cocaine" would be disingenuous, because it *can be* interpreted as such. To deny this truth for the sake of political correctness or fear of other people's criticism that this book "glorifies cocaine" or "glorifies the drug dealer" would cause the book to lose credibility. The denial would be just as disingenuous as telling a housewife who is lovingly cooking a meal on her gas stove for her family that that same gas stove could *not* be used to cook up powder cocaine into crack cocaine. The truth is that it most certainly *can*. Because that gas stove operates based on universal *principles*, it will work just as well for the drug dealer as it will for the housewife. The only difference is *intent* and *the product* each chooses to cook. The same holds true regarding the principles in this book. As you read, understand that you are the chef. You cook up what you want. But always remember, you are responsible for that which you prepare.

Speaking of the "housewife", that just might be the label that identifies *you*. Or you may be a fan of the more traditional style of "self-help" book. If so, you may initially scoff at the idea that you could learn anything about success from a *drug dealer*. As a matter of fact, you may feel that the principles employed by a drug dealer are the exact *opposite* of the principles of success. "Why would I read a success book about a drug dealer? I'm not trying to be a criminal." This may be 100% true. You may have no interest whatsoever in selling or using drugs. You may be an upstanding, law-abiding citizen, who has no plans to become involved with any type of illegal activity. Your success library may be stocked with the more "clean-cut" and traditional success authors such as Napoleon Hill, W. Clement Stone, or Og Mandino. Freeway Rick Ross may be the *last* person you'd consider adding to your collection. He's not likely to appear at the top of Oprah's Book Club and Bill Gates probably won't be recommending Freeway Rick as one of the authors on his summer reading list. And that's perfectly fine. This book is still for you. Because it is not imperative that one condone selling drugs or aligning themselves with the intent of selling drugs in order to benefit from the philosophy at the core of this book. Referring back to the example in the previous paragraph, the core of this book is about the *principles*—operating the gas stove—not whether the person using it is a "drug dealer" or a "housewife".

—Kolie Crutcher

Preface

Say the name "Ricky Ross" or "Freeway Rick"... What one word comes to mind?

Cocaine.

Yes, cocaine or "cocaina"—the name of that notorious white powder from South America—is what immediately comes to mind when you say the name of that notorious black man from South Central Los Angeles... *Freeway Ricky Ross.*

And so it is. This book is exactly what it appears to be—**a "success" or "self-help" book about, and based upon the principles of a drug dealer**. Notice I didn't say, "about... someone who *sold drugs"*—but "about... a *drug dealer.*" You may ask, "Well, what's the difference?" The difference is this: Freeway Ricky Ross was not someone who just sold some dope on the side to make a bit of extra money and help make ends meet. He was not someone who became nationally "known" for something legal, then later revealed that before he "made it", he had to sell drugs because there was no other option. No, when Rick Ross became "known", it was for one thing and one thing only—selling cocaine.

Rick's business enterprise has often been frowned upon by mainstream society because he didn't get rich by any of the traditionally "legal" methods, such as the stock market, real estate, professional sports or entertainment. Yet in terms of sheer revenue, one would be hard-pressed to find a businessman generating more cash than Freeway Rick in the 1980s. According to a federal prosecutor, Rick's fortune was estimated at over $600 million as he was bringing in a *daily* revenue of $1 million—$2-3 million on a "good day". To put this type of money into perspective, Magic Johnson made headlines in 1981 by signing a 25-year deal with the Los Angeles Lakers that paid him $25 million—or $1 million per year. To most people, this seemed to be an astonishing amount of money for 1981. But upon hearing this news, Rick's reaction was basically along the line of "A million per *year*…That's *all*?"

The fact that Rick Ross achieved on such an extraordinary level is even more remarkable when one takes into account the fact that *he was illiterate.* Not until the age of twenty-eight did Rick learn to read. And by that time, he was already incarcerated and out of the cocaine business. Although many people tout the United States of America as "the greatest country in the world", a major reason for this greatness is often overlooked. The United States' system of "free enterprise" is the crowning jewel of the world's economy. And Freeway Ricky Ross leveraged this system to become the biggest crack cocaine trafficker in United States history. But the system also leveraged Rick, as detailed by Gary Webb's explosive journalism that helped uncover the CIA's involvement in dealing drugs to fund a war in Central America. Though steadfast as the world's beacon of freedom and hope, the United States—*and several of its leaders*—are far from having their mighty hands free of cocaine residue.

Therefore, if we can highlight the remarkable achievements and success of the United States of America—*a drug dealing nation*—we can also highlight the remarkable achievements and success of Ricky Ross—*a former drug dealer*.

With that being said, it's been over two decades since Freeway Rick's last illegal drug deal. And in that time, he has become involved in many legal endeavors: a trucking business, a social media site, literacy non-profit organizations, women's hair weaves, public speaking, t-shirts, books and even legal marijuana.

And though many people genuinely commend Rick for his newfound legal businesses since his release from prison, a "The Real Rick Ross Is Not A Rapper" t-shirt is probably not what is inspiring you to read this book. The transition from prison into free society is a tough journey for most former inmates, and Rick is no exception. He has faced his fair share of struggles in rebuilding his enterprise by legal means. As a matter of fact, as you read these words, *you* may currently be more successful than Rick at selling your own t-shirts, or running your own small business—whatever that may be.

But even if you are currently doing what you do with more success than Rick Ross "the t-shirt dealer", it is highly unlikely that you are doing what you do with anywhere near the level of success of Rick Ross, "the drug dealer". *For some reason or reasons*, Rick Ross was the damn best who did it—selling cocaine, that is. And as we are all seeking to *improve ourselves* to become successful at what we do, we are naturally inclined to gain insight as to *how* and *why* someone else became the best at what they did. We want to know the keys to their success, so that we may understand and apply those keys towards improving our unique situation. That's the purpose of reading any self-help, self-improvement or success book. In that regard, this "self-improvement" book is no different.

At the same time, this self-improvement book—*The 21 Keys of Success*—is different. Most self-improvement books are written by or about "legal" businessmen, successful coaches, PhD's, politicians, polished speakers, entertainers, athletes, etc. And even a few are written by or about people who "sold drugs" for a brief stint before they made it big in their legal ventures. But "success" and "self-improvement" books are generally not written by or about individuals who are known *primarily* for the sale of cocaine. And so, *The 21 Keys of Success*—a "self-improvement" book detailing the principles of a MAJOR cocaine trafficker—falls into the category of a different kind of different. *This book is an anomaly*. And why does this matter? The reason it matters is because *success is also an anomaly*.

The rarity of success in society and the scarcity in which success is *actually* found in the lives of people means that real success lies in a realm *outside* the normal and rational tendencies that most people have and are comfortable practicing. *Success itself is a non-conforming occurrence*. Therefore, if you REALLY want to become a success, you too must become a non-conformist. You must move in a manner that is opposite of what 98-99% of the population considers "proper". And that's why this book is so different and powerful for those who really want to succeed. *That which you are seeking to become* ***is*** *that which you are studying to become it.*

As you begin reading this book, you should solidly embrace the fact that Freeway Ricky Ross is a former cocaine dealer. This is critically important to realize, because it is only from this perspective of truth that you may fully understand another truth: Rick Ross was not *only* a drug dealer…*he was an anomaly…just like success*. Success is an anomaly. And that truth is the power in this book, because as Gary Vaynerchuk once said, “If you want to be an anomaly… you gotta act like one.”

INTRODUCTION
"BUT THEY DIDN'T KNOW THE PRINCIPLES..."

December 3rd, 2011. New York, NY. Rick was only scheduled to be in town for a couple of days, which meant lots of interviews and appearances crammed into a very small time frame. New York City traffic being New York City traffic, it was a foregone conclusion that getting from Point A to Point B would take up a great deal of that precious time. Fortunately, after picking Rick up from JFK Airport, he had a telephone interview right before the meeting in Harlem. A telephone interview was the perfect use of time, as it was understood that Rick would simply call in to the radio station, speak to the host and answer questions from listeners who called in. This being the case, Rick could have this interview in the car as we were driving to the next meeting in Harlem.

Because traffic was flowing well and there was no construction, we made it uptown sooner than I expected. Furthermore, the usual headache of finding on-the-street parking in Harlem was a non-issue. On this day, we just happened to be in the right place at the right time. As we were about to turn right off of 125th Street onto St. Nicholas Avenue, we immediately saw in front of us white backing lights followed by the cutting wheels of a white sedan. This was the obvious sign of a car leaving the space in which it was parallel parked. Bingo!

After quickly pulling in as the last car parked on the block, we were right across the street from Rick's meeting, with thirty minutes to spare. This meant Rick could do his telephone interview as we sat in the parked car, in the relative peace of pedestrians passing by on the sidewalk (which was much preferable to the chaos of driving through Manhattan in the middle of the day). As I pushed the button to shut off the engine, I was still looking around to make sure we weren't too close to a fire hydrant. And Rick had already dialed in to the radio show.

Now certain that we would not be ticketed, I was especially glad that I could really listen to the interview instead of focusing on driving through the city. Even though I first interviewed Rick back in 2010 for *GET MONEY Magazine*, I always enjoyed listening to his interviews with other people because the details of his story were always inspiring and thought-provoking. Today would be no different. As customary, the host went through the pleasantries of introducing herself and thanking Rick for being a guest on the show. Then she began the interview:

Interviewer: My question is, learning that 42% of the prison population in this country is black men, what would you say led you to the path that took you there, and if there's two or three things you could name in your youth maybe you think could have been done differently...

Rick: I can tell you right off hand. It was one thing that led me there: a lack of knowledge. I went to the dope man and asked him how to make money. Very simple. I wasn't a bad guy. I wasn't crazy. Wasn't retarded or nothing like that... I saw a guy that…

Interviewer: Didn't you also play tennis?

Rick: I did play tennis. But I... the mistake that I made though, was that, I saw a guy who was driving around in Cadillacs and Mercedes Benzes, and wearing all the finest clothes, and I went to him and asked him, how can I make some money? And he was a dope dealer.... So you know what he did?...

Interviewer: What did he do?

Rick: *He gave me some dope.*

Interviewer: Wow... So how old were you?

Rick: Nineteen...

Interviewer: Nineteen. Ok.

Rick: And then he told me how to sell it... and what a great business it was.

Sitting next to Rick and listening to him recall the story of how he got started selling cocaine, I couldn't help but mentally flash back to the time in my life when *I* was nineteen. I recalled my specific state of mind. I thought about how eager I was to "be somebody". And of course, for a nineteen-year-old guy, "being somebody," meant having enough money to get a nice car. For me, all I wanted was a shiny yellow Corvette. Back then, I would have done almost anything to get the money to afford one—even sell drugs.

Remembering that Rick's initial goal in the cocaine business was $5,000 to fix up his car, I thought about how his eventual path contrasted with mine. After all, as nineteen-year-old guys, we basically had the same driving motivation—getting a nice car. But our paths did not follow the same track. Our paths separated… not because Rick was "a bad guy" and I was "a good guy". And it wasn't because Rick was around drugs and I wasn't. As I thought about it more, I saw that even though we had the same teenage aspirations, our paths separated because of two simple words: *perceived options.*

Long before I became a teenager dreaming of yellow Corvettes, I was a kid infatuated with books. Although I never remember a time when I *couldn't* read, my earliest memories were of lots of books being around me—my mother always reading to me. So by the time I started school, I never had to "learn how to read". As a matter of fact, as a four-year-old kid, I could read full books on a second-grade and third-grade level. I read so well that by the time I started school, my kindergarten teacher began inviting the teachers from the higher grades to sit around me and listen to me read on their lunch break. Once the administration heard about my reading ability, the school decided that the first grade would simply be a waste of time for me. I went from kindergarten directly into the second grade.

Fast-forward about fifteen years, and I was halfway through college—well on my way to receiving a degree in electrical engineering. Furthermore, I was a cooperative education student. This meant that every other semester (for three semesters), I was working at a major corporation and making more money as a nineteen-year-old student than most people who had already graduated. Although the co-op work effectively pushed my graduation date back by three semesters, my practical engineering experience (while still a student) all but guaranteed me a high-paying engineering salary at a company like AT&T or FedEx once I graduated. Not only would my salary double upon graduation, but I was also on track to make six figures before I was twenty-five and become some type of corporate vice-president before I was forty.

It was common knowledge that engineers were highly respected and made more money fresh out of college than any other major. And so the path I was on provided great assurance that I'd have a lot of money and "be somebody" very soon. From the companies I worked for, I already knew several engineers with 'Vettes. So even though I also knew a lot of people who sold drugs, I just kinda figured selling drugs wasn't the *only* way for me to get what I wanted. My logic was along the line of "I want a Corvette. Engineers drive 'Vettes. I'm in school to become an engineer. I'm going to have a 'Vette soon." That just made sense to me.

And so, I never really got into selling drugs. But my indifference to taking advantage of my opportunities to become a "D-Boy" was not because I was a "good guy". I didn't hesitate because I was "straight-minded", and I didn't "not sell drugs" because I was "sane". It wasn't because I was influenced by Nancy Reagan's old "Just Say No" campaign or some silly-ass commercial about an egg in a frying pan being people's brains on drugs. I wasn't concerned about drugs "causing harm to people or the community". I didn't care about any of that. My indifference on selling cocaine—which ended up being my decision to *not* sell cocaine—wasn't a moral or ethical decision. It was solely because I perceived I had other options. *I simply felt I had another option to get money, buy the things I wanted and "be somebody".*

But for the teenage Ricky Ross, whose dream of becoming a tennis star had all but vanished (because he couldn't read and was told he couldn't attend college), where were the other options? In a few short years, he would not have a tennis career *or* a college degree, and he knew it. If Ricky Ross ever wanted to "be somebody", or drive around in Cadillacs, Mercedes Benzes or Corvettes, *cocaine*—not electrical engineering—would have to be his major. And because he would not be studying on a tennis scholarship, he would have to take out a different type of student loan to further his education. That "loan" came in the form of a $50 rock of cocaine, fronted to him by a friend who introduced Rick to the drug.

As I snapped back to the present moment—the phone interview still in progress—I realized that although Rick and I had many similarities, we *perceived* different options for ourselves as teenagers. And if there was one line that divided our perceptions—the line that separated a path of college from a path of cocaine—it was *the ability to read.* The key of *literacy* opened the doors of college to me. Conversely, that very same key—turned in the opposite direction of *il*literacy—shut the doors of college to Rick.

But starting out on a certain path does not necessarily guarantee success or failure to any individual. And for Rick, the fact that he couldn't read did not prevent him from taking full advantage of what he *could* do. Although unable to attend college, class was still in session for nineteen-year-old Ricky Donnell Ross. He had been introduced to cocaine, and was now a freshman enrolled in "Cocaine 101". No, this wasn't USC, UCLA, or Long Beach State. But as with any course of study, there were *principles* that had to be understood before moving on to the more advanced levels within this newfound major. Fortunately for the illiterate Ross, a major in cocaine did not require understanding the principles of reading and writing, but arithmetic and weight instead. Ricky *knew* numbers. And although he started off slowly, he began to study cocaine with the diligence of an aspiring Summa Cum Laude. Rick became diligent in completing his assignments and spent all his time in the lab developing his understanding of the principles that would allow him to engineer the most powerful crack cocaine engine Los Angeles had ever seen. After a few years in, Ross' "cocaine machine" made his initial goal of $5,000 to fix up his car seem like spare change under the car seat. Rick had not only taken over the crack cocaine market in Los Angeles, but much of the nation as well. Mr. Ross was no longer a struggling freshman, but the Chief Engineer at Cocaine, Inc., re-writing the principles of the science of selling cocaine and making history (and a fortune) at the same time.

Although Rick did not discover the principles of success in a classroom on a college campus, he *did* discover them. To the chagrin of many, Rick's discovery of *keys of success through the sale of keys of cocaine* is not the "proper" way to display the effectiveness of these universal principles. However, the success of Rick Ross cannot be denied. As the interview continued…

Interviewer: But you just got caught up in the trap, you know. We've all seen New Jack City, where we've seen those guys rollin' around, you know… straight up in Harlem. I've had family members that have dated individuals, and they

made it look glamorous! Everybody back in the early '80s wanted to do what you was doing... but *they didn't come and make the type of money that you made*... because *you made 600 million bucks!!!*

Rick: But they didn't know the principles though... See, there's principles that you have to use in *any* business that you go into. And most people don't know the principles. I mean, that's why we're out here struggling right now. And that's what I do. I go around and I'm trying to give people the principles...

There are few entrepreneurs in American history who—starting with so little—went on to run an enterprise with such success. These principles—these keys—to the success of Freeway Ricky Ross are wrapped up in this book.

KEY 1
HUMBLENESS

BEING HUMBLE DOES NOT MEAN BEING WEAK OR A PUSHOVER. RATHER, YOU DO NOT ELEVATE YOURSELF ABOVE ANOTHER "JUST BECAUSE". YOU UNDERSTAND THAT YOU ARE NOT FUNDAMENTALLY GREATER THAN ANOTHER MAN. CONVERSELY, YOU UNDERSTAND THAT NO OTHER MAN IS FUNDAMENTALLY GREATER THAN YOU. FROM THIS PERSPECTIVE, YOU LIVE IN A MODE OF CONTINUOUS IMPROVEMENT BECAUSE YOU UNDERSTAND THE REALITY: *ALL MEN ARE CREATED EQUAL, BUT YOU CAN MAKE YOURSELF GREATER BY PURPOSEFULLY DEDICATING YOURSELF TO GREATNESS.* YOU THINK LIKE THE BOSS, YET YOU WORK WITH THE EFFORT AND DETERMINATION OF THE UNPAID INTERN.

"The reality is that here you are—this 'drug dealer'—and I find myself genuinely wanting to welcome you with open arms. I mean it's not supposed to be like that, but it is. And that's fucking amazing!"

–High-powered Hollywood Executive

TRUE STORY

The late 1970s and 1980s was the heyday for cocaine in America. As South American producers supplied the United States' insatiable appetite for "la cocaina", drug profits made by dealers were staggering. In the '80s, 2.2 pounds—1 kilogram (1 kilo or "key")—of pure Colombian cocaine cost about $1,000 to manufacture, and up to $4,000 to transport to Miami. This same "key"—once safely across the U.S. border—sold for a minimum of between $50,000 and $70,000. Prior to the late 1970s, large quantities of cocaine had been scarce in the U.S. As a result, there was plenty of money to be made in this emerging drug market. Of course, marijuana was still a popular drug among smugglers. But in the business of illegal drug dealing, success or failure often hinged on the smuggler's ability to prevent product from being detected by law enforcement. Consequently, a more compact and potent drug was the preferred product because it allowed a smuggler to reap the same amount (or more) of profit from a much smaller package.

For example, $70,000 worth of marijuana might weigh around 140 pounds and be impractical for a single person to conceal on their person. However, $70,000 worth of cocaine only weighed 2.2 pounds and would take up only about as much space as this book you are now holding. With such ease of concealment, even the local priests and parish nuns weren't above stashing a couple of keys on a flight from Bogota into the United States. The beauty of cocaine was that such a small quantity commanded such a big price. And at $70,000 per key, cocaine was *much* more lucrative than marijuana... *if one was willing to take the risk.* High risk, high reward was the cocaine game in the 1980s, and one of the most formidable players was quickly gaining notoriety down in Miami, Florida. No, it wasn't William Roberts. This cocaine "boss" was actually a woman. And her name was Griselda Blanco.

Griselda Blanco—also known as "The Godmother of Cocaine"—was born in Cartagena, Colombia in 1943. After a rough childhood and life of petty crime during her teens and early twenties, Blanco left Colombia and immigrated to Queens, NY. It was during this time in the mid-1970s when Blanco began to establish her cocaine business in the United States. But the early stages of Blanco's enterprise were not without its bumps in the road. After being indicted on federal drug conspiracy charges in 1975, Blanco fled back to Colombia before she could be arrested.

However, the awaiting fortune in cocaine profits was too inviting to keep Griselda Blanco away from the United States. So in the late 1970s she returned, this time settling in Miami. Coincidentally, it was around this same time when the extreme violence surrounding the cocaine trade became commonplace in South Florida. The paradise to which retirees flocked for relaxation and sunny beaches was now soaked in blood. In 1980, there were a record 573 murders in the city of Miami. In 1981, there were 621. Miami had fast become the nation's new murder capital. In order to keep pace with the number of dead bodies being found under the South Florida heat and humidity, the Miami-Dade County Coroner's office began renting refrigeration trucks as temporary storage facilities for murder victims. Many of these bodies were attributed to one Griselda Blanco. It is estimated that during her time as a drug trafficker, Blanco was responsible for some 200 murders.

As part of the Medellin Cartel, Blanco was known for her especially brutal tactics and unwavering violence towards rivals. Those who displeased Griselda Blanco found themselves dealt with swiftly and unmercifully. But Blanco's ruthless business model was not without its down side. Although The Godmother's network was generating an estimated $80,000,000 per month in cocaine revenue, her violent tactics and propensity to kill created many enemies who were especially eager to seek revenge. And in 1984—in an effort to escape the repeated attempts on her life—Blanco left Miami and settled in California.

But there are certain inherent and unavoidable costs of the drug business. One of the biggest is the fact that drug dealers are constantly at risk of being apprehended by the authorities. And while in California, on February 17, 1985, Blanco was arrested and held without bail. After her trial, she was convicted on drug charges and sentenced the maximum (at the time) of fifteen years. But because prosecutors also wanted to convict Blanco on murder charges from her time in Miami, they transported her back to Florida in 1994. During Blanco's time in prison, prosecutors gathered sufficient evidence to indict Blanco for murders in Miami, which could have given her life in prison or the death penalty. But the case fell apart due to a technicality involving a phone-sex scandal in the State Attorney's Office. Consequently, Blanco was able to make a deal for a light ten-year sentence. In June 2004, Blanco was released and deported back to Colombia. Griselda Blanco was free… or so it seemed.

On the night of September 3, 2012, after purchasing meat at a butcher shop in Medellin, Blanco was shot twice in the head by two gunmen on a motorbike. After openly killing Blanco, the gunman calmly got back onto the motorbike and rode off into the city. Griselda Blanco had been assassinated at the age of 69.

****

The next day, and 3,324 miles away from Medellin, in Long Beach, California, the headline flashed across my phone, "Queen of Cocaine Killed in Colombia". Before I got a chance to read the details, the breaking story was interrupted by an incoming call on my line. As soon as I hit the "Accept" button, the caller said, "Kolie, I'm downstairs!" and hung up. I threw on my blue Yankees hoodie, tossed my backpack across my shoulder and slammed the door behind me. As I jaunted down the stairs of the second floor at 3700 East Ocean Boulevard, I thought of the irony: *The 'Queen of Cocaine' had just been assassinated in her Colombian hometown, and I was about to hop into the car with the 'King of Cocaine' to make our daily rounds through his hometown.* But this drug lord's territory was not the "City of Eternal Spring" in Colombia. It was the freeways of Los Angeles—and his name was "Freeway Rick".

As I opened the door and jumped into the economy-sized grey Kia Rio, Rick was already on another call, and so he didn't say anything to me. We just took off. I wasn't sure where we were going, but I knew it would be a full day. As always, I was prepared for anything. For the first ten minutes of the drive, Rick was still on the phone. That gave me time to think about the death sentence just handed down to Griselda Blanco by the streets of Medellin. Most notably, I thought about how Griselda's *death* was in such stark contrast to the new *life* recently handed down to Freeway Rick.

After being sentenced to "life in prison without the possibility of parole" sixteen years earlier, Rick was now out on the street. And boy did the streets love Rick! The streets had always embraced Rick—even though he sold the same destructive white powder as did Griselda Blanco. Rick Ross and Griselda Blanco were similar in the fact that they were both infamous drug lords who played a major role in flooding

America's streets with tons of cocaine. But the similarities between Rick Ross and Griselda Blanco didn't end there. Despite their role in dealing a poison that destroyed many lives, both managed to encounter favorable technicalities in their court cases. These technicalities greatly reduced their prison time, and allowed them to avoid the extremely long sentences typically given to drug kingpins—sentences that would have effectively seen them die behind bars. And so, after having been through the court system and serving some time for trafficking cocaine, both Griselda Blanco and Rick Ross were *legally* free. Both were residing in their respective hometowns—no longer under the threat of arrest by the authorities.

Yet there were differences between Rick Ross and Griselda Blanco. Although Blanco was freed from prison because of a technicality based on a screw-up by the State Attorney's Office, Rick was freed because of a technicality that he discovered based on his own personal initiative. And *how* they got free was not the only difference in their freedom. *How freely they appeared* in public was completely different. After Griselda Blanco was released and deported back to Colombia in 2004, there weren't many reports of her being seen in public. In stark contrast, Rick was seen *everywhere* after his prison release in 2009. Rick came and went as he pleased, up and down the freeways of L.A., eating lunch and taking pictures in broad daylight—with no weapons or bodyguards—and going to meetings all around L.A.

On this particular day—one of the many I spent ridin' with Rick—the meeting on hand was with a particularly well-known executive at a Hollywood studio. The topic of discussion was mainly the financing of Rick's movie. I had gone to several of these types of "Hollywood executive" meetings with Rick. But this meeting stood out not so much because of the movie details, how much money was needed, or who should play the role of Rick Ross. All the meetings involved those topics. What stood out was the executive's reaction upon meeting Rick. After a few minutes of the normal pleasantries and a few minutes of getting a gist of some of the details of what Rick was trying to do with his movie, the executive gets this pleasantly surprised look on his face as he's shaking his head. And in disbelief, he says to Rick, "*The reality is that here you are—this 'drug dealer'—and I find myself genuinely wanting to welcome you with open arms. I mean it's not supposed to be like that, but it is. And that's fucking amazing!*"

The rest of the meeting went on as meetings go, with both sides gaining a clearer understanding of the project as a whole. Getting millions of dollars to fund a major movie isn't a one-meeting deal, but progress had been made.

After we all pulled off from the Hollywood studio lot, Rick and I rode back to South L.A. to see some people from the neighborhood that he had come up with. When we got to a familiar spot, Rick stopped the car and jumped out to say "what up" to some friends he hadn't seen in years. I had some e-mails to catch up on, so I stayed in the car for a few more minutes before getting out. But as I sat there, the words from the Hollywood executive whose office we just left played back in my head: *"The reality is that here you are—this 'drug dealer'—and I find myself genuinely wanting to welcome you with open arms. I mean it's not supposed to be like that, but it is. And that's fucking amazing!"*

As those words echoed, I began to think about how pleasantly surprised that executive was, and—more importantly—*why*; how that experience really *was* amazing… *for someone like him* who only knew *of* Rick Ross "the drug dealer". Of course for someone like myself, who had known Rick for a few years, or for anyone who had been around Rick for any appreciable amount of time, it was just natural to want to welcome him with open arms. Why? We knew Rick *the person.* And in growing to know Rick the person, any preconceived or unfounded notion of "the drug dealer" quickly evaporated.

For example, because of who Rick was, there was no fear that someone was going to open fire on Rick's Kia Rio while we were doing something as mundane as pumping gas or coming out of the Am/Pm convenience store with a couple of bags of pretzels. That *was* fucking amazing, because notorious cocaine kingpins generally don't have the luxury of running routine errands in public—even years after they have "retired" from the cocaine business. The recent assassination of Griselda Blanco was indication of this. For Blanco, what was intended to be a routine trip to the local butcher shop became the last errand she ran before she was publicly executed.

But the executive's surprised reaction upon meeting Rick Ross "the person", brought to light an interesting perspective that I had personally grown blind to—the result of having spent so much time around Rick. And yet, it was likely the perspective that most people in America actually had of him, since most people in America had never had the opportunity to ever meet Rick. And that perspective was simply this: *What it must be like for all those people who only knew of Rick Ross "the drug dealer"*. Someone with that perspective—a person having no experience with the *real* Rick Ross—would likely have in their mind the image of the stereotypical violent and ruthless drug dealer—someone with the image of a Griselda Blanco.

But even that initial thought of mine was hypocritical because *I* had never actually met Griselda Blanco. Although the media portrayed her as a ruthless "black widow", who is to say that she was viewed like that by everyone who genuinely knew her as a person? Was there *no one* whose personal opinion of her was that of a loving and compassionate woman? I'm sure there were people in her life—people close to her—who knew of a very different Griselda Blanco than the Griselda Blanco portrayed by the media. But as with all people, getting a grasp of another's true nature is often very difficult.

So although I was in no position to personally speak on the nature of Griselda Blanco, the *image* that the media portrayed of her got me thinking. The media often portrays drug dealers as using violence and intimidation to maintain their power. But two things can be true at the same time. The media's portrayal of Griselda Blanco as a "cold-hearted killer" appears accurate in the fact that she did have a great number of people killed. At the same time, the media's portrayal means little when it comes to her relationships with those whom she truly loved and who truly loved her. Life is paradoxical in that way. I knew it because I was often around Rick when he was playing with his two youngest children—Bricen and Jordan. With so much genuine love and joy evident between them in those moments, it was almost impossible to picture Rick as "Freeway Rick"—crack baron. No way could *this* be the guy whose relentless promotion of poisonous crack cocaine tore apart the fabric of so many black families during the 1980s and into the 1990s. And yet, he was.

So of course, someone not up-close and personal to the daily comings and goings and family interactions of Rick, can only image in their mind the generic "destroyer of lives" that is most often portrayed as one hears the term "drug dealer". And so I understood this rationale. It is why so many people find themselves utterly shocked that Rick doesn't carry himself as the typical "drug dealer". What an emotional twist, that upon meeting the most notorious crack cocaine dealer in United States history, you would feel like giving him a big hug and inviting him over for dinner!

This realization also got me reflecting back on all the "hoods" we had been in across the nation. Rick and I had been in Harlem, the Bronx, Queens, Brooklyn, Camden, NJ, hoods in Philadelphia, Detroit, and of course all around Los Angeles. It seemed like everywhere we went, we found ourselves in urban communities that had—at some point—been crippled by the crack cocaine that *he* pushed. These were communities where people's mothers, sisters, fathers, brothers, kids, uncles, aunts, dear friends, relatives and neighbors had had their lives destroyed by a small white rock that took from them everything that meant anything—*and then some*. And here was the man who played the biggest role in promoting this small white rock. Going a step further, Rick Ross was literally the face of crack cocaine in the United States.

However, I never witnessed a single person so much as give Rick a sideways look. In the cocaine game, things can get bent really fast—especially when someone feels crossed. And people have long memories when millions of dollars in coke money is in play. But from all the places we went, and with everyone knowing "the real Rick Ross" was in the building (word of

Rick's arrival travels fast in the 'hood), there has never been a rogue relative or disgruntled dealer seeking to exact revenge against The King of Crack Cocaine. It's all love. It's all respect. No bodyguards needed. No weapons needed. No bulletproof cars needed.

Now, am I saying that I have *not* heard and seen people extremely upset at Rick for "what he did to the black community by pushing cocaine"? No, of course I'm not saying that. On several occasions, I have heard people absolutely blast Rick for "selling out his community for a dollar" or calling Rick the scum of the earth because "their brother got hooked on that shit and it destroyed his life". Again, many of these people have seen their mothers, sisters, fathers, brothers, kids, uncles, aunts, dear friends, relatives and neighbors lives destroyed by that small white rock. However, there *is* a difference between the frustration and anger aimed at Freeway Rick Ross by family members who have lost loved ones because of their addiction to crack cocaine and the vengeance aimed at the typical "drug dealer" who uses violence as a business tool.

From the outside looking in, it would be natural for many to wonder why Freeway Ricky Ross hasn't suffered the same deadly fate as so many other "drug dealers" in Mexico, Colombia and our ghettos right here in the United States. In other words, **how can a man whose product destroyed the lives of *so many* people and is associated with *so much violence and death*, not have anyone out to kill him?** It seems that big-time cocaine dealers can never fully escape the threat of violence and death, even if they are no longer in the cocaine business or have already served their prison time. The threat is ever-present, because it only takes *one* person—feeling "some type of way" about something they perceived you did, and your life could be snuffed out. And yet, Rick doesn't have to hide out and live in fear of retaliation. Ironically, the key that allows Rick Ross to walk through any "dangerous" 'hood in America—with no bodyguards and no weapon—is the same key that opens to him the office doors of Hollywood's elite executives. The key is *humbleness.*

KEY TO SUCCESS

When a person says the word "drug dealer"—especially when that drug is *cocaine*—an image of a certain type of person often comes to mind. This person is someone who has the public image of a Griselda Blanco—ruthless, violent and unapologetic about murdering those who displease or oppose them. According to Al Singleton, a retired Miami police detective who was part of the federal task force that targeted the drug queen when she was at her most powerful, "Some people thought that Blanco felt she had to be more violent because she was a woman in a man's world, but I don't. I've been told by people who were close to her that this was just Griselda Blanco's nature." And when speaking of her preparation to play the role of Griselda Blanco in the film *Cocaine Godmother*, Catherine Zeta-Jones said, "I've tried not to homogenize her or find a sympathetic quality, because I don't think she had one."

Again, having no personal experience with Griselda Blanco, I don't know this to be true. However, from my experience with people, I've found that people's view of another's nature changes based on the nature of that particular relationship. I once interviewed Deirdre Marie Capone—the grand-niece of Al Capone. We—those who never knew or interacted with Al

Capone—can only know him as Chicago's most infamous gangster. He was "Public Enemy Number One". But to Deirdre Marie, she simply knew him as her warm and loving "Uncle Al". And so, when it comes to Griselda Blanco, "who she was" or "what she was like" is subjective and based on those who had first-hand experience with her.

But those who have seen Hollywood's portrayal of "drug dealers" in movies such as *New Jack City* and *Scarface* are certainly familiar with the sensationalized, aggressive and cut-throat drug dealers portrayed by Wesley Snipes and Al Pacino. And whether they are personified through Nino Brown or Tony Montana, a major cocaine trafficker's propensity for violence can be very real. It generally makes others uneasy and fearful. The physical and mental effects of cocaine itself mixed with the staggering amount of money at stake can make the cocaine business particularly violent. Especially in areas where life is cheap, killing is often viewed as just a necessary part of the business. Those not involved in the cocaine business generally seek to avoid "drug dealers" for this very reason. The last thing the "legit, law-abiding citizen" wants to do is welcome a "drug dealer" into their home, and extend him a welcoming invitation for dinner with their family.

But I've been there with Rick—in some of the most spacious and luxurious gated homes in Bel-Air and Malibu. Right there, eating dinner with a major network executive and his family—their kids running around barefoot and playing games in the next room. This is not the type of invite that a "legit" corporate network executive extends to a "drug dealer", and it's certainly not the type of comfort level generally exhibited. As a matter of fact, the opposite reaction is generally the case. The ruthless tactics of a Nino Brown or unbridled arrogance of a Tony Montana tend to instill fear in others and works to create many enemies. Their ultimate downfall becomes imminent. And the on-screen demise of these kingpins often occurs for the same reason that real-life drug lords meet their demise…pride.

It is often said that "pride goeth before destruction." In many ways, humbleness is the opposite of pride. And so it only stands to reason that if pride goeth before destruction, then humbleness goeth before success. And that is why the principle of humbleness is such a crucial key to the character of all who attain ultimate success.

In many regards, Freeway Rick Ross may be the most *successful* drug lord ever. Not simply based on money accumulated or influence, but based on current quality of life.

In 2018, Wikipedia defined a "drug lord" as follows:

'A drug lord, drug baron, kingpin, or narcotrafficker is a person who controls a sizable network of people involved in the illegal drug trade. Such figures are often difficult to bring to justice, as they are normally not directly in possession of something illegal, but are insulated from the actual trade in drugs by several layers of underlings. The prosecution of drug lords is therefore usually the result of carefully planned infiltration into their networks, often using informants from within the organization.'

The site then goes on to list the world's "notable drug lords" as follows:

- 1 Notable drug lords
- 1.1 Joaquín "El Chapo" Guzmán
- 1.2 Jorge Alberto Rodriguez
- 1.3 Pablo Escobar
- 1.4 Griselda Blanco
- 1.5 Roberto Suárez Gómez
- 1.6 Rick Ross
- 1.7 Manuel Noriega
- 1.8 Amado Carrillo Fuentes
- 1.9 Ramon Arellano Félix
- 1.10 Ismael Zambada García
- 1.11 Klaas Bruinsma
- 1.12 Arturo Beltran Leyva
- 1.13 Frank Lucas
- 1.14 Leroy Barnes
- 1.15 Zhenli Ye Gon
- 1.16 Christopher Coke
- 1.17 Demetrius Flenory

This is not necessarily the "right" or "wrong" listing of these 17 drug lords interpreted as #1 being "the most notable". Here, Rick is listed at #6. But there are sites that rank Rick as high as #3 all time as the most notorious drug kingpin ever, behind only El Chapo and Pablo Escobar. The actual listing order or "rankings" will always differ slightly depending on the source and who is asked. However, the important thing to realize is this: By any consensus, Rick is one of the most notorious drug lords of all time.

And when you look at the current status of the world's most notable drug lords, it looks like this:

- 1 Notable drug lords
- 1.1 Joaquín "El Chapo" Guzmán (PRISON)
- 1.2 Jorge Alberto Rodriguez (PRISON)
- 1.3 Pablo Escobar (DECEASED)
- 1.4 Griselda Blanco (DECEASED)
- 1.5 Roberto Suárez Gómez (DECEASED)
- 1.6 Rick Ross (ALIVE AND FREE)
- 1.7 Manuel Noriega (DECEASED)
- 1.8 Amado Carrillo Fuentes (DECEASED)
- 1.9 Ramon Arellano Félix (DECEASED)
- 1.10 Ismael Zambada García (WANTED FUGITIVE)
- 1.11 Klaas Bruinsma (DECEASED)
- 1.12 Arturo Beltran Leyva (DECEASED)
- 1.13 Frank Lucas (ALIVE AND FREE)
- 1.14 Leroy Barnes (WITNESS PROTECTION)
- 1.15 Zhenli Ye Gon (PRISON)
- 1.16 Christopher Coke (PRISON)
- 1.17 Demetrius Flenory (PRISON)

Rick Ross and Frank Lucas are the only ones on this list *not* dead, in prison, hiding out as a wanted fugitive or under witness protection. But a major difference between Rick and Frank Lucas is that Rick is thirty years younger and able to move around without a wheelchair. Taking everything into account—past notoriety, riches, influence obstacles overcome and current quality of life—perhaps no drug kingpin is as much of a *success* as Rick Ross.

This is not just a coincidence.

Why has the overall fate of Rick Ross—*despite being one of the world's most notorious drug lords*—been different? Why does Rick Ross—*despite being one of the world's most notorious drug lords*—still have the opportunity to have his life turn out to be labeled as a "SUCCESS"? What is the key to Rick Ross—*despite being one of the world's most notorious drug lords*—being able to move freely and not hide out as he pursues his own version of the American Dream?

The key: Humbleness. Humbleness unlocks the door to the rest of the Keys of Success that are detailed in this book. *If one lacks humbleness, the remaining twenty Keys are much more difficult to implement.*

When Rick was selling cocaine, he was definitely not a choirboy. Neither is he one today. But people genuinely liked him then and they genuinely like him now. Being genuinely liked by people is not necessarily about "being a good person" and "doing good deeds". Those factors can help. However, many people in this world "do good" simply because they are not brave enough to do what they really want to do. Often people do "good things" like give gifts or offer compliments that are not genuine. The ulterior motive behind the offer is actually to lower the recipient's defenses. This type of "good deeds" person always gives off a slight "smell" of being inauthentic, which others subconsciously pick up on and which subsequently nudges people away.

There is no reason to "act like" a good person. In reality, all people have within, an "element of irreducible selfishness". This quite simply means that our true desires often aren't as "good" as we portray in society or make a show of. When people do true and genuine good from their heart, they do those things without fanfare, spectacle or the need to be seen. Most adults already know or suspect this—that the motive behind most public good is not as genuine as it would at first appear. And so, when it comes to human relationships, people find it harder to relate to those "doing good deeds" than relating to those who simply accept them as they are. In other words, those who demonstrate that "there is no big me and little you". And this is what people feel when they meet the real Rick Ross.

Before we close this chapter, I'm going to re-emphasize the true spirit of the word "humble"—because everyone has heard of it, but most people have the wrong impression of the *spirit* of what it means to be humble.

Let's get this clear: An humble person is not someone who walks around, head bowed down, deferring to others. That's a person with low self-esteem. And they can never be a success. No, an humble person *thinks like the boss, yet works and gives effort like he's the unpaid intern trying to establish himself.* A person who is thinking and working in this manner simply doesn't have time to belittle others. Furthermore, those who do work for him know that he would not ask them to do anything that he would not be willing to do himself.

The humble person is continuously working like he still has something to prove to himself. He or she is dedicated to self-improvement, regardless of where he may currently be. We've all heard that success requires hard work. But between the prideful person and the humble person, who is going to be—at any particular time—working harder? It will always be the humble person, even though the prideful person may currently be "ahead". This feeling of having already "made it" causes the prideful person to "take his foot off the gas" so to speak—feeling entitled. That feeling of entitlement prevents one from seeing the common value in all persons.

On the contrary, when you are humble, you reach a certain level, but you don't slack off and have the feeling of "I've made it!" You continue to do what you've done to get where you are because you understand that we are all fundamentally the same. And any true advantage or benefit you gain will be a result of your hard work and effort, not simply because you are "better" than the next man. Many people greatly look forward to reaching a certain place in life just to "quit" or "retire". If this is the feeling you have, you are likely in the wrong business or profession. A commonality of the elites in any field is their desire to keep going—even after other people's perception that they've "made it".

Freeway Ricky Ross would have never been able to attain the level of success he experienced in the drug game without his sense of humbleness. Rick—although he was making millions of dollars daily—looked like his customers. He interacted with them. He blended in with the people who were buying his crack cocaine in South Central Los Angeles. By appearance, no one would mistake these people for multi-millionaires. And because he blended in so well, Rick was able to stay off the radar for a long time as he remained out of sight of law enforcement. This was more than a "cover". Rick's humbleness manifested in non-violent tactics as he supplied his dealers with an intangible asset that was more valuable than the cocaine: the "good will" of wanting to see them be successful based on the belief that "there is no big me and little you". This earned him the respect in the neighborhood—and eventually throughout the country—even though the product that was wrapped in good will ended up destroying many of those who ended up using it.

Rick's success as a drug dealer is not measured simply in terms of dollars signs. More accurately, it is measured in terms of health and quality of life *after* those days of selling cocaine were long gone. Rick's humbleness while involved in the cocaine business built him up a kind of "equity" that now affords him a quality of life free from all the revenge-based violence that very few former cocaine kingpins can ever seem to get away from. To this day, Rick still carries with him this sense of humbleness. It's who he is, and more than any other factor, it's the reason he is alive and lives in peace today.

In *New Jack City*, it was the "old fool" who killed Nino Brown. In *Scarface*, Tony Montana was blown away from behind after his pride escalated into an all-out war. As a person rises to success there will naturally be those who are envious and jealous. There is nothing that can be done to change this. However, employing unnecessary tactics to humiliate, dehumanize or bring violence against others will create enemies who will spend the rest of their lives seeking revenge.

Freeway Rick was, as described by journalist Jesse Katz, "a favorite son of the Colombian cartels." Rick was the Americano who was able to sell their product to a completely new market in the United States—the African-American community. Yet, Rick carried with him the key trait that somehow kept him insulated from the extreme violence of the Colombian cartels—the source of his cocaine. That trait also kept him insulated from the gang wars of the Bloods and Crips, who were selling his cocaine at the retail street level. That key trait is hard to describe, but one knows it when they see it. And the reality is—as the Hollywood exec said—here he is—this *drug dealer*—and so many find themselves genuinely wanting to welcome him with open arms. It's not supposed to be like that, but it is. And that's fucking amazing!

Summed up in one word, that key trait is *humbleness*—the first Key of Success.

KEY 2
HEALTH CONSCIOUSNESS

IN ORDER TO MAINTAIN THE EFFORT AND ENERGY TO WORK LONG HOURS, CONSTANTLY DEAL WITH ADVERSITY, TAKE ADVANTAGE OF OPPORTUNITIES AND BE PREPARED TO BEST APPLY THE PRINCIPLES OF SUCCESS, ONE MUST TAKE MEASURES TO ENSURE THAT HE IS NOT BETRAYED BY HIS OWN BODY. LITERALLY, YOUR BODY IS THE VEHICLE IN WHICH YOU TRAVEL THE PATH OF SUCCESS. NO AMOUNT OF MONEY, STATUS OR POWER CAN BE ENJOYED IF ONE DOES NOT HAVE THE PHYSICAL HEALTH TO EXPRESS ONESELF.

"I definitely feel like I'm half my age."
–Rick Ross

TRUE STORY

Back in 2010, before I ever set foot in California, we featured Rick on the cover of *GET MONEY Magazine*. And in December of that year—for the release of Rick's issue—we threw a "White Christmas" magazine release party in New York. Of course, what would a magazine release party be without the cover person being in attendance as the guest of honor? It would be like baking an apple pie with no apples. So well in advance, we planned to fly Rick out to New York for the "White Christmas". But at that time, Rick was still on parole. So he couldn't just hop a flight to New York without the trip being approved by his parole officer. Getting that trip approved was no easy task. But at the 11th hour, after providing Rick's P.O. all the details of the trip and after much back and forth paperwork, Rick was finally granted permission to fly to New York for the magazine release.

But we weren't *just* throwing a magazine release party. Wanting to make the very most of the trip and take full advantage of the fact that this would be Rick's first trip to New York since his release from prison, we planned magazine signings, speaking events, interviews and a multitude of media appearances around Manhattan, Brooklyn, Queens and the Bronx. The "White Christmas" 2010 trip to New York was a big deal!

Despite the major hurdles we encountered during the approval process, Rick Ross—the real Rick Ross—was coming to New York. Yet he would only be in town for three or four days before he was required to fly back to Los Angeles. Scarce on time, the last thing we needed was to allow the trip to get bogged down in the logistics of getting around the boroughs. So in order to comfortably move Rick around and make sure we were timely and efficient in getting him from place to place, we hired a car service to drive Rick (and a guest) around. We provided the car service company the full itinerary (including the address of his hotel and all the events) in advance so they could plan ahead in getting Rick where he needed to be when he needed to be there. We also advised them that once people knew that Rick was actually *in New York*, we'd have to be ready to jump on other media appearances and events on the fly. Having the car service was a huge benefit, because with so much on my plate—as the point of contact and coordinator for everything going on—getting Rick from Point A to Point B was one less thing I had to be concerned with.

Even so, staying on top of everything had me running at redline. As a parolee, Rick had to move according to the itinerary I provided his P.O. in our written request for his permission to travel. In part, permission was granted based on that itinerary. We couldn't change where he was staying and we couldn't travel outside of a certain radius from New York City. Any changes regarding where we were going or how Rick was being transported needed approval first. Rick also had to check in at a local U.S. Probation Parole Office while in New York. I was the person to whom Rick's travel to New York was granted, so I had a certain responsibility to keep on task with the itinerary. This was in addition to the normal planning headaches that go with organizing a major event with lots of people, other businesses and media involvement.

For two consecutive nights before the release party, I stayed up all night, without sleeping the following day. And even once Rick got to New York, I'd often be at one of the venues hours before Rick got there to iron out details, talk with management, make sure things were set up properly and double-check financial matters. Then, once Rick got there, everything got more hectic because so many people came to see him once word got out. So during that first trip to New York in December of 2010—during the "White Christmas"—I didn't really spend a lot of time *with* Rick.

Yet, despite my lack of time around Rick, I did notice that he was always ready to move and he never needed a break. He had lots of energy and he was quite comfortable zipping around from spot to spot amidst the hectic New York flow. No place in the United States *moves* at the speed of New York City. And it's not even close. So for people who come to New York from other parts of the country, it can be quite overwhelming at first. From my experience hosting other friends who visit New York—especially for the first time—they almost always needed a "break". Or after the first day or two, they really needed a day to "just relax" or "take it easy". *But not Rick.* Rick was always on "go" mode—always ready to "get it in" as he would say.

As I watched Rick move with ease, showing up fully engaged at spot after spot with no signs of fatigue, I was impressed. He was moving around like me—someone a lot younger and accustomed to moving around like a New Yorker. I knew Rick was a hustler, but drug dealing is a young man's sport for a reason. The body slows down with age, and that hustler's energy generally declines. Rick wasn't in his twenties or thirties anymore, but you couldn't tell by watching him move. I also knew that after all these events in New York had come to an end, Rick would be flying off to the next city to "get it in". That was just how he rolled. I thought to myself, **"How was a man in his fifties moving around like a man half his age?"** A few months later, I understood how.

After the flurry of events for the "White Christmas" had concluded, Rick flew back to Los Angeles as scheduled. But with the success of the trip and all the newly formed East Coast connections, I knew it was only a matter of time before we'd have Rick back in New York. And several months later in 2011, the opportunity presented itself. This time the trip was a bit different. Getting Rick approved to fly to New York wasn't quite as difficult as it had been the first time he came. Also, the amount of planning and coordination required was not on the scale of what had been required for the big "White Christmas" trip back in December 2010. So I wasn't being pulled in so many different directions with all the obligations and fires to put out. As a result, I had more time to actually spend *with* Rick. Also—and this was key—*this time he came alone*. This was key because it changed the way he got around in New York. On the first trip, Rick came with his lady, and because my car only had two seats, they couldn't both ride with me. So the car service we used on the first trip was not only a convenience that freed me up, but also a requirement. I would not have been able to drive two other people around in my car. But this time there was no car service. It was just me and Rick moving around in a two-seater—everywhere—*all day—for three days*. Little did I know that when I picked him up from the airport, that those three days of constantly *ridin' with Rick* in New York would answer my question of how this man in his fifties moved around with the energetic vitality of a young man. And I definitely didn't expect it to change the way I viewed *my* overall health.

Rick was a vegan. He didn't eat any meat or animal products. I had already known this about Rick for some time. I knew it when he first came to New York for the magazine release party. But Rick being a vegan didn't mean much to me during that first visit back in December 2010. Sure, as our guest of honor, we made sure we accommodated *his* diet. But when it was time for *me—Kolie Crutcher*—to eat, I had absolutely no interest in eating like Rick. I didn't care whether he was the "real" Rick Ross or not. What I needed was "real" food. I had known other people who were "vegan" or "vegetarians" and my attitude towards eliminating meat was "Oh, hell no! Not *me*!"

For me, there was nothing better than chicken wings and fries from Kennedy's Fried Chicken, literally a five-second jaunt across the street from my apartment in the Bronx. And Kennedy's wasn't just *my* preference. Kennedy's wings and fries was an absolute *must* for most people who came to visit me from out of town. Once they tried those wings and fries, they wanted them every day. The food was addictive. If it wasn't the chicken and fries, it was a big plain or pepperoni slice of pizza. And the Chinese food spot was right next to Kennedy's. General Tso's chicken and fries was a close second as my meal of choice. Of course, the bodega was right next to the Chinese food spot. Wash it all down with an ice-cold—and I mean *ice-cold*—22-oz Heineken beer. Those ice-cold Heinekens were not even kept in the regular glass display refrigerator with all the other cold drinks. No. They were kept in a special white floor freezer that housed *only* Heinekens and Coronas inside. And such was the sustenance of a young magazine publisher living in the Bronx.

Of course, this was not the healthiest choice of food, but it was so *convenient* in the neighborhood and it tasted so great. Plus, I didn't figure that my diet really mattered. I was always moving. All of my walking, backpacking, train-hopping, working out and jogging kept me slim and ripped. I could afford to eat anything I wanted. I could afford to drink anything I wanted. And just because I could, I would often drink a ½ pint of Seagram's Gin (of course the liquor store was close by too) mixed with fruit punch and Seagram's ginger ale, and *then*… go work out; sets of dips and push-ups, followed by a brisk run from 168th Street to 161st St - Yankee Stadium—and back.

Ok, what's my point of saying all that? My point is that although I thought I was in "great shape" as far as my weight and ability to work out, I was far from my *best.* And I didn't realize this until Rick came back to New York in 2011.

As soon as I picked Rick up from the airport, we started "gettin' it in". We were at this place for an interview; that place to sign magazines. We had some snacks—pretzels, nuts, juice—throughout the day. But we really didn't stop for food until later that evening after we had finished most of the meetings and interviews. I found a vegan spot close to Rick's hotel in Harlem. We went there and Rick ordered. At first I was just going to let him order his food while I looked for another place for me to eat—some place with *real* food. But I didn't leave. I stayed with Rick. Partly to save time and partly because the food actually looked and smelled great, I ordered the same thing Rick ordered. And to my surprise I really liked it! It wasn't what I expected at all. The food was tasty and flavorful. Also, I could get completely full without feeling weighed down after the meal. I was shocked at how much we ate, without the "itis" kicking in.

After we ate, we took some food to go, and met up with some people that called Rick while we were in the restaurant. They had driven up from Philadelphia to meet with Rick. By the time we got done with everything, and got back to Rick's hotel, it was going on 1 AM. Rick's room had two beds, so I just stayed in his room. To drop him off at his hotel, take my car back to the parking garage and then go back to my place in the Bronx would have wasted a lot of time. Not to mention the fact that I was exhausted and we were getting up in just a few hours to do it all over again.

The next morning, I hopped up at 5 AM. Rick was already up, getting ready to shower. I was thinking he may have needed to sleep in a bit, especially with all running around we did the previous day and considering that we never really rested from the time his flight landed until we got in late at night. But Rick was up and at it again. At 5 AM, Rick was ready to start the day. Once again, it was another full day. And once again, it was another day of vegan food. Each day, we ate at vegan restaurants and I tried something new each time. Each time my meal was delicious. Never feeling tired or sluggish, we were here, we were there, and we were everywhere. We'd get back late, and be up early. I was shocked at how Rick was able to keep up with me. It was almost like *I* needed to keep up with *him*. I was already in the habit of waking up early—around 5 AM. And when I got up, Rick was up. And it wasn't like we were coming back early and then going to bed at 8 or 9 o'clock to get up at 5 AM. We'd get back at midnight or 1 AM (or later), and hop right back up at 5 AM. And now, it was actually getting easier for me to get up at 5 AM too. I felt different—lighter, more focused and more eager to start the day. When Rick came to New York the first time, I wondered, **"How was a man in his fifties moving around like a man half his age?"** And now, after being with him non-stop for a couple of days, I was starting to understand how.

For three days straight, we "got it in"; hitting as many spots as possible and making the most of all opportunities before Rick had to fly out. And for three days straight we ate nothing but vegan food—no meat or animal products. As I was driving Rick to the airport to catch his flight back to L.A., I noticed that I was getting hungry and I was thinking about going to the vegan spot later in the evening after I dropped Rick off. This thought surprised me a bit because in the past, my hunger would have led me to Kennedy's for wings and fries. But not this time. After three days of not eating any meat or animal products, I felt a unique lightness and a different level of energy that I hadn't felt before. I really loved how I felt. And equally important, I didn't crave the taste of chicken and fries that I was used to eating. Vegan food was just as delicious and fulfilling, but it didn't leave me feeling in any way sluggish after the meal. I actually looked forward to getting vegan meals. This time I was going to the vegan spot, not because it was the only place *Rick* could eat, but because it was the place *I* wanted to eat. For the first time, I thought, "Wow, I can actually keep eating like this and make it a part of my lifestyle."

This new lighter and healthier feeling showed me that despite my slim and muscled physique, I hadn't been operating at my best. I could have been better, *but my diet wasn't the best.* I hadn't been operating at maximum energy efficiency. Although I could stay up late, grind it out and get up early up in the morning, my stomach sometimes bothered me and I wasn't operating at my peak performance as far as my energy efficiency. Sure, if need be, I could go three days with no sleep. However, the thing that was allowing me to keep up with a hectic New York grind—despite my constant intake of wings, fries and Heinekens—was my *youth.* But Rick was able to move with the same energy, despite being in his fifties. This stood out to me in New York. So even before I went to California and found myself ridin' with Rick every day, Rick's principle of healthy eating caught my attention. At that time, I wasn't thinking of it as "KEY 2 – HEALTH CONSCIOUSNESS" for a book. I was only aware of how I felt based on *my* personal experience.

And from that point, when I saw the conscious application of these healthy habits in Rick's lifestyle, I realized the development of these habits—this health consciousness—was key to his success. Despite being in his fifties, he moved around like he was in his twenties. And here's what I realized about myself. Because of my youth *I didn't have to consciously do anything* to move with lots of energy. But here's what that also meant: Later on, once I got older, *I wouldn't be able to do anything* to prevent myself from losing that energy either. However, if I consciously started developing those healthy habits—that health consciousness—while I was still young, I could use those healthy habits to still provide me energy when I got older.

KEY TO SUCCESS

By the time I first went to Los Angeles in the summer of 2012, I understood how Rick—despite being in his fifties—was able to move around like he was in his twenties. Although his age may have had *some* influence over his energy and vitality, his health consciousness had a much greater influence over that energy level and vitality. In other words, his health consciousness shaved about 20-25 years off the age declared on his birth certificate. This was the impression I got from the previous time I spent ridin' with Rick in New York. So later, during the many months I spent ridin' around Los Angeles with Rick, it was no surprise what we'd be eating on a daily basis. To be clear, food and eating was never high on the priority list. It was business first. We ate to live. We didn't live to eat. Rick and I would often go the whole day without stopping for a big meal. We'd take some snacks in the morning, and as we rode from one meeting to the next appointment, we would quickly grab bags of pretzels, nuts and bottles of cranberry juice at the Am/Pm when we stopped for gas. But to stop and take an hour out in the middle of the day for the sole purpose of eating was something we just didn't do.

On the occasions when we *did* take time out of the day to go to a restaurant and "sit for a meal", the meal itself was not the objective of the restaurant visit. The priority was the meeting or interview that was going on during the meal. Sometimes it was just convenient to meet up at a restaurant, especially if it was during the time when most people stop working to have lunch. For example, when Jesse Katz was shadowing Rick for his May 2013 *Los Angeles Magazine* article titled "Freeway Rick Is Dreaming", part of the interview and some of the photos for the piece took place at a Denny's restaurant in Van Nuys, California. And even then, with all the various meal choices on the menu, Rick ate simply—oatmeal and tea with lemon and honey. Although he could have opted for something more "hearty", Rick's frugal choice of lunch signified his basic thought: *Even though we're at a restaurant, I'm here to work, not eat.*

If you've ever been in an office environment, you know about the "2 o'clock itis". Basically, that's the feeling of sluggishness and lethargy that kicks in around 2 PM, after finishing that big lunch around 1 PM. At that point—especially when you're sitting in front of a computer—the only thing you look forward to is getting off at 5 PM. The consummation of a big meal in the middle of the day is very counterproductive, because the big meal weighs you down and makes you feel like taking a nap instead of working.

Is it necessary to radically change your diet to become a vegan or a vegetarian? No. There is nothing inherently wrong with eating meat. And Rick doesn't push his eating habits onto other people. If you're around Rick and you want to eat a big box of greasy fried chicken, that's your business. You won't get a lecture from him about how you "shouldn't be eating like that" and you won't feel like he thinks his way of eating is better than yours. Rick's choice to be a vegan was his choice because that works for him. Furthermore, Rick doesn't smoke and he has a drink only on very rare occasions. But concerning your personal health consciousness, you don't necessarily have to go so far as giving up meat from your diet or totally eliminating alcohol. They key is moderation.

Below are ten things you should strive to do with the goal of developing them into lifestyle habits. Once you can incorporate these habits into your lifestyle, you will have set a great foundation for health consciousness.

1. Drink plenty of water
2. Limit the intake of foods high in sodium (salt), sugar, and saturated fat
3. Eat plenty of fruits and vegetables
4. Avoid overeating by eating smaller-sized portions of meals
5. Quit smoking
6. Exercise regularly
7. Limit the intake of alcohol
8. Avoid dependency on narcotics
9. Think optimistically
10. Manage stress

Of course, if this book were solely dedicated to health and physical fitness, we could list many other specialized "health tips" beneficial in improving overall health. However, in most instances, if a person is able to regularly incorporate these ten basic habits into their lifestyle, they will generally have a great foundation for their overall health. Once this solid foundation of health becomes established, other—more specialized habits—will be easier to incorporate if desired. And while people do encounter health issues and diseases that are beyond their control, a body and mind that has already been conditioned for health has a much better chance of fighting off those types of unforeseen health issues and diseases. Healthy habits can oftentimes weaken or lessen the effects of an illness or disease—if it doesn't prevent it in the first place. All things being equal, a healthy body can fight disease better than an unhealthy body.

Health is one of those funny things, because you can't truly miss it until it is gone. As I was finishing up the process of writing this book, I went away to Colombia, South America. Wanting a late night snack, I went across the street from my hotel and bought what I *thought* to be a simple mix bag of pretzels and tortilla chips. I didn't know that there were also fried pork rinds mixed in with the snack mix. In the middle of the night, I got the worst stomachache I've ever had. The entire next day I had absolutely no energy, no appetite, and no desire to do anything but lay down. I didn't want to write, go to the gym, listen to music, or venture out to spend time with the new friends I had recently made in Cartagena. I felt absolutely drained—like a shell of skin. My energy was so low, getting up to go to the bathroom was a challenge. I had obviously come down with food poisoning, and at that point there was nothing I could do but lay in bed to let my body fight it and recover.

Ironically, the very next day was one of the best days of my life! Why? Well, because the previous twenty-four hours had been so awful. I had regained all of my energy. The spark was back in my eyes and the pep was back in my step. Just having the energy to go for a walk was something that I had always taken for granted. But never again would I pass on an opportunity to be grateful for my health and vitality. And part of that gratefulness is shown by giving the consistent efforts necessary to maintain and improve that health and vitality.

I tell this story because it is very difficult to appreciate your health and energy on an everyday basis. Health is a free gift that is almost always there. For me, since I changed my diet back in 2011, I may have caught a "common cold" *once*. "Flu season" means nothing to me. I just don't get sick. I can be around sick people without catching their cold. That wasn't always the case. Before my change of diet, I might catch a cold or get a sore throat a couple of times a year—basically like most people. But now, I have no sick days. I just don't *believe in* catching the flu or getting a common cold. And that's a direct result of health consciousness.

If I do feel bad, it is because of something acutely wrong that I ingested—like the bad fried pork rinds in Colombia. But even in such a situation, my pre-established health consciousness ensures that I'm not down for long. A blessing in disguise, I was grateful for the temporary illness in Colombia, because it reminded me of how extremely important it is to cherish that irreplaceable gift of human vitality. Although we will all get older and slow down with time, Rick shows us that there is no need to slow down prematurely because of neglect or the lack of discipline to eat foods good for your health and energy. If a man in his fifties can move around like a guy in his twenties, what's your excuse? There is no excuse! Develop your health consciousness and you will develop yourself into an energetic hustler who can keep "gettin' it in" for decades—not just in your twenties.

KEY 3
BE A MAN OF THE PEOPLE

THERE CAN BE NO SUCCESS OR CREATION OF WEALTH WITHOUT SERVING OTHER PEOPLE. HOWEVER, THE INITIAL GROUP OF PEOPLE TO WHOM YOU BEST SERVE IS NOT ARBITRARY. EVERY SUCCESSFUL MAN BEGINS BY SERVING A CERTAIN GROUP OF PEOPLE—"HIS PEOPLE"—WITH THE PRODUCT OR SERVICE THAT BEST EMBODIES WHO HE IS. IN THIS WAY, HIS SERVICE IS GENUINE, AND THE PEOPLE WHO PURCHASE FROM HIM DON'T FEEL LIKE SIMPLY DOLLAR SIGNS. RATHER, THEY FEEL AS THOUGH THEY ARE PART OF SOMETHING BIGGER. THE LEADER IS ONE OF THEM. SOON, "OTHER GROUPS" SEE THIS MOMENTUM AND JOIN THE MOVEMENT TOO.

"I used to believe God put me here to supply everyone with cocaine."

–Rick Ross

TRUE STORY

I'll never forget a lunch meeting with Rick and several other people at a Manhattan restaurant. The lunch had not been planned beforehand. A friend of Rick's had a couple of friends who were in town and wanted to meet Rick to discuss some possible business ventures. As it just so happened, Rick's previous meeting ended early and there was some time before the next appointment. So he had a bit of time to meet for a quick lunch meeting since we were already in the area. At any rate, when you have those type of "on the fly" lunch meetings and people are short on time, it sometimes happens that you get people together at the table who wouldn't normally be sitting together at the same table.

In this instance, the "unlikely guest" was a friend of mine. She was from a small town, but would come down to New York to work on the weekends. She had family in New York, so she usually relaxed at her people's apartment before going to work later that night. She worked at a local gentleman's club and would often take the bus down to New York to make a quick couple of grand dancing over the weekend. She was young and new—only having been a dancer for a couple of weeks.

But this particular weekend, there had been some type of mix-up about when she was coming to New York. Therefore, when she got to the Port Authority, her people had not got off work yet. And she did not have the key to their apartment. She called me to see if she could stay at my place, but I told her I wouldn't be home until late. Because she really didn't know her way around and didn't know anyone else in New York, I told her that she could tag along with me for the afternoon. I gave her the address of the restaurant and told her to meet me there.

It didn't take her long to arrive. Rick and I had not gone into the restaurant yet because it was a nice day and we were waiting on a few more people to come. But once everybody arrived, we went in. As we all went inside and got seated, there was a look of "Great! We made it!" on the faces of the ladies who just got there. Again, this was an impromptu meeting and they didn't expect to be eating lunch with Rick Ross today. These ladies were a bit more mature and more professionally accomplished. They wanted to discuss the possibility of a literacy program.

Some bread had been brought to the table, but our waitress had not arrived yet. So there was some polite small talk around the table. Noticing my friend and her backpack, one of the ladies at the table casually asked, "So… what do you do?" Obviously seeing her as young and a bit immature, I suppose she was expecting her to say something like, "I'm a student."

Of course, I was now amused because I was the only one at the table who knew what she did; that she wasn't a student. But I had also known her for several years, so I knew her before she started dancing. Also, being a guy, I definitely didn't think there was anything wrong with her choice of profession. I was also amused because I was anxious to see the look on those other ladies faces… if he answered truthfully. They just didn't seem like the type of women who thought highly of "exotic dancers". Their conversation was a bit uppity and they were well-wrapped into the image of traditional education.

With no hesitation, and just as our waitress approached the table, my friend responded "I'm a stripper!" In that moment, you could feel the mood of the other "professional" women at table deflate to a sort of unimpressed "who invited her?" The uncomfortable silence and glances away highlighted their belief that my friend was now somehow "lesser than" they were.

But the silence didn't last long. Because Rick—as he's tearing a bite out of a piece of hot bread says, "Oh yea? That's good! That's real good! Strippers make good money! Strippers make good money!" In that moment, the mood of the table changed back into the light and jovial atmosphere that was present beforehand. Without saying so, and without making an awkward social situation worse, the message was clear: We're not judging people at this table… There are no "little yous" and "big me" here because there's good in *everybody*.

As I experienced that brief exchange and saw how Rick's attitude towards the young lady (who was at first considered "lesser than") changed the mood of the lunch, I gleaned a key to Rick's success as a drug dealer. Despite being illiterate, Rick had hundreds of people working for him in a business that can be downright cut-throat. Yet he managed to run his operation with remarkable efficiency. Why? This was possible in large part because Rick was (and still is) truly a man of the people. Rick had a rapport with the concerns of ordinary people. Those people whom society may deem as "less than" were accepted as equals by Rick. This is a rare quality, but one that generally causes people to go that extra mile that they wouldn't travel for someone who they can sense looks down upon them.

KEY TO SUCCESS

In the 2013 movie *Man of Steel*, just before the final fight scene between General Zod and Superman, Zod states the following:

"I exist, only to protect Krypton. That is the sole purpose for which I was born. And every action I take, no matter how violent or how cruel... is for the greater good of my people. And now... I have no people."

So that you may fully grasp the underlying *spirit* of KEY 3, it is well worth your time to watch that short clip in *Man of Steel*. The clip is easy to find online. Simply go to YouTube and type in "man of steel final fight", and you can watch it.

As you continue reading this chapter, think on the spirit of the scene during the first minute of the clip. Oftentimes, a picture (or in this case, a moving picture) really *is* worth a thousand words. In General Zod's brief monologue that occurs before the fight scene, the true spirit of commitment and accountability that Zod has for the people of Krypton—*his* people—can be felt by the viewer, almost as a tangible force. It is the same spirit of commitment and accountability that Superman has for the people of Earth—*his* people. So although Zod and Superman were not committed to the *same* people, they were both "a man of the people". And this is why the final fight between the "villain" and the "hero" is so compelling. Of course, Hollywood plays up the "good guy versus the bad guy" theme. In real life, the roles of the "bad guy" and the "good guy" are often interchangeable or unclear, but neither is effective in the absence of deep commitment. As we live our lives, it is not so much the spirit of "doing good" or "doing bad" that compels us. But rather, it is the underlying spirit of *commitment* to "our people" that carries weight.

This is mentioned, because it is with that same underlying spirit of commitment and accountability that Freeway Ricky Ross sold cocaine. Rick *believed* that he was put on the earth for the sole purpose of supplying everyone—including all his people—with cocaine. That steadfast belief permeated every move he made. As Rick put it, "I was afraid people were going to run out of cocaine." So Rick hustled as hard as he could, giving maximum effort day in and day out. His aim was to ensure that the people he felt personally responsible for and accountable to, did not run out of product for their customers; that they were taken care of. And whether you label him as the "villain" or the "hero", the key is that Rick was a man of the people. For a man of the people, running out of the people's product would have been a huge disappointment. After all, God *did* put Rick Ross here on earth to supply everyone with cocaine. That was the sole purpose for which he was born—*or so he felt.*

Now, here is where many people may be left scratching their heads as they ask the question, *"How can a man who got rich by selling his people an addictive product that destroyed many of their lives be considered a 'man of the people'?"* This is a great question, because someone who hasn't been around Rick might likely consider him—a drug dealer—anything *but* a "man of the people". Of course, the moral debate over how much praise and adulation should be given to an individual who did "wrong" in such a remarkable way, will forever be argued. Because as completely paradoxical as the statement sounds, it is true: *Rick Ross sold cocaine the "right" way.* And where truth resides, there is always something to be learned. Therefore, the focus is on highlighting the *way* Rick moved, not necessarily *what* he moved.

Again, the moral debate is a never-ending discussion, and one that Rick has never shied away from during interviews and speaking engagements. As a matter of fact, he is quite at ease conversing with those who wish to excoriate him for being "the bad guy". Rick seems extremely comfortable with this conversation because he seems to understand the reality of all people—including himself: *There is always some good in the "worst" of us, and always some bad in the "best" of us.*

As a society, we tend to label things as "right" or "wrong". And we tend to label people as "good" or "bad", without realizing that this type of generalized labeling is for our own mental expediency and convenience. Because life is a constant stream of complex encounters, comprised of difficult situations, things and people, labeling gives us less to have to think about. Once a person is labeled as "good" ("man of God" and "man of Country" are "good" labels), we want to assume everything they do is somehow good. Yet, the never-ending headline of "good" people caught doing bad things shows us otherwise.

In the same vein, once a person is labeled "bad" ("drug dealer" is a "bad" label), we want to assume that everything they do is somehow bad. And this is not true either. As I heard an old-timer from the neighborhood tell Rick, "You know why they love you? They love you because for every million you made selling cocaine, another $7 million came through the community. That's money that would not have been here—not in this community—had it not been for you. That's why they love you." Indeed, as a drug dealer, Rick Ross may have been the "bad" guy who did the "wrong" thing. But as a man of the people, *he did it in the "right" way.*

****

In the late 1970s and early 1980s, powder cocaine was expensive, often costing between $300 and $350 per gram. Of course, middle and lower-class people simply could not afford to pay such a steep price for a coke high. Therefore, powder cocaine was viewed mainly as a party drug snorted by rich white people—musicians, actors and entertainers in Hollywood or traders on Wall Street. In this sense, cocaine use was largely "segregated"—too exclusive and expensive for blacks—as it was available only in its high-priced powder form. Keep in mind, $300 in 1980 was a lot more money that it is today.

During this time, the majority of the cocaine being shipped into to the United States (landing in Miami) was coming through the Dominican Republic and the Bahamas. But soon there was a huge excess of powder cocaine on these islands, which caused the price to drop substantially. Faced with dropping prices for their illegal product, drug dealers made a decision to convert the powder to "crack", a solid smokeable form of cocaine that could be sold in smaller quantities and to more people.

The recipe was simple: By mixing in baking soda and water to powder cocaine, then artfully cooking it, the hydrochloride portion of the cocaine was removed with the baking soda. Left behind was a large insoluble cocaine cookie or rock. The large rock could then be broken down into smaller rocks of cocaine, convenient to carry and ready to smoke due to its low vaporizing temperature. This new form of cocaine—also known as "ready rock"—gave users an intense and immediate high when smoked. It was cheap, simple to produce, ready to use, and very profitable.

But even though the recipe had been developed, "crack" or ready rock was not yet a widespread commodity in the United States. Cocaine was still mainly seen in its expensive powder form. And therefore, the cocaine "color barrier" was still largely in place. *But then Ricky Ross came along*. Rick—because of the principles he employed to distribute crack—became the main driving force that made this new smokeable form of cocaine readily available to his people. And *his* people were the economically disadvantaged African-American community—a group to whom cocaine was formerly deemed "too expensive" for. Of course, whites smoked ready rock too, but Rick's focus—living in South Central L.A.—was the people closest to him. As early as 1981, reports of "crack" use were coming out of several major cities, including Los Angeles, Oakland, Houston and Miami.

In large part because of the enterprising nature and astute resourcefulness of Freeway Rick, ready rock cocaine quickly spread across the nation. A cocaine high in some 'hoods would soon cost as little as $5. *Cocaine—previously reserved as "the white man's drug"—was now available to everyone*, people of all races and socioeconomic classes. So now, the lower-class black man in South Central could get high off cocaine, just like the upper echelon rich white man in Hollywood. *The cocaine color barrier had been broken. Cocaine was now integrated.*

Looking at the spread of crack through the lens of the "integration of cocaine" may help clue us in to the deepest underlying motivation of Freeway Rick. As Rick stated, "I used to believe God put me here to supply *everyone* with cocaine." Obviously compelled by something much deeper than the average drug dealer's motivation for money, cars, jewelry and women, Rick's "calling from God" launched him to a level of success that no other dealer of his era reached. For a man to be *so* profoundly dedicated to a cause—any cause—is rare. And in these rare instances, the priming for such dedication often takes root early in childhood. So although Rick's cause—the widespread introduction of cocaine into the black community—did not sprout until the 1980s, the soil may have actually been tilled and seeded two decades earlier, in the young fertile mind of small black boy growing up in the South. In the 1960s, "equality" and "integration" were the dominant motivating factors for many black people in America, and it was no different for the Ross family.

****

Ricky Donnell Ross was born in rural Arp, Texas in 1960, and spent the first three years of his life there. Being a small child in the South during a time when blacks were not allowed access to the same things as whites—separate bathrooms and water fountains, for example—likely left a lasting impression on the psyche of the young Ross. In his autobiography Rick states, "Back in the '60s, Texas was considered a racist state, because blacks were still having to say 'yes, sir' and 'no, sir' to white folks. California offered Southern blacks more opportunities, and Mom wanted to give us the best shot at a good life. The only opportunity she had in Arp was limited, and that was cleaning houses."

Although the move to California took the Ross family out of a "racist state", the move did not shield young Ricky Ross from the impression that blacks in America were simply *not* supposed to have the same access and privileges as white people. Rick recalls, "I think that's when she [his mother] learned that by leaving Texas she couldn't necessarily escape racism; despite the California sunshine, palm trees, and positive image, our skin was still black. One of my earliest memories was during our first weeks in Cali when mom took me with her to fill out job applications. It was a "whites only" restaurant and we had to enter the business from the back alley because blacks weren't allowed to walk through the front entrance."

Now, as long as I have known Rick, the absolute worst thing you can say (or imply) to him is "you can't do that"—especially if he feels that your *reason* for thinking "he can't" is simply because he's black. Rick Ross believes in Rick Ross, period. And although the unprecedented success in the drug game and "insurmountable" adversities that Rick Ross overcame has no doubt strengthened his belief that nothing is impossible, the fact that his earliest childhood memories were those of "you can't" likely primed this steel-like determination he later exhibited as an adult. Those early memories of being excluded because blacks "were not good enough" lay dormant, but not dead.

As a child, he could do nothing to provide blacks equality via a seat at the white man's restaurant. But when cocaine came along in the 1980s, Ricky Ross—now an adult—*could* do something to provide blacks equality...via the white man's drug. Cocaine—the exclusive and glamorous "white man's drug" that people said, "...would never sell. It's too expensive for blacks" was now under the command of a man *unusually motivated* to include "his people" in on the action. Cocaine signified status, wealth and privilege—something largely denied to blacks in America. And Rick Ross—remembering that he had always been denied a seat at the white man's table, took full advantage of his opportunity to put his people on—providing blacks a seat at the luxurious cocaine buffet of the 1980s.

Ever curious as to the unique motivations of people who made insane amounts of money—I wondered the same of Rick.

What was motivating Rick deep down? What was he out to prove?

Could it be that Rick's earliest childhood memory—that experience of himself, his mother and people who looked like them (blacks)—being refused service at the "whites only" restaurant embedded an inordinate sense of responsibility to serve his people the "whites only" drug—cocaine? This thought process is not something that I have ever heard Rick verbalize. But in a nation that has historically taken extensive measures to exclude the black man from those "better things" reserved for "whites only", the irony of a poor illiterate black kid making a fortune off the white man's drug is the type of story that would seem completely made up—had it not been true.

Throughout the history of America—a nation whose proclamation is "that all men are created equal"—certain measures have been put in place to ensure that *the black man* does not view himself as an equal to the white man. I use the terms "the black man" and "the white man" as generic terms to emphasize the underlying premise of these measures. And that is this: If you take two men, one black and one white, *knowing nothing about either of them except their skin color*, "the white man" is automatically assumed to be superior to "the black man". Case closed. And it is from this position of *false inherent inferiority* that every black man has operated since the first African slaves were brought to Jamestown, Virginia in 1619.

Fundamentally, slavery cannot exist and flourish for any appreciable amount of time unless one group (the slave owners) claims inherent *superiority* over the other group (the slaves). At the same time, the slave owners also aim to impart a sense of inherent *inferiority* onto the slaves. And so, in America, the underlying notion that white people are somehow superior to black people is a false idea baked into the American psyche and cultural ideology. It was baked in when fair-skinned Europeans came to the North American continent and killed off the original inhabitants who were already there. The *original* "Americans" were of dark and copper-colored complexion. It was baked in when Africans were being brought to America as slaves. It remained through the generations as evidenced by the period of segregation and Jim Crow. But whether displayed brutally through slavery, overtly through segregation, or covertly through racism, the aim was to impart a sense of false inherent inferiority onto the minds of black people.

Now, the term *false inherent inferiority* is extremely important because, as the age-old adage states, "The truth shall set you free." The truth is that "the black man" is not *inherently* inferior to "the white man". Now—and this is key—*a* particular black man *may* be inferior to *a* particular white man when the two men are compared to each other in something specific. But, if he is, the *reason* for the inferiority is due to something that could just as easily cause a white man to be inferior to a black man as well. For example, if a particular black man is playing chess against a particular white man, and that white man wins every—or most—of the time, then we can say that particular white man is a superior chess player as compared to that particular black man. But the *reason* for his superiority comes down to factors that a black man *could* also utilize to become a superior chess player over a white man—namely dedication and practice playing chess. And so this type of "superiority" is okay because it is isolated on a person-by-person case, and *merit-based* on factors equally available to all.

However, what slavery (and its derivatives of racism, segregation and bigotry) champion is the idea that an *entire group of people* (the white people), are superior to another *entire group* of people (the black people), *based on a factor that neither group ever had control over or could ever change*—skin color. The race game—unlike the game of chess—employs a *non*-merit-based superiority scale. In the game of chess a black man can practice and dedicate himself to chess and become a superior chess player over a white man. But in the game of slavery, segregation and racism in America, there is no amount of practice or dedication that can make a black man superior over a white man. *The* black man—based solely on the fact that he is black—is always inferior to *the* white man. That was "the rule" originally put into place by "the laws of America" due to slavery.

Now, even though that was the law put into place by man (white men), the laws of *nature* say otherwise: The black man is *not* inherently inferior to the white man. And because the laws of nature are the true laws that govern the universe, they slowly win out (over time) against those unjust and false narrative-based laws put into place by man. As a result, after flourishing for centuries, slavery no longer exists in America.

But each step of the way—as the laws of nature slowly eclipse the unjust laws of man—those men who benefit from the false narrative fight to keep that false narrative in place. And each step of the way, when the black man argues the false narrative of his inherent inferiority, and figuratively "looks the white man in the eye" (blacks were once forbidden to look whites in the eye—literally) as an equal, a *racist* white man feels he must bring everyone's attention back to the original rule: *The* black man—based solely on the fact that he is black—is always inferior to *the* white man. And although the brutality of slavery is something that even racist white people probably don't condone today, a racist still harbors the spirit of that original rule that put slavery into place. *But that rule was false.* It was through the proclamation of truth—*all men* (black and white) are created equal—that blacks were granted "freedom". And it is through the continued proclamation of that truth that blacks fought the remnants of slavery—segregation and racism. It was not long ago when blacks could not:

- Drink from the "whites only" water fountain
- Go to the "whites only" bathroom
- Go to the "whites only" diner
- Learn to read (reading was for "whites only")
- Go to the "whites only" school
- Gaze or whistle at the "whites only" woman

Seeing the utter hypocrisy that certain things—the proclaimed "good" things—were for "whites only", was Rick somehow motivated to dismantle the false narratives of segregation and racism through his cornering and mastering the "whites only" drug—cocaine?

Motivated by greed? Yes. Motivated by power? Yes. Motivated by selfishness? Yes. To pretend as though Rick was not motivated by greed, money and selfishness would be disingenuous. But what was Rick *really* fueled by? "**What was**

motivating Rick deep down? What was he really out to prove?" While the subtle intricacies of the very deepest motivation of a person can never be truly known—even within self—it was very evident that Rick is generally motivated by the truth. And while there are many truths, for Rick—the truth of equality stood head and shoulders above the rest. Rick Ross was motivated by the truth in equality, and as a black man in America, he was naturally motivated to shine the light of truth highlighting *equality for the black man.*

I've often heard Rick say, "I want to show that a black man can do anything a white man can do." That's the truth. *The black man is equal to the white man because the factor that separates men as inferior or superior is not some factor beyond his control (such as skin color), but rather it is the factor that is within his control—the ability to think and dream*. Rick is a dreamer. But he is one of the very few people I've met who understands the reality of dreams: As human beings having the capacity to dream, we are limited only by that same capacity. In other words, the ability to dream of something is the *proof* that it is indeed possible. If that thing were not possible, then you would not have the ability to dream it. Rick is a dreamer and a realist at the same time, because he knows the truth that *dreams are real.* Stated another way, *it is impossible to dream of something that is impossible to achieve.* You've heard it before, but if you can dream it, you can achieve it. And *all* men (red, yellow, black and white)—being born with the innate capacity to dream—are therefore created equal.

It is often said that crack cocaine "exploded" in America's inner cities. And in this sense, the match that sparked the "Crack Epidemic" of the '80s and early '90s may have very well been one little sentence: *"It'll never sell, it's too expensive"*. In light of hearing this "challenge", and already sitting on a powder keg of "you can't" from early childhood, could it have been the opportunity to show "I can" that fueled an obsessive dream for one Ricky Donnell Ross? The difference between Rick and other "dreamers" was that Rick *believed* his dream. Just as he said, "I used to believe God put me here to supply everyone with cocaine."

And because he believed his dream, he achieved his dream. Unfortunately, Rick Ross' dream became America's real-life nightmare.

This new form of smokeable cocaine took off like wildfire, and so began the United States' "Crack Era" of the '80s and '90s. Freeway Ricky Ross strategically cornered this new market, and in the process, got rich off cocaine.

Of course, we've seen this principle applied in business models before, albeit with different products. *Do not let the fact that the product—cocaine—is deemed "illegal" dissuade you from understanding the principle by which that product turns to profit. Products change, but principles remain the same.* Throughout history, when high-priced, high-demand products are made affordable to "everyday people", riches generally follow. Henry Ford was celebrated as a genius of industry for his role in manufacturing an automobile that was affordable to the everyday workingman (not just the rich). Before 1908, when Henry Ford came along with his "Model T"—a "car for the common man"—the automobile was something that only rich people could afford.

The same holds true in the computer industry. Today, nearly everyone has a computer (or has access to a computer) of some type. But in the 1970s computers took up whole rooms and cost hundreds of thousands of dollars. Back then, the average person simply could not afford a computer. Even though those early computers were nowhere near as fast or powerful as the iPhones we carry around in our pockets today, the price tag (and physical size) made them impractical for all but a few large entities and corporations. However, Steve Jobs had a different vision for the computer. Said Jobs, "We started out to get a computer in the hands of everyday people, and we succeeded beyond our wildest dreams." Jobs too, was celebrated as a genius in the computer industry for his role in manufacturing a personal computer that was affordable to the everyday workingman (not just the rich).

And when it comes to cocaine in the 1980s, Rick Ross is celebrated for his role in the manufacture and distribution of "crack" cocaine that was affordable to the everyday workingman (not just the rich). It is worth noting that Henry Ford did not invent the automobile. But he *was* the visionary pioneer of the system and principles (including raising the wages of his workers) that made the automobile affordable to everyday people. Steve Jobs did not invent the personal computer. But he *was* the visionary pioneer of the system and principles that made the personal computer affordable to everyday people. And in the same fashion, Rick Ross did not invent the recipe for "crack" cocaine. But he *was* the visionary pioneer of the system and principles that got this affordable cocaine to everyday people. The lesson here is simple: *Find a reliable method and system to make a very expensive product affordable to everyday people, and you're on the path to riches.* **Cars, computers, or cocaine... the principle works for any product.**

And here it is that you—the reader—must understand that it is not *just* your product that will get you rich. In the early 1900s, there were many people who were attempting to manufacture and sell cars. There was only one Henry Ford. In the 1970s, there were many people attempting to design and sell computers. There was only one Steve Jobs. And in the 1980s, there were many people attempting to cook up and sell cocaine. There was only one Rick Ross. And so, while the product is important, it is the *principles behind the product* that bring in the big profits and make you legendary.

The key that unlocks the door to your profits is the *spirit* in which you serve the legions of people you are attempting to make your product accessible to. This is what being a man of the people is about. Without that deep sense of accountability to all those people you serve, you'll never discover that reliable method. You'll likely give up when you face adversity or quit short of that "Aha!" moment.

Here is a good time to clarify what we mean by a *man of the people*. Often, we hear about an individual being a "people-person". This individual is many times viewed as good-natured, friendly, chatty, and loquacious. Furthermore, they generally enjoy being around and interacting with other people. But being a "people-person" is not the same as being a *man of the people*. A "man of the people" may not be remotely endearing or chatty, yet he does have that rare quality, that deep sense of personal accountability to the people he serves through his product or with whom he interacts. It's that quality we want our politicians to possess—accountability to the people they serve or represent—but which they often lack.

When Rick Ross was selling cocaine, he was a "man of the people". That quality is still a part of who he is today. When it is time to come through and deliver on what he says he will give to the people—be it "good", "bad", "legal" or "illegal"—no effort is too great to ensure that he will come through on delivering his product *to those who want it.* And as I rode with Rick, I saw this spirit of commitment and accountability to people in action every day. If Rick was supposed to supply an interview, he always delivered. If Rick was supposed to supply an appearance at an event, he always delivered. If Rick was supposed to pick you up or drop you off, he always came through. Being a man of the people isn't just about showing up. It's more than that. It's more that you are showing up to bring something of immense value that is going to help the people. Of course, in hindsight, Rick can see that his product did not bring long-term value to his customers and those who sold for him. Many of Rick's guys—big time crack dealers across the nation—are still in prison today. And many of their customers are dead or still hooked on crack. However, when you know better, you do better. And today, Rick is employing this principle in a way that ensures his *new* customers get a product that is long-term beneficial, leading them to freedom instead of prison. Remember, a key—turned one way—will *lock you in.* But that same key—turned the opposite way—will *set you free!*

As you apply this key of success to your life, you must understand the value of what you are bringing. When you know they want or need what you have or can supply, you place yourself in the way of a stream of revenue. The fewer who can supply the people, the larger that stream is for you. The more people you can supply, the larger that stream is for you. In order to be successful in any entrepreneurial endeavor—whether you are selling cocaine or cosmetics—there is a certain *special* relationship that must exist between you, your product and your customers. This is called the special "holy trinity". But what about it is so "special"?

Well, do you think Henry Ford just thought it would be "great" if he could produce an automobile that was affordable to the masses? No. In the mind of Henry Ford, the relationship between Ford, the automobile, and the drivers of the automobile was a unique kinship. What about Steve Jobs? How do you think he viewed the personal computer? Was it something that would be "wonderful" if he could get computers to everyone? No. These pioneers of modern industry felt a deep sense of accountability to bring the best products and services to their customers. Ironically, neither Ford nor Jobs were known as particularly warm "people persons". Yet, their personal accountability to supply their customers with the best and most reliable products (regardless of their motivation to do so) made them respected in a unique way.

And here we see gleaming examples of the "holy trinity". The founder feels an unyielding personal responsibility to ensure that his customers get their product. This feeling is so deep that it is just part of who they are. It transcends a "goal" and it transcends doing it for the money.

Henry Ford was driven by an impelling feeling that he—and he alone—was the chosen one. Ford felt hand-picked by God to deliver to the world the first affordable automobile. If he didn't do it, then no one else could, and it may never come about.

And so when Rick Ross says that he used to believe that God put him here to supply everyone with cocaine, the average person may have a reactionary scoff at the statement as "immoral" or "unethical". However, it is much more preferable to deal with a person who feels a deep sense of accountability and resoluteness to do something others don't agree with, than to deal with a person who has a weak sense of accountability and resoluteness to "do right" or do something that many people agree with. Why? The reason is because the man of weak resolution will never get the "right thing" done anyway. While the man of accountability, while he may at first "do wrong", he at least has the opportunity to someday "do right".

People often speak of having a "mission". But no person can have a true mission unless they feel that sense of personal responsibility to bring people along—common people—and connect with their needs. You work so hard because you are the last hope. If you don't supply the demand, no one will. And that is why *you* are so important.

What makes Superman special? Of course, Superman is on a mission. But why is he always there? Why is he always saving the day? Because Superman knows that *there is no one* else who can provide the service he provides. There *is no one else* who can run faster than a locomotive. There *is no one else* who can leap tall buildings with a single bound. If you're falling off a skyscraper, the cops and the fire department won't make it there before you hit the concrete. But one person *can*… Superman.

And so, as we close this chapter, the goal is not to inspire you to go out and start selling cocaine. Rather, the goal is to inspire you to go out and do what you do—whatever that may be—with the spirit of absolute commitment and accountability to those you do it for. Who are the people you serve? Who are "your guys"? Who are the people who need and depend on you? Take on the responsibility of being the one they look to. It is often said that with great power comes great responsibility. But it is likewise true that *with great responsibility comes great power*. Superman knew that the people of Metropolis needed him and depended on him to save them when they were in trouble. He felt accountable to ensure their safety. In the 1980s Rick Ross believed that people needed and depended on him to supply them with their cocaine. He felt accountable to ensure they didn't run out. Today, Rick Ross knows that what the people actually needed him to supply them was not the product (cocaine), but rather the *principles behind the product*. And that is what he is now supplying. You can get rich off the product, but you *stay* rich off the principles. Serve your customers in this fashion—as a man of the people—and you will hold one of the most important Keys of success for any endeavor you choose. And always remember, a key—turned one way—will *lock you in*. But that same key—turned the opposite way—will *set you free!*

KEY 4
CREATE A COLD MENTAL ATMOSPHERE – THE "SNOWMAN" EFFECT

EVERYONE ENCOUNTERS ADVERSITY, OBSTACLES AND PROBLEMS THAT FALL UPON HIS LIFE. FOR MOST PEOPLE, THEIR ADVERSITY RAINS DOWN ON THEIR MIND LIKE A SUMMER DELUGE, WASHING AWAY THEIR HOPES AND DREAMS AND DROWNING THEM IN MISERY. BUT A SELECT FEW HAVE LEARNED TO CREATE A MENTAL ATMOSPHERE WHERE THE TEMPERATURE IS MUCH "COLDER". AS A RESULT, WHEN THE PRECIPITATION OF ADVERSITY FALLS, IT DOES NOT COME DOWN AS A RAIN THAT DROWNS THEM, BUT RATHER AS A BEAUTIFUL "SNOW". FROM THIS SNOW, THEY BUILD A GREAT MONUMENT THAT REMAINS LONG AFTER THE STORM PASSES—A "SNOWMAN".

"I try not to let things stay on my mind."
—Rick Ross

TRUE STORY

During my first month in L.A., I had to fly back to New York to finish off some minor renovations on my condo in the Bronx. There were a few lingering issues that needed completion before the final inspection and new tenant occupancy. Well, as coincidence would have it, Rick also had to fly to New York around that time. It was the weekend of a certain awards show in New York, and someone had got Rick tickets to attend. Although the timing was close, Rick got a flight and flew to New York, just for the show. I had already arrived in New York, so I picked Rick up from the airport and he stayed at my condo the night before the show. The place was empty, but we just needed a spot to lay our head for a couple of hours and get a quick rest.

The next day, as we were coordinating some logistics regarding getting to the event, Rick called the person who had actually got his ticket. But something was wrong. Someone had made a mistake (or someone changed their mind about Rick being in attendance at the awards show), because Rick no longer had a ticket or an invitation to attend the show. And no one had bothered to inform Rick of this change of plans before he hopped a flight and traveled all the way across the country from Los Angeles for the sole purpose of attending this planned event. How disappointing!

As we stood there in the kitchen of that empty Bronx apartment, surrounded by nothing but the smell of fresh paint, the level of the initial disappointment was palpable. In regards to an explanation about why Rick could not attend, the only thing the girl on the other end of the phone could say was, "I'm sorry".

But think about it. This was not like showing up for dinner at a restaurant a few miles from where you live and them telling you that your reservation was lost. Nor was this like the hotel not being able to find your reservation. This was a flight taken clear across the country for nothing—and no real explanation as to why the plans had changed, what happened or how the situation might be remedied. Yet Rick did not curse out the young lady on the other end of the phone or slam the phone to the floor in anger. *Obviously disappointed*, and with no one around but me, the realization of the moment simply sunk in. Rick is a human being, and of course he was disappointed—maybe even embarrassed. However, he didn't try to avoid the situation. It was what it was.

In that moment, I learned a lot about character. Bad situations and disappointments are a part of life. None of us are totally immune from them. And in this bad situation, Rick simply (after giving the situation some thought), got on the phone and started arranging his travel plans back to Los Angeles. For the rest of that afternoon, until it was time to leave for the airport, Rick helped me clean and paint the condo. And if someone had walked in and saw us working, they would have thought that fixing up the condo was what he came to New York to do. There was no hint or evidence of the major disappointment that he had just experienced. Rick's attitude regarding the situation was not negative. His mood was not one of defeat. There was no complaining. There was none of the "that's fucked up" attitude, etc., which would have been completely understood given the circumstance. There was just an individual doing the best job he could in the moment—with no regard for a circumstance that was now out of his control.

That night, as I was driving Rick back to the airport, even I was a bit somber about the situation. I thought to myself, "Wow, how disappointing tonight must be for Rick. Instead of flying back to L.A. after attending the awards, the only thing he got done here in New York was patching some drywall and touching up some paint."

To this day, I don't know the exact reason why Rick was not allowed to attend that awards show. According to the girl on the phone, there was simply nothing more she could do. Rick just couldn't attend... even though he had flown from L.A. to New York based on prior information that was obviously reliable enough to make him feel comfortable enough to make such a trip. You mean Rick's invite was no longer good? The *real* Rick Ross, who had flown all the way from L.A., was now not invited? Wow!

But although there was nothing he could do to change that circumstance, the mental atmosphere around Rick remained positive—as if this temporary "rain on his parade" had no real or lasting effect on the enthusiasm with which he moved. The rain on Rick's parade had changed over to a different form of precipitation. And Rick—rather than being soaked in a soggy puddle of misery—was now building something useful from the freshly fallen *snow* as it accumulated. He was building a mental "snowman".

KEY TO SUCCESS

"Think positive..."

"Stay up..."

"Keep a positive mental attitude..."

We hear these mantras and others similar to them all the time. However, in the course of our everyday journey through life, we often struggle just to acquire the basics of food, shelter and clothing (before even taking into consideration our attempts at living the "good life"). Due to this struggle, it may appear "unrealistic" or "futile" to maintain a "positive mental attitude". It can be quite easy to "get down" or quietly "give up hope" on the possibility that we can truly have things go our way and live the life we want. We believe so many things to be stacked against us—things over which we seemingly have little or no control. The more we realize this, the gloomier our outlook on life generally becomes. We see the gray clouds rolling in and hear the thunder begin to rumble. And as we get older, many of us subtly feel it quite foolish to "think positive", as our little inner voice echoes, "What's the use?"

Earlier in life, it was often easy to have a great outlook on our bright, sunny future. Sheltered from the harsher realities of life, our youthful ignorance and inexperience gave us a sense that our dreams of accomplishment would happen like they do in the movies. Those we looked up to in the movies or on television made success look easy, and so we got the impression that it would be easy for us too. Of course, we didn't yet realize that a master makes the difficult *appear* effortless.

But as we age and enter into adulthood, we tend to experience more setbacks, difficulties, disappointments, unfavorable conditions and tough situations. Those hardships eat away at our once positive mindset. Our confidence in "I" fades. And because the general mood and thinking that exists in the world is based on fear, we soon find ourselves swept up in the current of negative thinking that carries most people through life, with the crushing waterfalls of failure lurking downstream.

People often talk about the importance of having a "positive mental attitude" when it comes to life in general, and especially when it comes to dealing with adversity. But the nature of this "positivity" is generally misleading. Many times, the picture painted of the "positive" person is one of a happy-go-lucky, bubbly person mindlessly spewing anecdotes and catchy success quotes they saw on a motivational poster hanging in the break room at their job. Yet, these are generally not the people of the greatest and most noteworthy achievements. When real adversity hits them (as it hits us all), that poster on the wall isn't enough to keep them from mentally drowning.

So, how does one maintain a "positive mental attitude" and avoid getting swept up in the world's current of negativity? Well, having a positive mental attitude isn't accomplished through catchy phrases or smooth anecdotes. It's not maintained with the forcing of smiles and trying to "fake it till you make it". And it certainly isn't acquired by spending thousands of dollars to attend lectures and seminars by so-called self-help "gurus". The foundation of a positive mental attitude is actually something much simpler.

During the extensive time I spent ridin' with Rick, I daily sat in the presence of a man who—over the course of his life—had been hit with the type of adversity that crumbles most men to mere ashes of their former selves, and forces them to give up. Yet, he was always moving forward without blinking an eye. I had often *heard* people talk the term "positive mental attitude", but I *saw* it embodied in Rick. And when I saw it—when I saw Rick walking the principle that most everyone else just talked—the difference was like the experience of having a *real* glass of cold water on a hot summer day versus having a *photo* of a glass of cold water on a hot summer day. As the one having the experience, you understand the difference in a way that words cannot explain.

While Rick navigated through his daily affairs, there was no "rah rah!" or extra fist pumping. There was no manufactured tone of a high school pep rally with his daily affairs. Instead, there was just a calm, confident, steady forward movement; one that was inner-directed by his own thinking *instead of* being swayed by outside circumstances and adversities. And because this is *not* the response that most people have to adversity, I figured that Rick must *know something* most people don't know. I couldn't "prove" that he indeed knew something. But based on observing Rick and how he moved through adversity, I could find no justifiable reason, other than him being in possession of some knowledge that was unknown to most everyone else. But what was it? **What did Rick know about the nature of an individual's inner thinking that no one else knew?**

Based on his actions, my conclusion of what Rick must have known was this: **A man's *inner* thinking (which he controls) possess some type of power—a power that outranks all other *outer* circumstances (which he does not control).**

A MAN'S INNER THOUGHTS HAVE **POWER** IN HIS LIFE BECAUSE THEY ARE **UNIQUE**. And *that* power is the power that ultimately determines *that* man's lot in life!

That must be the secret knowledge that Rick was operating on! Regardless of the outer adversity, Rick always maintained a genuine positive mental attitude (or cold mental atmosphere, as we now call it) because he understood that *the true power that controlled his life was his inner thoughts. And those inner thoughts had that type of power* ***because they were unique to him***. Outer situations, circumstances and ideas—because they were not unique to *him*—had no ultimate power in *his* life—lest he be foolish enough to take them on and adopt them as his own. As a principle, that's worth repeating: *The true power that* *controls your life is your inner thoughts. And those inner thoughts have that type of power* ***because they are unique to you***. Outer situations, circumstances and ideas—because they are not unique to *you*—have no ultimate power in *your* life—lest you be foolish enough to take them on and adopt them as your own.

By "unique", is meant that what you generate in thought and mood is under your control, and *no one else's*. **No one can stop you from thinking exactly as you please or force you to think something you don't want to think**. As trivial as it may sound, *you* are an individual separate from other individuals for a *reason*. Consequently, your thoughts and mood are as unique to you as your fingerprint or DNA. Who knows why no two people have the exact same DNA or fingerprints? The important thing is that anything that is unique to you is an advantage to you. Why? Because the law of supply and demand mandates that if there is only one of something, it is more valuable than if there exists multiples of the same thing.

The fact that your DNA and fingerprint are unique to you is beyond your control. Your thoughts and mood are unique to you *because* no one else but you can control them (unless you allow them to). In other words, your thinking is the equivalent of your mental fingerprint that you can fashion exactly as you please. This is your uniqueness. This is your power. When you choose to not be in control of your thinking (which is what happens when you allow outer circumstances and other people to dictate what you think and how you feel), you give up that uniqueness—and consequently you give up the *power* linked to that uniqueness.

The thing I notice (and respect) about Rick is that his actions seem to reflect an understanding of the bare essence of this truth. Rick doesn't seem to "react" to what other people do or say. His actions seem to be in line with the *belief* that "you become what you think about", as opposed to that phrase being mere lip service. In essence, his belief that "you *become* what you think about" and "you *control* what you think about" means "You *control* what you *become*." It's as simple as the equation:

If A = B,
and
B = C,
then
A = C

In other words, if two seemingly unequal (or unrelated) things are equal (or related) to the same thing in the same way, then that which at first seemed to be unequal (or unrelated) is actually equal (or related).

If you **become** <u>what</u> you <u>think about</u>,
and
you **control** <u>what</u> you <u>think about</u>,
then
You **control** what you **become**.

Although Rick couldn't read until he was twenty-eight years old, one does not accumulate a fortune of over $600 million unless he is good with math. And so when Rick states, "I try not to let things stay on my mind", that simple statement carries great meaning because it is backed by his unique mastery of an equation that never fails—yet only 1 in 1,000 utilize to their benefit. Ultimately, *you* control what *you* become.

However, something within the psyche of man takes great comfort in looking towards *outside* factors as the reason for where he ends up in life. Human nature is generally apt to be up, active and moving around when "things are going good". But when "things are bad" and when the situations in life are not ideal, what separates winners and losers is the ability to keep going… even when the part of you that "feels" doesn't feel like it. It seemed that in a way, having and maintaining a "positive mental attitude"—which manifests itself in the ability to keep the mind and body moving forward, absent the obvious motivating factors—required a certain detachment, a certain character trait that might easily be misunderstood as coldness or even *heartlessness*.

But it is not that a person is cold or heartless in the sense that they are evil or looking to cause harm. Instead, they have slowly come to realize that *they cannot allow themselves to be beholden to all those temporary negative occurrences they will face in life*, because the only way those temporary negative occurrences will have any long-lasting power in THEIR life is if THEY dwell on them. If not, they pass. Tough times don't last. Tough people do. An individual must develop the mental toughness to think their own thoughts and project their thinking forward in the face of thoughts from elsewhere that would suggest otherwise. If you ride your emotions through life without being in control of those same emotions, you'll be on an out of control roller coaster. And when temporary situations beyond your control go south, you feel it impossible to move forward.

Your mentality, therefore, can be considered as your atmosphere. Your mentality surrounds you. And this toughness—this *coldness*—is the mental atmosphere you want to cultivate. Think about it like this: On earth, as your rise in altitude, the atmosphere becomes colder. Anyone who has been in the mountains has experienced this phenomenon firsthand. In the same fashion, as you *raise the level of your thinking*, the temperature of your mental atmosphere becomes colder. There are definite benefits to developing a "cold" mental atmosphere, which will be discussed more in KEY 15 - *Compartmentalized Focus*.

The situation in the Bronx stood out because there was absolutely nothing around to distract from the "disappointment" of the moment. Imagine the echo of a completely empty apartment and two grown men just standing there with nothing to do but digest the situation. And not only digest the situation, but digest it exactly as it was—no sugar coating that shit. Everything Rick had planned to do was based around that event, and now it was no more. It wasn't like Rick was in L.A., where he could just hop in his car and go to "Plan B", finding something else to do in his hometown. Already tired from the first flight to get to New York, he had to turn right back around, knowing the trip had been for naught. There was nothing else for him to do in New York, and no time to plan anything of significance. And the emptiness surrounding us in the apartment was only exaggerated by the fact that we didn't even have a place to sit down to help absorb some of the shock and disappointment.

But that was not the only time I have seen Rick deal with a tough situation. I've seen Rick lose his mother's home to foreclosure. I've seen Rick have people whom he truly cared about leave him. I've seen Rick betrayed by family members. I've seen Rick lose court cases. I've seen Rick lose money and be prevented from traveling to make money because he did not get permission from his P.O. I've seen Rick defeated, talked about, and embarrassed in ways that are tough to write and speak about. And on top of these struggles, there's the struggle that he's had to deal with *every single day* I've known him: Waking up to start his day, knowing that another man has stolen his name and likeness, is making money from it, *but refusing to even acknowledging his existence.*

Of course, these adversities can be viewed as "minor inconveniences" when compared to facing the possibility of life without parole. However, the way in which Rick handles these minor inconveniences is a reflection of how he dealt with his life sentence. Many people in that situation would have just given up hope.

To be clear: Rick does not have a cold *heart*. He has a cold *mind*. And there is a huge difference. A person with a cold heart simply doesn't care about other people and their well-being, and that's not who I know Rick to be.

I use these low points from Rick's life, not to "put his business out there" or highlight his tough times, but because it is no true demonstration of a person's embodiment of a "positive mental attitude" if all they have in life is smooth sailing. Anyone can "be positive" when the winds of life are favorable and at their back. But what about your attitude when life gets tough? The truest test of whether or not a person is actually in possession of a positive mental attitude is when he must navigate through the storms of life. Just as the true test of a sailor is not his ability to navigate the ship in smooth water, but rather when there is a raging storm at sea.

A unique aspect of my time ridin' with Rick is that my experience was not through the eyes of someone initially looking to write a book about the experience or conduct an interview. At the time, I had just completed a previous book. So my intent was promoting that work and experiencing the city of Los Angeles. Consequently, as opposed to "looking for something to write about" while we rode, I simply experienced what was going on. And even after I started making mental notes of situations that stuck out or made me think, Rick himself didn't know that a book was being written, because I didn't even know that I'd later write this book. Because my initial intent of ridin' with Rick was not "to write a book", I was able to witness Rick in his natural state, without gathering information as a "journalist" for the purpose of a "production". Things change ever so slightly when we are being "interviewed" or we are doing something for production. When we are being filmed or recorded, it is human nature that our demeanor changes slightly. Of course, later on I did tell Rick, "You know I'm thinking about writing a book about the success principles and how you applied them daily as we rode around L.A." He thought it was great idea. And because Rick is basically the same all the time, he had no problem with anything I chose to write about. He never tried to have me "include this" or "don't include that" or "edit that". All that Rick said was "Don't hold back."

Rick knew I had seen him struggle. Rick knew I had seen his mother lose the house—the same house where we made occasional pit stops in the middle of the day as we rode around L.A. He knew I was there when people close to him left. He knew I was there when he was living in a cramped one-bedroom, apartment in Long Beach. Including Rick, there were three adults and two young kids living in that apartment. And even though it wasn't the ideal living situation (at one point, fleas got in and were biting his kids), Rick always showed his gratitude to V and Ms. Judy (R.I.P.) for renting to him at a much reduced rate.

It takes a special person to allow another man to see him struggle through so many tough times in his personal life. And not once did Rick say, "don't tell anyone about that", nor did he ever attempt to make any excuse about his situation. Most of us want to "put our best foot forward" when we present ourselves to others. But what I've learned is that others are more inspired by our struggles, because *everyone* struggles at some point with something. But we tend to hide our struggles and exaggerate our accomplishments. It's ok to struggle, have hard times, and to temporarily fail. Like Internet billionaire entrepreneur Drew Houston said, "Don't worry about failure; you only have to be right once."

Throughout the course of life, shit happens. Mistakes will be made. Unexpected situations beyond your control will pop up. Setbacks will occur—even when you're earnestly working hard and moving in the right direction. When so-called adversity strikes, your job is not to sit there, bitch, moan and complain about it. In this mindset, you're akin to a person standing in the middle of a rainstorm and complaining about how wet they're getting. What must be understood is that the situation itself is what it is—H_2O. However, your inner thinking—your mindset—toward it is the "temperature" that determines whether you experience that H_2O as rain or snow. *The same clouds that pour rain on the coastline bring snow in the mountains.* As you rise in elevation, the temperature drops and rain changes over to snow.

Raise your mental elevation. Your mental altitude is your mental attitude. At this higher mental elevation, you will see your rain change over to snow. And once you have mental snow instead of rain, you will see the situation differently. Instead of feeling like an irritated wet adult, you are more of a kid playing in the snow. Here is where you build something of value from your adversity—a snowman. And what's so inspiring is this: *the bigger your adversity, the bigger your snowman.*

Positive thinking doesn't make the good things happen in your life. Positive thinking makes the things that happen in your life good.

Because of the complexities of life—the uncountable number of variables that are beyond our control—there has never existed a truly successful individual who does not practice this principle in some form. Those who cannot learn to create mental snowmen are simply washed away by the unpredictable storms of life.

To end this chapter, listen to this story about the Chinese farmer, as told by Alan Watts:

Once upon a time, there was a Chinese farmer who lost a horse—ran away. And all the neighbors came around that evening and said, "That's too bad." And he said, "Maybe."

The next day, the horse came back and brought seven wild horses with it. And all the neighbors came around and said, "Why, that's great, isn't it." And he said, "Maybe."

The next day, his son, who was attempting to tame one of these horses and was riding it and was thrown and broke his leg. And all the neighbors came around in the evening and said, "Well, that's too bad, isn't it." And the farmer said, "Maybe."

And the next day, the conscription officers came around looking for people for the army and they rejected his son because he had a broken leg. And all the neighbors came around that evening and said, "Isn't that wonderful." And he said, "Maybe."

Watts continues,

The whole process of nature is an integrated process of immense complexity and it is really impossible to tell whether anything that happens in it is good or bad... because you never know what will be the consequences of a misfortune. Or, you never know what will be the consequences of good fortune.

This being the case, what ultimately determines your life as "good" or "bad" is not the things that happen to you. The determining factor is your positive mental attitude towards those things. In other words, you have the power to *make all things work together for your good*, by choosing to create and maintain a cold mental atmosphere.

KEY 5
MISSION-MINDEDNESS

IT IS NOT ENOUGH TO DESIRE TO BE GREAT. IN ORDER TO SUCCEED, YOU MUST DEVELOP THE DESIRE TO BE THE GREATEST. THE AVERAGE MAN DOES WHAT HE DOES BECAUSE IT PAYS HIM ENOUGH TO GET BY AND MAKE A LIVING. THE TRULY SUCCESSFUL MAN—THE MISSION-MINDED MAN—DOES WHAT HE DOES BECAUSE HE BELIEVES HE CAN BE THE BEST WHO EVER DID IT!

"I didn't sleep much. I was on a mission. I thought they were gonna run out of cocaine."

–Rick Ross

TRUE STORY

During my time in L.A., I wasn't the only one ridin' with Rick. Author and journalist Mike Sager was in Los Angeles doing a feature story on Rick for *Esquire* Magazine's 80th Anniversary Issue. Also, as mentioned earlier, journalist Jesse Katz was along for many of the rides. On this particular day, Jesse was along for the ride as we were going to see one of Rick's long-time friends from the neighborhood—Cornell Ward. Far removed from his hustling days with Rick, Cornell was now a football coach. And as we had done at so many schools while I was in L.A. with Rick, we were going to speak to the students about the importance of education. This day the school was Los Angeles High and the students were football players who were gathered in the bleachers after their practice. The topic was generally about becoming the best person you can be and avoiding the pitfalls of drugs. It was mainly Rick speaking, but I got a chance to speak briefly as well.

After we left the school, we drove back to Rick's old neighborhood. It was at this point that Rick started to show everyone in the car where he and Cornell used to sell cocaine. We were about to turn onto 87th, when the question was casually asked, "So Rick, as you were out here in these streets in your day, were you out late or up early?"

As Rick seemed to reminiscently snap back to 1985, he paused for brief moment, and then replied, *"Both. I didn't sleep much. I was on a mission. I thought they were gonna run out of cocaine."*

At that point, there was silence in the car. No one else said a word. The gravity of what Rick had just said needed some time to really sink in. It wasn't so much *what* he said, as much as it was *how* he said it. Even though Rick was *more than 20 years removed from his last drug deal*, when he answered that question, everyone in the car *knew* (in case there was any doubt before) that they were in the presence of someone who was *serious* about moving cocaine. Not only was he serious about moving cocaine, but he considered himself to be the greatest at it. This was a real drug kingpin—the real Rick Ross.

When I heard Rick express his reasoning as to why he didn't sleep much—*"I thought they were gonna run out of cocaine"*—his words didn't strike me as the words of a "selfish drug dealer" trying to get quick money. Ironically, his words sounded more like what you would hear from the director of FEMA or the chief meteorologist on CNN as they are urging people to evacuate the coastline before the arrival of a major hurricane. As the storm is approaching, government officials, news anchors and those responsible for getting potentially life-saving information to the public speak and work with a certain sense of urgency. In these situations, everything they do and say feels serious. The reason: *They worry that people are going to run out of time to evacuate before the deadly storm hits.* Emergency officials and meteorologists are on a mission to save as many lives as they can by doing their job. And no one is more qualified for the mission than *they* are qualified. Consequently, they work tirelessly around the clock, knowing that the information and warnings they provide directly result in lives being saved. If they do not persist and work diligently to keep up with the forecast and supply the public with accurate warnings, people die. During such matters of life and death, *something* in the human tenor, posture and movement lets everyone around know that this is a serious situation. It was with that same *something* that Rick Ross spoke about keeping up with the demand for cocaine.

And here was the fascinating dichotomy of Rick Ross. He was selling a harmful product that was playing a role in *killing* people. However, Rick's work ethic and mission-mindedness to not fall short of his aim under any circumstance is rarely seen from the human spirit unless they are trying to *save lives*. On one hand, what he was doing by selling cocaine was "bad". Yet at the same time, the determination and consistency Rick demonstrated as he did the "bad" thing was undeniably admirable. In a world where so many people give just enough effort to save face, the rare individual who goes all out—be it for "good" or "bad"—stands apart. Although it is not "politically correct" to state, the truth of the matter is this: With the exception of certain crimes against innocent people, the man who gives a 100% effort towards "crime" garners significantly more notoriety than the man who gives a 50% effort towards "doing good". Effort is king, and in order to give all-out effort, you must be mission-minded.

KEY TO SUCCESS

If anyone ever wondered about "the secret" of Freeway Ricky Ross' greatness as a drug dealer (which can clue you in to the secret of greatness in your field too, as these principles are universal), it is summed up in this one sentence: *I thought they were gonna run out of cocaine.* In order to fully understand the gravity of this statement, one must first understand exactly why Rick felt that running out of cocaine would be unacceptable.

Sure, running out means selling a lot. And from the average person's perspective, if you're already rich and you run out, you just run out, right? People run out of things all the time. For most people, this may not be a big deal, especially if they've already had prior success and now have enough money to buy the material things they want. But from Rick's perspective, running out of cocaine—no matter how much he had already sold—was simply unacceptable. And it was unacceptable for the same reason it would be unacceptable for Dunkin' Donuts to run out of donuts, or Pizza Hut to run out of pizza, or The Coca-Cola Company to run out of cola: *That's what they do.*

The sole reason those companies exist is to sell that one thing and sell it better than anyone else. As we highlighted in KEY 3, Rick Ross was compelled by something deeper than the average drug dealer's desire for money, cars and jewelry. As he put it, "I believed God put me here to be the dope man." Think about it. If God Himself put you here for the sole purpose of selling one thing—*yet you run out*—you're just as useless as The Coca-Cola Company with no cola. MISSION FAILED! With this in mind, you work tirelessly to ensure that this *never* happens. You feel as though the deepest and innermost perception of who you are is linked to "that thing you do". Without it, there simply *is* no you. Now, you are no longer just working to make money; you are working with your ever-present mission in mind. So with Rick's belief that God put him here to sell cocaine, selling cocaine was all that mattered to Rick. While other dealers wanted to be *a* dope boy, Rick wanted to be *the* dope man. That was his mission.

Some would argue that this type of obsessive connection to "what you do" is detrimental to living a "well-rounded" life. I would agree. But "well-rounded" is often code for "average". And this book is about being a success, not about being average. Average people chase money—but never catch up. Mission-minded people chase their mission—and the money comes to them.

People want to be successful, but at the same time, the majority of people are so bothered by temporary defeat that they give up. Doing this, they essentially become "okay" with not achieving what they set out to do long-term in life. Most people give up on their dreams when they see that achieving their dream is not easy. Going to interviews with Rick is always interesting, but especially when the topic of "easy money" comes up. Rick is quick to debunk the notion that selling drugs is the way to make "easy money". He will quickly correct the interviewer by notifying them, "Selling drugs is anything *but* easy." Rick sees that this idea of "easy money" through selling drugs is widely held and sometimes unknowingly spread by interview questions or statements that glamorize the lifestyle of the drug dealer. At the same time, the "easy money" notion leaves out the myriad of difficulties real drug dealers face on a constant basis. Although the lifestyle of the drug dealer is glorified as fast money and easy riches, the reality of the drug game is often quite different.

Even Rick was not immune to the harsh struggle. Getting beat out of his first deal, he lost both the drugs and the money. On top of that, he still had to figure out how to get more product. Also, many people don't realize that in the beginning stages, Rick sold cocaine for free. He did this for several months. He could have given up—taking the average person's attitude of "I'm not being paid enough." But this would not have furthered his ultimate mission. In order to "make it", you MUST place yourself in a position where NOT achieving what you set out to do is simply not an option. So even if you fail in the short term, you would rather die than quit for good.

Let's say that in the short term, you lose, get beat or you don't accomplish what you set out to accomplish. If you have a true mission, your immediate short-term loss is okay because you will not allow yourself to quit because of that temporary setback. You're in it for the long haul because what you do is inextricably linked to your sense of existence. In this mindset, you don't take temporary loss seriously, because you won't accept it as final. Sometimes—many times, in fact—you will lose. Just like Rick got beat out of his first drug deal. You won't always get to where you want to get, when you want to get there on the first try. And it has to eat you up inside, *but not so you quit*. Rather, so that you get better, learn more and give even more effort the next time around. The mission-minded person is not okay with losing long term. The mission-minded person is not okay with coming in second place. The mission-minded person is not okay with the silver medal. The mission-minded person is not okay with the notion that anyone is better at what they do than they are. This mindset allows him to move through the numerous temporary losses with more enthusiasm than the average man, who gets discouraged as he associates himself with his short-term losses.

One day in 2011, as I was talking to Rick on the phone, we got on the topic of how the issue of *GET MONEY Magazine* with him on the cover was selling. I was selling copies in New York. Rick was selling copies in L.A. I had been doing really well that week, and after I told him how many copies I had sold, his immediate response was, "You didn't sell more than me!" *That's* the mindset of a person who is mission-minded. Under no circumstance is it okay for them to *not* be on top.

Understand this: The difference between the average man and the successful man is not *what* he does; it's *why* he does it. **The average man does what he does because it pays him enough money to get by and make a living. The successful man does what he does because he believes he can be the best who ever did it!** And because *why* he does what he does is different, *how* he does what he does is different as well. This is the reason that two different people can work at the same thing, yet produce completely different results. This is the difference between a painting by an average unknown artist and a painting by a Leonardo da Vinci. This is the difference between a composition by an average unknown music composer and a classic by Beethoven. Think about this: Do you think Rick Ross was the only drug dealer out on the streets pushing crack in the 1980s? No, of course he wasn't. But the average drug dealer sold cocaine *just* because of the money. Rick sold cocaine not just for the money, but because he believed he could be the best who ever did it. Rick was on a mission to be the greatest drug dealer in American history.

In order to be a success in life (which is presumably why you are reading this book), you must not only have the desire to be great, but you must have the desire to be *THE GREATEST!* If you work with the mission-mindedness to become the greatest at what you do, you will soon find that getting money will no longer be a problem for you. Speaking of money, the reason that most people continue to work jobs they hate (even though they would much rather be doing "something else"), is because that "something else" that they would rather be doing does not currently provide them a dependable paycheck. And because that "something else" does not currently provide them a dependable paycheck, they give all of their time and effort to the job instead. But because they give all of their time and effort to the job (so they can get the dependable paycheck), they never develop their "something else" to the point where it takes over and becomes their mission.

One must think of that "something else" as their mission in order to become financially free. You must be in it for the long haul. It is highly likely that in the beginning, your mission will not provide as much or as steady of an income as would a job. But being mission-minded means you have made a decision to do what you do because you believe you can one day be considered the greatest who ever did it. Anything outside of that which you have chosen as "your mission" is a waste of time.

Understanding this is absolutely crucial to becoming a success in life. Going outside of your mission just to make money is like cheating on your wife or husband. You may get away with it once or a few times, but if you make it a habit, you will find your relationship with the one you love ruined. So stop cheating on your mission with a job you hate. In the end, it "ain't worth it". "Legal" money is just as bad as "illegal" money, if you have to give up the essence of who you are to get it.

NOTE: While settling in to your mission, know that you are not striving to be the greatest at *everything*, just the greatest at one thing—your thing. As you examine yourself and take inventory of your unique talent and what you truly love to do, ask yourself what is the one thing that you can imagine yourself as being the greatest who ever did that particular thing? Find your narrow lane and own it. On this planet, that's your task: To discover who you really are and what you are here to be the greatest at. Then spend your time *actually working* to become the greatest at it. The result of spending your time in this manner is something called "happiness". And if you aren't spending your time in this manner, you will feel that you are not living up to your true potential. Regardless of the amount of money you may get from doing other things, you will feel unhappy and you won't understand why. In essence, *becoming fully engaged as you strive to become the greatest* is what makes life worth living.

Outwardly portraying this mission-mindedness often makes other people uncomfortable. The prevailing mindset in society is that because there are so many people and so many obstacles in this tough world, the goal is to just "get by". But "getting by" is not how we are supposed to live our entire lives. Although most of us feel that we are basically dumped onto this planet as minuscule "nobodies" who are forced to do anything just to scrape by, that initial struggle can help you hone in on what you can do to live the way you *really* want to live. **Because you are unique to anyone else on the planet, you are also uniquely qualified to do something better than anyone else on the planet.** You just have to figure out what that something is and give your *all* making sure that in that one category, your name eventually sits at the top as #1. It doesn't have to be something "popular". It doesn't have to be something that makes you recognizable to others as "famous". It just has to be true and fulfilling to you.

Whether you realize it or not, there are more choices of things to do than there are people on the planet. Even though there are almost 8 billion people on earth, your unique choices are unlimited. Maybe what you choose to do—your particular niche or style—doesn't exist yet. What's to stop you from doing it? The aim of this book is not to inspire you to become a better drug dealer. The aim of this book is to inspire you to be the BEST at whatever *you* determine to be *your* mission in life. If you focus your thoughts on this one simple question—"At what can I become the greatest who ever did it?"—the focus, dedication and excitement you put into your work will eventually raise you to the top of your field.

If you don't take the time and effort to do some honest self-evaluation, taking the mission-minded position of being "the greatest who ever did something" sounds unrealistic. But your self-awareness will allow you to see the practicality of this mental position. *Why should any person come in second place at the thing they themselves are most uniquely qualified to do?* It's like someone looking better in a suit that was tailor-made for you. There's simply no way that is possible *if* you give your best effort to look good in that suit. Think of your mission as your suit. The mission-minded person is not fixated on money. He is fixated on becoming the greatest, and he already has an advantage, should he simply develop the courage to just *be himself* and put on the suit that was made for him, instead of thinking that what everyone else is wearing is the way to dress. As you become the greatest version of yourself—your true self—you will also naturally grow to become the greatest who ever did what you do, because no one should ever be better than you at the thing you are most uniquely qualified to do.

Here's a simple question that can get you thinking more about your mission. Tell yourself: "Towards the end or after my career, when someone Googles 'greatest ________________________ (your profession or field here) ever', my picture should pop up." Now, answer the question, "What would this profession or field be to fill in the blank?" Be as specific as possible, based on the qualities unique to you (especially those you're born with) and what you love to do (not what you think pays a lot of money). Maybe it shows up as an individual. Maybe it shows up as the head of a company. You don't have to rush to come up with your answer. Rather, set aside time each day, thinking about this in a quiet and relaxed state—preferably first thing in the morning when your mind is clearest. Turn off the television and get away from all your "Likes" and "Followers" on social media. You want to get away from all the distractions that bleed away your individuality. Dedicating time to routinely think about this will allow the picture of your mission to slowly begin to develop in your mind and heart.

The point is that consistently thinking of yourself as striving to be the "greatest ________________ ever" gives such a gravity and vigor to your actions that spending time doing anything outside of "what you do" starts to seem like a waste of time. When you feel this to be the case, you know you are living with a mission-mindedness. This is not something made up. Rick was open about the fact that when he was selling cocaine, he moved past the desire of just wanting to get some extra money. He didn't want to just sell drugs. No. As he stated in his autobiography, Rick Ross wanted to be "…not only the biggest, but also the best, drug dealer in the City of Angels, if not in all of America. Nothing else would do for me. I guess it was something I'd gotten from tennis, an overbearing need to be number one. When you have a goal like that, and you can visualize it, feel it, almost smell it, you do whatever you can to get there."

Rick continued, "For once, I'd found something that just maybe I could be the greatest at. In tennis, everybody wants to be number one. Heck, in any sport they do. I brought that same mentality into the drug game, and I didn't want anyone or anything to stop me from climbing to the top."

When you have a moment, do a Google search for "greatest crack cocaine dealer ever". Under the "Images" tab, whose picture do you see?

We're not saying that you have to sell drugs to be great. But what we are saying is that you can learn a lot about greatness from a person who was the greatest at what he did.

KEY 6
GAIN INDEPENDENCE BY NOT WORKING FOR MONEY

MONEY IS A CONTROL MECHANISM. THEREFORE, IF YOU GET INTO THE HABIT OF WORKING FOR MONEY, YOU CAN EASILY BE CONTROLLED AND YOU WILL NEVER TRULY BE FREE. YOU MUST GAIN YOUR INDEPENDENCE BY NOT WORKING FOR MONEY. INSTEAD, WORK FOR THE LOVE OF WHAT YOU DO, AND MAKE THE MONEY WORK FOR YOU.

"If you work for money, you can be controlled."
–Rick Ross

TRUE STORY

Part of this book was written while I was in Colombia, South America. I felt that spending a few months traveling a foreign country would prove very helpful for my writing process. Although routine is important to create good habits, familiarity can sometimes dull the creative spirit. So even though I was only slightly familiar with one person in Colombia and I only understood a few words in Spanish, I knew that leaving the United States and everything familiar to me was an adventure that would daily sharpen my senses and prompt me to think outside the conventional box. Multiplied out over the course of a few months, the creative part of my mind would grow a lot stronger from the experience. So off I went! But I had no clue that my conventional thinking about money and what money actually *was* would be shattered on my first full day in Colombia.

My flight touched down in Bogota on a Saturday night. After taking a pre-arranged taxi to the hotel (which had also been booked in advance), I got some much-needed sleep. On Sunday morning, I awoke bright and early, eager to stroll around the neighborhood and get acquainted with my brand new environment. But when I opened my suitcase to get my toothbrush, I noticed that I had forgotten to pack one. No problem though, because I was in the biggest city in Colombia. Bogota has a population of almost 8 million people. And there was a shopping center close by, within walking distance. I started walking, and after about a thirty-minute leisurely stroll, I ran into what looked to be the equivalent of a small Walgreens in the United States. I walked in and when I saw an employee, I put my hand close to my mouth and gestured like I was brushing my teeth (I didn't know how to say "toothbrush" in Spanish). "Ahhh", she politely replied and gestured for me to follow her. And there they were—el cepillo de dientes—toothbrushes. "BINGO!" I thought. I picked out my el cepillo de dientes, along with some snacks, and took them all up to the counter.

The clerk scanned my items and rambled some price—in "mil pesos"—that I didn't understand. But from my experience, a toothbrush, and a couple bags of almonds and pretzels shouldn't have cost more than $10. So I took out a $10 bill and handed it to him. But he shook his head, "No." I was a bit shocked, but ok, maybe the cost was more like $10 and some change. It couldn't be more than $12 though. So I took the $10 bill back and handed him a $20 bill instead. Surely that would be enough. And even if he was charging me extra because I was using American dollars instead of Colombian pesos, I felt certain I'd get some change back. But he refused again. "Pesos!" This took me by surprise. Although I knew that the preferred currency to pay was the Colombian peso (COP), I didn't think they would flat out *refuse* the "Almighty" American dollar. Maybe it was just this store? Surely, stores in Colombia would accept payment in American dollars and simply convert it to Colombian pesos at their convenience. So I went to another store a few blocks down. But the result was the same. I was refused again.

As I went from store to store—each time getting more and more desperate—the reality was sinking in: I would be unable to use any of my "Almighty" American dollars to purchase anything at any store in Colombia. This was my reality, despite the fact that I was in the huge capital city of Bogota. And my problem was compounded by the fact that it was Sunday. This meant that none of the money exchange businesses—such as Western Union—were open. After a couple of futile hours trying to find a store that would allow me to make a purchase, my stomach was growling and I was insanely thirsty. I was even further irritated because I could taste that my teeth were in desperate need of a brushing. I had plenty of money in my pockets, but I couldn't eat.

That's when it became crystal clear to me. What I had heard Rick say several years back echoed in my head… "If you work for money, you can be controlled." Of course, I had heard him say this before—many times in fact. But now in the midst of this extremely uncomfortable situation, I understood what he really meant. For the first time, I was experiencing a situation where I could clearly see money for what it *really* was: a CONTROL MECHANISM! The reason that people who work for money *can* be controlled is because money IS the means by which people are controlled. Although people are led to believe that money is food, shelter, clothing, comfort, etc., it is not. For the first time, I realized that money was *not* food and comfort, because I had a pocket full of American dollars, yet I was starving. I had a pocket full of American dollars, yet I couldn't get a toothbrush to clean my teeth. Of course, in America, I had been in positions before where I was uncomfortable or couldn't eat because I had *no* money, but all that did was reinforce the false notion that money was food and comfort. In those situations, I thought, "If I only had some money, I could eat and be comfortable." My whole life I had been hypnotized into believing that money was real; that I could pull out a $20 bill and eat with it. And now, all of a sudden, I couldn't. The spell was broken. So this is what money *really* was—primarily a control mechanism. And that is why Rick said, "If you work for money, you can be controlled."

KEY TO SUCCESS

In 1963, Tanzanian secondary student Erasto Mpemba noticed something particularly strange. When freezing ice cream mix that was hot in cookery classes, he noticed that it froze *before* the cold mix. This observation—that a hot substance could actually freeze *before* a cold substance—was counterintuitive. It would seem that the cold substance—needing less of a temperature reduction than the hot substance to reach the freezing point—would be the one to freeze first. But this was not the case. Soon after, Mpemba became a student at Mkwawa Secondary School in Iringa, Tanzania. During a class, guest Dr. Denis G. Osborne from the University College in Dar es Salaam gave a lecture on physics. After the talk concluded, Mpemba asked Dr. Osborne, "If you take two similar containers with equal volumes of water, one at 35 °C (95 °F) and the other at 100 °C (212 °F), and put them into a freezer, the one that started at 100 °C (212 °F) freezes first. Why?" Although Mpemba's teacher and classmates frowned upon the question, Dr. Osborne later tested the question and confirmed Mpemba's observation. In 1969, Mpemba and Osborne published the results together.

The strange phenomenon—in which *hot water can freeze faster than cold water*—became known as the "Mpemba effect". More precisely:

There exists a set of initial parameters, and a pair of temperatures, such that given two bodies of water identical in these parameters, and differing only in initial uniform temperatures, the hot one will freeze sooner.

So what's the point of telling the story of Erasto Mpemba? Although we won't get into the detailed thermodynamic principles in this book, the Mpemba effect is an example of how a phenomenon that seems strange and counterintuitive to our conventional way of thinking may be disregarded as impossible… *when the principles behind it are not understood.* And if you are reading this book right now, I am almost certain that you are looking for it to address your one burning obsession: *How do I get money?* To be clear, in this context, "get money" does not mean getting enough just to "get by". "Get money" means having true financial abundance. You—along with the rest of us—desire to experience the phenomenon that is "getting money". And yet, "getting money" seems to be a rather strange phenomenon, as so few truly experience the process or see it take place firsthand.

Referring back to the story of Erasto Mpemba, the majority of us are like Mpemba's classmates and teacher. Because we so rarely have the opportunity to study and observe a person in the process of *really* getting money, we can only use our conventional way of thinking (much of which is molded by advertising and mass media) to explain how *we think* they did it. And because we don't understand the principles behind the phenomenon of getting money, if how they really "got it" doesn't line up with our conventional thinking of how people get money, we laugh it off or dismiss it as "Oh, *that* can't be how they got rich." But as strange, unlikely or counterintuitive as it may seem, the underlying principle behind the science of getting money is this:

To get money, you must understand that money isn't real.

What! Anyone using "conventional" wisdom knows *that* doesn't make any sense. "Money isn't real?!" The notion that you get *more* money by adopting the mindset that money isn't real is just as counterintuitive as the notion that you can freeze water *faster* by first making it hotter! And yet, if the principle behind getting money *were* intuitive and was guided by conventional wisdom, why are so few people actually rich?

Everywhere you turn, everyone is running around, frantically trying to attain money. But why is this? At first glance, it's obvious: Money is necessary to buy food and have a place to live (along with numerous other comforts). On the surface, this makes perfect sense. It's seems so "obvious" that no one really questions the need for money. But in this frantic struggle to attain that coveted dollar, we miss a crucial step. We overlook the fact that *how we set out to attain money is far more important than how much money we set out to attain.*

In life, things are either real or not. And across the board, here is the difference:

> With real things, what's important is getting it.
> With things not real, what's important is *how* you get it.

Money falls into the category of not real. My "financial hardship" in Colombia made this crystal clear to me. But as you are likely not in such a dilemma right now, let's look at the nature of money a bit closer:

There are very few *real* things in this world. When you have something real, it affects you with the same significance no matter where you are. Water is real. If you purchase a bottle of water in LaGuardia Airport and drink half of it because you are thirsty, you don't have to convert the remaining water into something else to quench your thirst when you land in Bogota. The exact same water that quenches your thirst in the United States will quench your thirst in Colombia. Oxygen is real. Regardless of what country you travel, oxygen is necessary to breathe. When you land in a foreign country, your lungs don't suddenly prefer to take in carbon monoxide instead of oxygen. Love is real. Love is a feeling that is felt the same 'round the world, whether written as "love" (English), "amor" (Spanish) or "amour" (French).

However, a dollar is not real. Possessing a dollar in a Colombian convenience store does not affect you with the same significance as it does in an American convenience store. While having a dollar in an American convenience store will get you a bottle of water to quench your thirst, having a dollar in a Colombian convenience store will simply leave you thirsty.

Another example is spoken language. Spoken language is not real. Depending on your location in the world, the language spoken may be different. Money and spoken language are similar in the fact that their *effectiveness* in different locations is dependent upon your ability to *convert* or *translate* them into something else. If you speak English and have dollars from the United States, you will be ineffective in Colombia unless you convert to Spanish and Colombian pesos.

The fact that you have to change or convert your money over from American dollars to Colombian pesos is a clue that money is not real. Along the same line, you have to change or convert your language from English to Spanish. And if you have to change it, convert it, or translate it because it doesn't mean the same thing to everyone, it is not real. By this very nature, *things that are not real can easily be manipulated and used to manipulate*. A person communicating with you using spoken language can lie to you and you wouldn't know that he is lying. But if a person communicates to you with love, a genuine smile or sudden laughter, you can feel it as real—regardless of what language either of you speak.

You've probably heard the saying, "The best things in life are free." The "best" things are the *real* things. And real things are free. Think about it. How much does the oxygen we breathe cost? How much does love cost? How about true friendship? And even food and water—how much do they cost… *really?* Sure, because most of us live in a modern society, it is much more *convenient* to exchange money for food and water. But water flows freely on this planet and food grows in abundance. Since the beginning of time, no animal placed on this planet has ever earned one red cent, and yet, for millions of years Mother Nature has supplied a bounty of sustenance for these animals to flourish.

At the same time, humans are not animals. So learning to "live off the grid" is not necessary. You don't have to go to the extreme of foraging for berries or growing your own potatoes and cabbage. You don't have to rely on the local stream to catch fish, bathe and gather drinking water. Attempting to live a lifestyle devoid of money is not the way to go for the vast majority of mankind. Animals—because they do not possess a mind as such—don't really have the capacity to feel "poverty". Give a roll of $100 bills to a dog and he will treat it the same as a rolled up newspaper; used to be chewed up and urinated on. But because money is a creation of man's mind, humans—having a mind—are subject to feel the negative effects of lack of money. This is especially true today, at a time when most people live in an area where the infrastructure has been put in place to make *purchasing* food and water easier (in exchange for money, of course), but that same infrastructure makes it nearly impossible to "live off the land" without using money.

And so we humans find ourselves in a bit of a conundrum. We really don't *need* money, because the literal money itself (by the way, it's just paper) does nothing to keep us alive. In this regard, a $100 bill is about as useful to a man as a leaf on a tree.

However, we really *do* need money, because we live in and have grown accustomed to an advanced society that has cut off our ability to live decently without money. So what's the solution? Well, we can't avoid the fact that modern society has been built up around us the way that it has, making it basically unrealistic to survive without money. Furthermore, none of us really *want* to trade away the conveniences made possible by this modern society. We light our homes at the flip of a switch. We get clean water at the turn of a faucet. We cook our food with the turn of a knob. We connect with people on the other side of the world with the click of a mouse. So we need to attain money for these comforts.

However, the fact that society has been built up around us such that we cannot realistically survive without money *does not change the fact that money is not real.* And as we noted earlier, with things that are not real, what's ultimately important is not just getting it, but rather *how* you set out to get it. **How you set out to get money is the key**. As a human with a mind living in a modern society, it is unrealistic to survive—let alone succeed—without money. But what society doesn't tell you—the little secret—is that *the intent of your work* broadly differentiates money into two types: 1) Direct money and 2) indirect money. Direct money is money gotten solely for the sake of getting money, as another man (boss or supervisor at a job) directly and quickly pays you for the time and effort you recently gave. Indirect money doesn't come within a short time of your efforts, and it doesn't come from a person. *Instead of working for money from a man, you work for the love of what you do.* And money comes later… *from the market.* This indirect money is the key to gaining your true financial independence in a world where having money is an absolute must.

True independence comes—not as a result of how much *money* you get from doing your work—but rather how much *love* you get from doing your work.

Once you understand this, you can reposition yourself properly to money. This repositioning consists of focusing your efforts on the love (the real thing) of what you do, instead of focusing on money. By focusing on the love of what you do—money from the market will begin to seek *you* out—instead of you always chasing it. If you go about it the other way—always working just to have money—you slowly become a slave to money, dependent on another man and constantly finding yourself engaged in activity you don't really like doing. And even though you don't like what you have to do to get the money, you keep doing it because you need the money. Of course, you'd like to stop (since you'd rather be doing something else), but you know that if you stop working, the money flow stops. So if you're working a job you don't enjoy, but you do it "just to pay the bills", you're basically screwed. You hate what you do, but you can't stop doing it. *You are being controlled.*

It's just as Rick said: "If you work for money, you can be controlled." And way too many people are in this situation. Way too many people work *for* money, meaning *their only or primary reason they do what they do is to get a paycheck.* They have no love whatsoever for doing what they do. They dread Monday mornings and live only for the weekends. Sadly, the majority of people have just accepted their fate: Misery for money is "just the way it is". People feel somehow *obligated* to sacrifice years of happiness as the cost of a barely decent existence on this planet. Soon, begrudgingly "working for money" becomes normalized as just something humans *have* to do—like eating, sleeping and going to the bathroom. But if you spend your best and most energetic "working years" of your life (generally early 20s through early 50s) resentfully working this way, you simply will not be a success. Thirty years of misery in exchange for a paycheck just to keep a roof over your head and food in your stomach is a waste of human potential. Life on this earth would have been better experienced as a squirrel or a rabbit.

As I rode with Rick, I always heard him say two things that really stuck out—although I didn't quite understand the deep meaning at the time: *"If you take their money, they think they own you"*, and *"If you work for money, you can be controlled."* Those phrases didn't click for me until I was walking around in Bogota with a pocketful of dollars—but hungrier than I had ever been in my life. Consequently, this Key has been one of the most difficult principles to grasp. We are all led to believe that money is real. But it's not. I learned that lesson the hard way in Colombia. At the end of the day, I thought, "Wow! I'm walking around Colombia with more money in my pocket than many people right next to me make in a month, and *I'm the one starving*. This is unreal!!" But it wasn't the *situation* that was unreal. It was *the money in my pocket* that was unreal. If money were real, I wouldn't have been walking around hungry in Bogota, Colombia with a pocket full of cash. My real need to eat, drink and brush my teeth didn't suddenly disappear just because I got on a plane and left the United States. Yet I couldn't pull a $20 bill out of my pocket and eat it.

We stated earlier in this chapter that money is primarily a control mechanism. But let's take a closer look at what's happening. A government prints up a currency on a piece of paper that has virtually no value. Then they assign an arbitrary value to that worthless piece of paper by labeling it. In other words, the paper (technically linen and fibers) that a $100 bill is made of is not 100 times more valuable than the paper they use to make a $1 bill. They just add some zeros, change the design, use different ink, and place a different president's face on the front. But these things don't make a $100 bill inherently more *valuable* than a $1 bill. If you had to do something practical with money—like burn a pile of cash to stay warm—a pile of $100 bills does not burn 100 times as long as a pile of $1 bills. If money were *real*, a $100 bill would provide much more heat than a $1 bill when burned.

Contrast the burning of cash with the burning of a real natural resource, such as coal. Let's say I have two pieces of coal, and each weighs one pound. On one piece, I write "100" and on the other piece, I write "1". I burn both pieces to stay warm. Which piece burns longer and gives more heat? Neither. They burn the same. We can do the same thing with water. Let's say I have two separate gallons of water. One gallon is labeled "100" and is being held in a green container. The other gallon is labeled "1" and being held in a clear container. When you are thirsty in the middle of the desert, do you prefer one more than the other? No, of course you don't. They quench thirst the same. The label or color of the container is irrelevant.

So a government can print as many or as few bills as they want, and label them as they please to assign value to money. In Colombia, the currency is labeled as Colombian pesos (COP). In the United States, it's labeled as U.S. Dollars (USD). But the principle behind each bill is the same. Now, for the people of a certain country—be it the United States, Colombia or wherever—that country's system says, "The only way you can eat, is if you give us back this currency *we have already created.* But… the only way you can get the currency in the first place is to *work* for it." And being a citizen of that country, you are subject to that country's economic system. Yet, you don't realize how you are being controlled as labor.

Now, in the big picture, this control of labor is of great value for the development of modern society and infrastructure. *Someone* has to give their labor to build up the roads, tunnels, bridges, pipes, cables, buildings, homes, automobiles, etc., that make society run smoothly. And in exchange for that labor, those "someones" are given money. And with that money, they can purchase others' labor or goods as they see fit. But, we can't forget that the actual money that is being circulated through the system to buy real goods and labor is just paper with virtually no value. And when *that's* what everybody is working for, the system can be manipulated and people can be controlled.

You may desire to become financially free, but you cannot do so until you realize the reality of *how* you are presently being controlled. The strings that control you are basically invisible because they've been there since birth, and because we so associate money with "real things" that we honestly believe it is real. It is not.

Activities such as robbing banks, selling drugs and counterfeiting money is "illegal" largely because they are ways of getting money that circumvent the control the government (who prints the money) wants to have over you (your labor) in exchange for you to have that money. This is labor that is necessary to build up the very society and system that the government governs. When people do not provide labor in exchange for money, government becomes irrelevant.

Therefore, there is a monetary system in place and the basis of that system is that the majority of citizens must work for money in order for the system to operate. This is the case, despite the fact that those doing the work would rather be doing something else. But because this direct method (exchanging labor for money) is the only way most people know to attain money, most people remain working. And so the system continues to flourish, as the laborers remain controlled by the money they need.

Now, this is not to say that the "control" the government exercises over its citizens using money does not provide benefits that we all take part in. The system—of using money as a control mechanism—is actually necessary for the basic functionality of the masses. It is sort of a "necessary evil" in order to have a functioning society. At the same time, not everyone in society is on the side that is being controlled by money. A few—a very small percentage—use money to do the controlling. And because the vast majority of people will never understand how the money they seek is indeed a control mechanism, the vast majority will continue to work for money. And because the vast majority of people will continue to work for money, the oil in the engine of the system remains and ensures that society will continue to grow and operate smoothly. It's a well-hidden fact that is quite frankly necessary to keep people blind about. Again, it is a necessary evil of existence of people on this planet.

Of course, if everyone suddenly applied KEY 6 and stopped working for money, society would immediately come to a grinding halt. And that would be a disaster for everyone—those being controlled and those doing the controlling. As of this point in the history of mankind, we have not found a way for people to comfortably exist and progress unless it is within a society where the majority of citizens are working for money. And so, things are set up in this world to ensure—by any means necessary—that the vast majority of people believe that they MUST work directly for money.

But, if you—as an individual—want to be free in this world, you must get out of the habit of working for money. You must work for the love of what you do, and learn how to make money work for you. You may—and probably have—heard this before. But even so, it is likely that your current position in life is such that you must still work some type of job, where you directly exchange time and labor for money. This is not to say that one should up and quit their job, neglect rent and bills and starve. The money you get from your employer is useful because you pay for your food, clothing, shelter, transportation, utilities, phone bill, taxes, tuition, other bills and many other things that make your basic existence here on earth possible. We all must use money to pay for our daily needs and basic level of functionality on this planet. None of us are different in that regard.

But here's the problem: It is very likely that in the course of spending your money, you don't use any of that money to purchase things that will put money back into your pocket *after you purchase them*. In other words, once you spend a dollar, you never see that dollar again. You don't spend a dollar that will reappear in a few years *and* bring a dime or a quarter with it. And you really don't think about making these types of purchases, because you are trained to expect your income to come from your employer. This is a mistake in the long term! Why? It is a long-term mistake because the money from your employer is given to you in exchange for your labor, which is going to run out. As physical beings, we all get tired, and we all get old and get to the point where we can no longer provide the labor that an employer will pay for. This is especially true when we feel forced to work at something we really don't enjoy. Then what? But, if you can get in the habit of having your money work for you (in which case, your money makes money), you will soon see that money doesn't get tired or need to retire when it gets old. As a matter of fact, the older the money, the harder it works. This is the opposite of how human labor functions. The older human labor gets, the less hard it can work, and the more often it needs to take breaks. And soon, old human labor must retire. And at this point of retirement, the labor is no longer of use to the employer. The result: No more income is generated by that person accustomed to trading their time for money.

Before that happens, you've got to slowly transition into investing a percentage of the money you get from your job into purchasing assets that provide you some type of financial return. The bigger the percentage, the better will be the long-term return for you. And that starts with the simple desire to accumulate long-term wealth (by purchasing assets) instead of satisfying the desire for short-term instant gratification. When you hand over your money to purchase an asset, you really don't "get anything" as far as gratification at the moment you purchase. You simply have put your money somewhere where it can grow peacefully, out of sight and out of mind. This is rather uneventful and it doesn't make us excited in the moment. Liabilities, on the other hand, excite us because we get immediate pleasure from our purchase. Purchasing a new car, a vacation, nice clothes, jewelry, shiny toys of all kinds, gives us a rush of excitement in the moment and make it easy to want to spend. However, after we spend, that money is gone. And it is never seen again, because the instant gratification that we just purchased (the liability) doesn't put money back into our pocket.

When it comes to financial matters, those who are apt to spend the majority of their money on liabilities never grasp the concept of gaining their independence by not working for money. Consequently, they work at jobs or seek careers where they trade their time and labor in exchange for an hourly wage, yearly salary or some agreed upon amount, based on their "labor" or "time on the job". If they produce a certain amount, work for a certain period of time or otherwise meet certain obligations that have been predetermined by their employer, their employer gives them money in return.

And so, because the employer is determining how you use your time during that period where they are paying you, they basically control you. Understand that it's not just the task you have to perform, but you have to do it the way *they* want you to do it. Your individuality takes a back seat to the company policies, dress code, standards of conduct, etc. And if you spend the entirety of your working years doing something you don't love—simply for the sake of getting a paycheck—you have been controlled, and you have been robbed of your independence as a unique expression of humankind.

The end goal is to free up your time to continuously work at what you love. But because working at what you love is the *indirect* method of attaining money, you're not going to see a paycheck from it after two weeks. Hell, you might not see a paycheck after two years! So, how do you eat, while you are working at what you love? It's a combination of 1) cutting back your lifestyle in conjunction with 2) using the money you save to purchasing assets that can generate income to cover that new modest lifestyle. You may have to keep working a job of some sort to initially purchase those assets. But that's fine because you are positioning yourself to have those assets generate the income to cover your basic living expenses and free you up to work at what you love. If you're really working at what you love, why do you need a plush lifestyle right now anyway? Live simply now, so you have more money to purchase assets, and have more time to work at what you love. Although you won't see money directly or fast, the only way to get rich and keep your independence is by working at what you love doing. Once money finally comes to you from doing what you love, it floods in, more than making up for all the prior lean years when you prioritized love over money.

Don't work for money. Work for the love of what you do, and let the money come to you.

KEY 7
SELF-RELIANCE & PERSONAL INITIATIVE

REGARDLESS OF ANY WELL INTENTIONS, GOOD WILL OR FAVORS DONE ON YOUR BEHALF BY ANOTHER, YOUR SUCCESS IS YOUR RESPONSIBILITY, NO ONE ELSE'S. YOU WERE GIVEN AN INDEPENDENT MIND WITH THE ABILITY TO CONTROL YOUR OWN THOUGHTS FOR THE PURPOSE OF GUIDING YOURSELF TO SUCCESS. WHILE OTHERS MAY BE INFLUENCED TO HELP YOU SUCCEED, THE RESPONSIBILITY TO SUCCEED CANNOT BE PUT OFF ON ANOTHER. FURTHERMORE, NO ONE WILL FOR LONG HELP A MAN WHO THEY DEEM HAS NEITHER THE ABILITY NOR INITIATIVE TO FIRST HELP HIMSELF.

"Anytime someone wants something for you more than you want it for yourself, you're in trouble."
–Rick Ross' former lawyer

TRUE STORY

While I was in L.A. with Rick, we visited many college campuses and Rick spoke to many students. I particularly enjoyed hearing him recall his legal encounters to law students, because they readily related to the system that Rick was battling against. On one such occasion, Rick spoke to a group of law students at the University of Southern California. As Rick talked about the struggle to regain his freedom, he recalled this bit of advice given to him by his lawyer years ago: *"Anytime someone wants something for you more than you want it for yourself, you're in trouble."* At the time this advice was given to Rick, he was still in federal prison, serving his life sentence. "It was worth all the money I had paid him up to that point," Ross recalled. "Up until that point, I had been relying on my lawyer to get me out of prison. I figured that since the lawyer lived in Beverly Hills, had graduated from Harvard Law School and supposedly knew law, he was *responsible* for getting me out of prison. But *I* was the one who was still in prison. *I* was still not a free man, and it looked like *I* would be serving the remainder of my life behind prison bars. And ultimately, that was *my* problem… not my lawyer's problem. To drive the point home, on one occasion, my lawyer also told me, 'Tonight, I'm going home to my wife and kids. *What will you be doing?*'"

It was at that point, Rick Ross knew, that if he ever wanted to get out of prison, *something had to change.* And that change—whatever it might be—wasn't coming from his lawyer.

KEY TO SUCCESS

The late, *great*, Steve Jobs once said, "Everything around you that you call life was made up by people that were no smarter than you. And you can change it, you can influence it, you can build your own things that other people can use. Once you learn that, you will never be the same again." I italicized *great*, because the significant thing that made Jobs great—as he admitted in this quote—was his understanding that *no other person is inherently smarter than another*. And consequently, *he* was just as qualified to do *anything* as any other person. When you grasp this, you no longer perceive yourself as a disadvantaged victim in life.

The disadvantaged victim mentality causes you to believe that *other people* are somehow smarter that you, and therefore have the ability to bring you up to a place in life that you cannot bring yourself. And consequently, you slowly begin to hold other people *responsible* for your position in life—be it good or bad. Sadly, many people have this type of mentality. It is a common reason so very few people actually succeed.

Rick Ross admittedly had this disadvantaged victim mentality during part of his time in prison. Being locked up and knowing he was probably going to spend the rest of his life behind bars, Rick was often down and spent lots of time feeling sorry for himself. He blamed those around him for his situation. Rick blamed the police, he blamed the courts, he blamed Danilo Blandon, and he especially blamed his lawyer. And why did Rick blame his lawyer so much? Well, it only made sense at the time, because as Rick recalled, "I used to think my lawyer was smarter than me. But now I know that's not true."

Understand: When you take on the mentality that another person is "smarter" than you—or "richer" or "prettier" or "whatever-er"—you are not only creating a false narrative in your head, but you are also holding that person subtly responsible for using their "advantage" (as you see it) to help you out. And when they don't do it, you become bitter, angry and frustrated. You feel like the disadvantaged victim who needs help, but can't get it.

However, the best help you are ever going to get in this world is always going to come from *you*. Why? Because no other person is inherently smarter than you, and everything changes the moment you realize this. Rick Ross realized this when his lawyer told him *"Anytime someone wants something for you more than you want it for yourself, you're in trouble."* That was the changing point—Rick Ross' point of realization. Rick finally understood that the key to unlock his prison cell was not a physical key held by any lawyer, judge or P.O. Instead, it was a *mental key* that he *always* had access to, but was not using in the right direction. That key was called *personal initiative*.

And from that point of realization, Rick began turning that mental key of personal initiative to develop steadfast self-reliance. Rick Ross began relying on Rick Ross (not his lawyer) to free Rick Ross. He began spending as much time as he could in the law library trying to figure out the details of his case and exactly *why* he was sentenced to serve so much time. He had heard of the "Three Strikes" law, but now he had to figure out how it applied to him if he ever wanted to see the outside world again. By means of his diligent personal initiative and self-reliance, Rick Ross found the *actual sentence* in the law books that stated he was *not* supposed to be serving a life sentence for the crime he committed. His case did not meet the qualification for "3 Strikes Law".

However, when he brought this clause to the attention of his lawyer, the lawyer responded that it didn't apply to Rick. Yet Rick again took the initiative to bring it up during his petition, and he won! The percentage of inmates who beat a life sentence is astonishingly slim, and those who do, win because of the initiative they take to free themselves.

This key stayed with Rick as a free man. As I rode around L.A. with Rick, one thing he always stressed was this: **Just because a person has a particular skill in a certain area—**

such as law—does not mean they are going to necessarily use that skill to benefit *you*. Once you ponder the significance of this truth, you'll recognize that *ability* does not equate to *responsibility*.

Rick Ross is a free man today not because he paid his lawyer millions of dollars to win his case, but because he used his own initiative and took responsibility for finding how he could get himself out of prison. He found the exact sentence in a law book that freed him because he stayed in the law library and diligently worked at understanding the law, himself, and his case. He knew that it was—at the end of the day—*his* responsibility to free himself, *because he was the one sitting in prison*. Had Rick Ross not taken the initiative to study his own case, understanding his responsibility to fight for himself, he would still be in prison today.

This process that Rick went through to overturn his life sentence is crucially important for any person who wants to be a "success" in life. Few situations in life are as bleak as serving life in prison. And so as each of us face life's challenges, we should be encouraged that we absolutely have what it takes to overcome—*if we can practice personal initiative instead of relying on others to solve our problems for us*. If you wait on someone else to "hook you up", "put you on" or "take care of you", you're going to be waiting around, in the same spot, for a long time without making any real progress. When dealing with others, you must grasp the reality that *ability* does not equate to *responsibility*. Rick Ross doesn't wait on anyone to do anything for him, and neither should you. Rick's prison experience showed him firsthand the power of personal initiative. And he knows it is the reason he is walking the streets as a free man today.

I often say of Rick, he 'smells of independence'. What I mean by that is that when you're with or around Rick, you can just sense that you are around a person who *ain't waitin'* around for you. Now, for people who know the story about how Rick overturned his life sentence by not waitin' around for anybody, it is clear why this man doesn't believe in waiting on people. But for some people, Rick's deep-rooted belief in personal initiative and self-reliance is mistaken for rudeness. Here's a few example of what I mean:

- When you're ridin' with Rick, and you get to where you are going and stop to get out, *Rick will just get out and go in.* Rick is not going to wait on you to see if you made it into the building or even turn around to see if you made it out of the car. You will make it in when you make it in, and that's that. And when it's time to go, if you're not ready, you're just gonna be left. (Ironically, if he tells you he is going to pick you up or drop you off, you can bet on him being there.)
- If you're talking to Rick face to face, and his phone rings, he'll just answer his phone without acknowledging you—even if you're in mid-sentence.
- If you're talking on the phone to Rick, and he's got another call, he'll say "Hold on", but he won't wait for you to say anything before clicks over.
- When Rick is on the phone, when he's done talking, he immediately hangs up.

- Rick will walk out of the room without saying "Goodbye".

Now, I mention all these examples because our society has encouraged most of us to pad our words and actions towards each other with all sorts of niceties (that we don't really mean) to get in "good favor" with people who can help us out. But all too often, what this false "politeness" really does is help weaken our own self-reliance, because we subtly feel like how we act towards others is the *key* to our ultimate success or failure. It is not. They key to success is our very own personal initiative. Success waits for no man. And if you wait on any man, success will leave the both of you. The beauty in this is that it's also why no man can *stop* you from succeeding—if you're truly determined to make it. Of course, if you want to be nice and cordial, that's fine, but not in an effort to win people over to do for you what you should be doing for yourself. Most people haven't yet grasped the belief that EVERY INDIVIDUAL IS SOLELY RESPONSIBLE FOR HIS OR HER OWN SUCCESS OR FAILURE.

But with Rick Ross, you're dealing with an individual who has deeply **internalized** this principle of personal initiative because he *knows* that without his self-reliance, he would still be locked away in a prison cell. Hence, one can then understand why this type of person sees all the "padded niceties" that most people use in their speech and actions to get people to do things for them is really a waste of time.

Initiative and self-reliance are closely related. There were many times when Rick and I would be at the gas station and a guy would come up asking for money. Rick's reply: "Come on man…Why you ain't got $1 in your pocket? You supposed to keep *some* money on you." Rick was not harsh or selfish. Instead, his intent was to get people to think about exactly why they felt unable to rely on themselves to do for themselves. When people would come asking for small amounts of money *just to get by*, Rick saw their problem not as needing money, but needing initiative and self-reliance. It cannot be overstated that Rick *knew* that he'd still be in prison had he not had the ability to rely on himself. And he knows that millions of people today are still locked in their own mental prisons because they don't know how to use their key to freedom—personal initiative.

The sentence in the law book that Rick found to overturn his life sentence was incidental. It had been there the whole time. But it was of no use to Rick *until* he used his very own personal initiative to find it. That was the key. That's what freed Rick Ross. And that key of personal initiative will free you too, from any of life's difficult situations. But you must use it, and learn to rely upon yourself… to free yourself.

KEY 8
THE RE-UP

AFTER HAVING A BIT OF INITIAL SUCCESS IN BUSINESS, MOST PEOPLE DO THE WRONG THING WITH THE MONEY. INSTEAD OF REINVESTING THEIR PROFITS BACK INTO THE BUSINESS TO BUY LARGER QUANTITIES OF PRODUCT AT BETTER PRICES, THEY WASTE THEIR PROFITS ON LUXURY ITEMS. THESE LUXURY ITEMS—SUCH AS CARS, JEWELRY, AND EXPENSIVE CLOTHES—DO NOT GENERATE INCOME, YET THEY REQUIRE ADDITIONAL MONEY TO MAINTAIN. IN ORDER TO FULLY LEVERAGE YOUR BUSINESS, YOU MUST PUT THE SMALL DOLLARS BACK TO WORK SO THAT THEY ATTRACT AND GROW BIGGER DOLLARS.

"Danilo was trying to get to me. All those Nicaraguans were trying to get to me because I was the only one with the money. Nobody else had a million dollars. Other dudes might get a key and make $5,000 profit. I'd get keys for $48,000 and triple my money, because I was buying so much."

—Rick Ross

TRUE STORY

After his once-promising tennis career didn't pan out, the 18-year-old Ross couldn't see many options to make something of his life. He couldn't read. He wasn't going to college, and he had to grapple with the dilemma of trying to make money in South Central Los Angeles, where most people just didn't appear to have a lot of money. The situation seemed bleak. But things changed the day Mike—an old friend of Rick's—turned him on to a small amount of rock-like powder, supposedly worth no less than $50. Although *taking* the drug did nothing for Rick, the idea that something so small could *sell* for so much intrigued and excited him. So shortly after Rick's introduction to cocaine, he and another friend (Ollie) officially started out in the drug business. The initial investment they needed? It was just $125 apiece to get started.

Although Rick Ross eventually became the most notable drug dealer to come out of L.A., he definitely wasn't the first. As a matter of fact, before Rick ever touched his first rock, two of his other friends were already selling drugs. One of his friends was selling PCP, and the other was selling marijuana. Rick knew that they had some money because they had already been selling drugs. And because they already had money, Rick figured they would be great candidates to turn on to the cocaine game.

So Rick got them going in the cocaine business. They did pretty good starting out and when they all got up to about $8,000, each one made a decision on what to do with their money. One of Rick's friends bought a Cadillac. The other bought a van. Rick, on the other hand, *bought eight more ounces of cocaine*. While the cars that his friends bought were nice, and brought a sense of initial happiness, Rick noticed something: *"They had to keep putting more and more money into maintaining those cars, but those cars weren't making them any money,"* Rick recalled. *"On top of that, I noticed that all the guys who had new cars and clothes were working for me."*

Rick's decision to **reinvest** his profits back into buying more cocaine meant that he could now buy larger quantities of cocaine. And because Rick was buying larger quantities of cocaine, his supplier began to give him a discount of $300 per ounce. His two friends on the other hand, never saved up enough money to purchase in large quantities, so they would never receive any discount. Eventually, Rick's supplier no longer wanted to sell to Rick's other two friends because they could only buy ounces. The supplier told them that if they wanted to buy ounces, then they would have to buy them from Rick.

KEY TO SUCCESS

Everyone who is in business with a product to sell must re-up in some way, form or fashion. Once customers buy, you must replenish your supply so that you can sell to more customers. If one starts out with 100 widgets and then sells 50 of those widgets in two days, he must very soon re-up the supply of widgets if he wants to keep selling them. If not, he will soon be out of business. There's nothing difficult about understanding this. *But most people don't re-up properly.* Most people buy small quantities of product and make a relatively small—if any—profit when they sell. Then, they take those small profits and put the money towards buying things like cars, clothes, jewelry and other things that don't make them any more money. And lo and behold, when it's time to buy more product—when it's time to re-up—they are paying the exact same price they paid last time, because they again only have enough money to buy small quantities. This purchase of small quantities again forces them to pay a higher price. And this cycle of no growth continues until the business eventually dies.

Most businesses fail because resources are not properly and efficiently managed in a way that allows profits to grow. Andrew Carnegie—the richest man in the world for a period during the early 20th century—ran U.S. Steel under the belief that *if you take care of the pennies, the profits will take care of themselves.*

In order to not be constantly dependent on other people for the things you need, it is absolutely crucial that you habitually set aside your money and resources so that you can reinvest back into yourself and your business. If you never learn to flip a little into a lot, everything that you purchase will be bought at retail price, leaving you no room for any real profit.

This efficiency translates into your time and all of your resources of value. Those people who squander money, time and other resources will never be financially free because they can never set aside enough money to purchase in bulk. *The best prices are reserved for those who purchase in large quantities.* And the better the price at which you purchase, the better the price at which you can afford to sell. And the better your prices, the more people want to buy from you. So not only do you have the option of increasing your profit margin on each sale, but you also have the option of being an affordable and attractive buy to more customers. And if you can constantly reinvest into yourself to the point where you begin buying in huge quantities, you can lower prices to the point where no other sellers can compete. Early on, this was a principle that Rick Ross deeply understood and religiously applied. It was the key that turned $125 into $600 million.

Some people might say that Rick was "lucky" to eventually run into Danilo Blandon and begin getting his cocaine at those remarkably low prices. "Well, if Rick was not getting his drugs from Blandon at such a cheap price, and instead had to pay the same price as everyone else, then Rick would have never been able to make such huge profits," some would argue. However, the reality of the situation is that Rick made his own luck, because *it was Blandon who was trying to get to Rick.* Why? Because Rick was the one who had the money to buy fifty to one hundred kilos at a time. Rick didn't just get a chance to hook up with Blandon because Blandon *liked* Rick. Danilo Blandon didn't care if the person was named "Rick Ross", "Peter", "Paul" or "George"... any John Doe would have sufficed. It could have easily been someone else. But it could *not* have been someone who only had enough money to buy a brick or two. At that level of the game, a kilo would be a waste of time. As a matter of fact, Rick had to pay $60,000 just to meet with Blandon. In turn, Blandon also paid $60,000 to meet with Rick.

So as it turned out, it was the person who applied the re-up principle that attracted Danilo Blandon's attention. By re-ing up—from $50 worth of cocaine to three grams, to a ½ ounce to an ounce to a pound to a kilo and so on and so forth—Rick went from scraping up a few hundred dollars to cop an eight-track to moving one hundred kilograms of cocaine per day. The person with the money was who Blandon was looking for. And that person was Rick Ross, because Rick knew that the principle of reinvesting back into himself to re-up was the crucial key to getting more keys of cocaine. And it is the crucial key to you as well, whatever your business may be.

As Rick noted in his autobiography, "Guys who I thought were doing better than me were becoming my workers." The reason they were becoming Rick's workers is because they were violating the re-up principle. For young entrepreneurs, the re-up is one of the most violated keys to success. Everyone has heard that "It's not how much you make… It's how much you keep." Maybe the saying should be "It's not how much you make… It's how much you keep *in the business*." You can learn a lot from a drug dealer, because a successful drug dealer is a master at the re-up principle.

Unfortunately, many people will continue to miss the underlying importance of this principle just because we are talking about cocaine.

But whatever you are buying or producing to sell to others, the more you buy, the cheaper the price. And the cheaper the price, the greater can be your potential profit margin. Furthermore, you can afford to sell to others for less, which brings you more customers. On the other hand, if you never grasp an understanding and maintain the discipline to apply KEY 8, you suffocate your ability to grow your business.

Most people believe the purpose of cocaine money is to buy flashy cars, purchase expensive jewelry, and get beautiful women. No. In reality, the purpose of cocaine money is to buy more cocaine. In other words, if you are a drug dealer, the money you make from selling drugs should go towards *buying more drugs*. If you sell t-shirts, the money you make from selling t-shirts should go towards *buying more t-shirts*. If you sell M&M's, the money you make from selling M&M's should go towards *buying more M&M's*. Once you get to a certain point, where your money is making money that's making money, then… you can start to buy some of those luxuries (liabilities) should you so choose.

When it comes to developing the discipline to make this re-up principle a *habit*, a drug dealer like Rick is perhaps the best person to learn from. Why? Drugs dealers are often arrested or killed because their fancy lifestyle and luxury items—purchased with coke money—attracts unnecessary attention. So for Rick, continuously reinvesting profits to buy larger quantities of cocaine was not only a smart move to grow his business, but it was also a smart move to keep his freedom and his life. This "extra incentive" to re-up would not have been there had Rick been selling t-shirts or books back in the 1980s. Had Rick blown his "t-shirt money" or "book money" on fancy clothes or expensive jewelry, the *worst* that could have happened is that he lost his money and went out of business. But because Rick was selling illegal cocaine, the stakes were much higher. The more Rick spent on visible signs of his illegal riches, the more he unnecessarily jeopardized his life and freedom. As a result, the importance Rick placed on putting his money back into the business so it wasn't *seen* created in him an incredibly strong re-up game that remains to this day. Consequently, modeling your *legal* re-up game after this former drug dealer can place you head and shoulders above the competition, most of whom don't truly understand the gravity of having a strong re-up game.

In closing this chapter, it is perhaps no mere coincidence that Rick excelled in tennis before he ever got started in the cocaine business. If there's one irrefutable common denominator of success in both business and sports, it's discipline. A tennis player must have the discipline to hit thousands of tennis balls each day if they want to develop that killer serve and formidable backhand. In business, that day-in, day-out discipline displays itself in the form of a proper re-up game. A business owner must take those actions day-in and day-out to create that disciplined self—one who puts the money back into the business instead of buying a new car or fancy watch.

It doesn't matter whether you're selling Girl Scout cookies or crack cocaine. If you make sales, and then immediately head to the mall to "get fly", go to the showroom to dump money into a new whip or hit the club to pop bottles for models, you aren't going to be in business very long. The re-up isn't glamorous or sexy, but a business simply cannot succeed without proper implementation of this principle as a cornerstone of its culture.

KEY 9
MOVE EFFICIENTLY BY KEEPING A LOW PROFILE

YOU'VE ONLY GOT 24 HOURS IN THE DAY. IN ORDER TO MAXIMIZE YOUR TIME, YOU MUST MOVE EFFICIENTLY. THE KEY TO THIS EFFICIENCY IS LEARNING TO KEEP A LOW PROFILE AND NOT GETTING SLOWED BY YOUR OWN DESIRE TO "APPEAR SUCCESSFUL". MOST PEOPLE ONLY HAVE THE INTENT OF APPEARING TO BE A SUCCESS. INSTEAD, MAKE YOUR MOVES WITH THE INTENT OF ACTUALLY BEING A SUCCESS. AT FIRST, OTHERS CAN'T TELL THE DIFFERENCE. BUT AS TIME PASSES, YOUR GROWTH INCREASES EXPONENTIALLY BECAUSE ALL OF YOUR EFFORT HAS BEEN PUT INTO ACTUALLY BECOMING THE SUCCESS THAT EVERYONE ELSE CAN ONLY APPEAR TO BE.

"Eliminate as much stuff that isn't beneficial out of your life, because if it isn't bringing you up, it's bringing you down."
–Rick Ross

TRUE STORY

One night I went to an informal gathering in Baldwin Hills with Rick. Also with us that night was Rick's legal consultant at the time. The dress was pretty casual, but I remember that the view looking out over the Los Angeles skyline was really nice. Hosting the gathering was Jody Armour, the Roy P. Crocker Professor of Law at the University of Southern California. This was his place. And because this was the professor's place, many of the people in attendance were current students at USC. These students were some of the future leaders of Los Angeles, and the United States, for that matter. The gathering seemed to be something that Professor Armour held from time to time, to allow students a comfortable atmosphere away from campus where they could network, discuss topics concerning them as young college students and generally express themselves in a non-judgmental environment.

But whatever the purpose of the gathering, one thing was clear: These young minds were highly educated, and the sale of crack cocaine did not appear to be their means of choice to "make it" in life. Being there that night also highlighted one of the fascinating aspects about ridin' with Rick. At 5 PM we might be in a gang neighborhood in South Central talking to killers and drug dealers, and by 8 PM that same day, we could be in a posh Baldwin Hills loft talking to future doctors and lawyers. Yet, no matter where we were, to Rick, people were people. He would speak to a hardened criminal who just came home the same way he would speak to a stellar student at USC who just graduated valedictorian of her high school.

And so, on this particular night, as the professor thanked everyone for coming and encouraged us all to make ourselves feel at home, he was particularly excited. For on this night, there was a special guest in attendance… Rick Ross… the *real Rick Ross*. And although these students didn't come to USC to learn how to calculate cocaine purity based on how much came back when it was cooked up, the African-American experience in the United States is incomplete without the story of Freeway Ricky

Ross. And by the end of the night, this reality was even more evident.

Several people spoke that night, including the professor. Of course, Rick spoke last. And afterwards, the floor was opened up for questions. The students had many questions for Rick. Even though they were young college students, because most were also from the Los Angeles area, they were much more up to speed on Rick's story than young college students in other parts of the country. Many of their parents, aunts and uncles were in the streets during Rick's heyday, and so they had heard of the legend of "Freeway" Ricky Ross from them firsthand. And they knew that the real Rick Ross was from *their* hometown—L.A—*not* Miami. That being the case, the tone of the students was more of "we've been waiting to meet you" as opposed to, "Wait a minute… you're not the *rapper*?"

Towards the end of the question and answer session, one young lady—very bright and articulate—stood out in particular. As she spoke about her experience thus far at USC, it was apparent that although she had been fairly successful in her studies, she was a bit bothered by something. As she stated, "No matter what I do and no matter how good I am in my classes, I always feel the need to *show* that I'm successful. How do I *show people* that I'm really a success?"

Rick's answer to the young lady was quite simple: "You don't have to *show* you are successful", Rick told her. "Just *be* successful."

As the young lady just stood there, waiting for Rick to say more, it was clear that she didn't get the point. Maybe she was expecting some fancy, over-worded professorial answer, because Rick's answer seemed to bounce right off her highly educated head. When the longevity of the silence confirmed that "Just *be* successful" was Rick's final answer to her question, she slowly replied, "I know, but …"

Rick smiled. And he just repeated his answer. "Just *be* successful."

Now, I don't know if she actually ever "got it", but in that brief exchange between the young USC student and Rick, I clearly realized the thing that was holding her—as well as untold numbers of "highly qualified" people—back from being successful…

Themselves.

That night, it suddenly hit me: Most people have the terrible habit of trying to *show* everyone around them that they are indeed a success, instead of just *being* a success. In putting so much effort into *showing* some level of accomplishment to others, they are moving inefficiently through life—ultimately working against themselves. **The key was to move efficiently by simply working to *be* successful, instead of working to *appear to be* successful.**

KEY TO SUCCESS

In the movie *The Departed*, Billy Costigan (Leonardo DiCaprio) is being interviewed by Sergeant Digman (Mark Walhberg) and Captain Queenan (Martin Sheen) for the Massachusetts State Police. During the interview, Captain

Queenan says to Costigan, "We have a question. Do you want to be a cop, or do you want to *appear* to be a cop? It's an honest question. A lot of guys want to *appear* to be cops—a gun, badge; pretend they're on TV..." Although Queenan's question about "wanting to be a cop" is a scene from a movie, the underlying motivation has real-life importance to any individual who "wants to be a success". It is here that you must ask yourself the same important question regarding success: Do you want to *be* a success, or do you want to *appear* to be a success?" It's an honest question. A lot of people want to appear to be a success—a fancy car, an expensive watch; pretend they're on TV...

The average person puts as much—if not *more*—effort into trying to show other people the appearance of success as they put into simply *being* a success. In doing so, they waste valuable time, resources and energy. And thus, they remain average. But just like there's a difference between wanting to be a cop and wanting to *appear* to be a cop, there's a difference—a *big* difference—between wanting to be a success and wanting to *appear* to be a success.

The successful person puts all his or her effort into *being* a success. And that efficiency of their effort is why they ultimately become successful. Although it doesn't sound like much of a difference, the difference between "being" and "appearing to be" is truly like night and day. And it's the difference between the few among the ranks of the "successes" and the masses among the ranks of the "average".

Today especially, as we strive to *show* our success, *prove* how successful we are, or otherwise *give the appearance* of success to others, we are taking time and energy away from the actual process of *becoming* a success. In our world of "Likes" and "Followers" as our modern social currency, this concept is somewhat difficult for people to grasp. But real success comes to you because of what you do, not because of what other people think you do. Real success comes to you because of what you think of yourself, not what other people think of you. You can fool people on Instagram or Snapchat, but you can't fool success.

It is often said that "real recognizes real". This is very true. **When an individual persistently incorporates the *principles* of success into their everyday life, *THE PROCESS of applying those principles* is "being a success".** And as a law, the indicators of success will—over time—recognize that individual, and become attracted to them. This is real success recognizing a person who "smells like" real success, because they have been figuratively "bathing" in the principles of success for so long. In reality, you become a success before any other person realizes it. So, if you're using other people's opinion of you as the measure of your success, you are going about the process of becoming successful the wrong way.

This *should be* great news because it means that the only person you really have to convince of your greatness is yourself, not everyone else. This is a much more efficient way to move mentally over the long haul. Why constantly run yourself ragged trying to impress your worth onto the minds of a whole bunch of other people (because *their* opinion is how you measure *your* success)? All you really need to do is impress your self-worth onto a single mind—yours. At the end of the day, what other people *really* think about you is simply a mirror of what you really think about yourself anyway. And so, while it is human nature to be liked by our fellow man, the smart and efficient way to get long-term "Likes" is to truly like *you*.

Think about it like this. Have you ever noticed that the fastest sports cars—the Corvettes, the Ferraris, the Lamborghinis, and such—sit extremely low to the ground? In other words they have a very *low profile.* Why is this? Well, quite simply, the underlying principle that allows a Ferrari to accelerate to over 200 mph is the same principle that allowed Freeway Rick Ross to accelerate to a fortune of over $600 million: *Move efficiently by keeping a low profile.*

Without getting all into the physics and aerodynamics, in order for an automobile to accelerate to speeds of 200+ mph, there are a lot of factors that it must overcome. For instance, the weight of the car, the friction of the road, and of course, air resistance, all tend to slow it down or prevent it from accelerating. A 600-horsepower engine just wastes a bunch of fuel if the car is bulky, with a high profile that catches all the air as it travels. A car that sits too high gives too much of an area for the air to push against as it moves, and therefore the car cannot efficiently accelerate to high speeds. Another problem occurs if the car is not low enough to the ground, because air can easily get underneath and cause the car to flip at high speeds. And so, while all the people easily see a gleaming yellow Lamborghini or bright red Ferrari, to the air—which can set up resistance to slow it down—*the car is barely seen.*

Understand: You don't want to be *seen* by anything that can slow you down or prevent you from accelerating. You simply can't move efficiently if things are always slowing you down and holding you up. And things WILL definitely slow you down if you don't keep a low profile. *In order to keep a low profile, you've got to get out of the habit of trying to show and prove your success to other people.* Giving them the impression that you are successful is not what makes you a true success. So why bother? When you move like that, you're wasting energy that could be going towards actually becoming the success that you want to be.

Instead, you want to move like a low profile sports car—barely visible to the air, two seats, and no room for a bunch of extra people and baggage. As Rick put it, "Eliminate as much stuff that isn't beneficial out of your life, because if it isn't bringing you up, it's bringing you down." Rick was able to move so efficiently as a drug dealer because he was barely seen by anything or anyone who could slow him down. He wore regular tennis shoes, sweatshirts and Levi's, unlike the other dealers (who actually worked for him) who tended to be bright and flashy with new cars, expensive jewelry, and beautiful women all around them. What those guys were doing was actually slowing down their progress in the drug game. They were moving inefficiently because they had the habit of wanting to *show* other people their success and flaunt a high-profile lifestyle. And unseen to everyone, here was the real success—the boss—walking around in a low-key, unimpressive manner. Looking like a customer instead of a kingpin, Rick moved with extreme efficiency and thus accelerated past his flashy contemporaries. While the cars, clothes and jewelry were nice, and brought an initial happiness, Rick noticed something. He said, "They had to keep putting more and more money into maintaining those cars, but the cars weren't making them any money," Rick recalled. "On top of that, I noticed that all the guys who had new cars and clothes were working for me."

As you move towards your ultimate goals in life, you will have many obstacles to overcome. Of course, we know that the drug game is filled with competing dealers, robbers, envious people, rats and police. Those are some of your resistances if your business is selling cocaine. But even if your endeavors are completely legal, you'll still have resistance to overcome. Granted, those resistances may be of a different nature, depending on your business of choice. But they will always be present in some form. According to your situation and unique form in which you encounter those resistances, you set your low profile to avoid getting slowed down. As you make moves and conduct business, periodically ask yourself, "Do I want to *be* a success (by diligently practicing the principles of success, regardless of the opinions of others) or do I want to *appear* to be a success (by trying to show and prove my success to others)?" Know that by wanting to *appear* to be a success, you are setting up unnecessary resistance and slowing yourself down. This is not the efficient means of movement that accelerates you to the top of your business or profession.

To close out this chapter, keep this fact in mind. *Most people talk too much.* Don't be one of the "most people". I mention this specifically because no matter what business you're in, talking too much *almost always* sets up resistance to you and keeps you from moving efficiently. Each unnecessary word you speak is like a mini parachute that is opening up and slowing you down. Just think about those high-powered Top Fuel dragsters that reach speeds of 335 mph and travel 1,000 feet in just 3.64 seconds. When they finish the race, parachutes open behind the dragster to provide air resistance and help slow them down. If not for those parachutes and the resistance they provide, it would take too long for the dragster to slow down from such high speeds.

Well, in your life, you're not trying to slow down! So stop opening your parachute (your mouth) so much, and just get to work! People won't notice you much at first, but that's fine. The time will come when you get so good at what you do, others can't help but notice. Why? Because people who are really good at what they do are in short supply. It is then, once you've accelerated past the pack, when you can do your talking, if you so please.

You speak things into existence by your words *to yourself*—your inner thought conversations. There *is* power in your words, but you dissipate this power the moment you go around telling everybody what you plan to do before it's done. If you must tell it to anyone, tell it to yourself. It is much more efficient to spend thirty minutes having a good conversation with yourself about your great qualities and grand plans than spending hours trying to impress others by telling them about all the wonderful things you intend to do and the lofty dreams you seek to fulfill. If you—instead of trying to show and prove your success to others—simply keep your mouth closed and go to work employing the principles of success, you'll find that you'll begin moving with much more ease and efficiency. And soon, you'll find yourself at the top of your field—whatever your chosen endeavor may be. **The key here is this: Instead of moving *in*efficiently by working to *appear* to be successful, move efficiently by simply working to *be* successful.**

KEY 10
MAKE YOUR NAME CARRY WEIGHT

YOUR NAME CAN BE IN PLACES WHILE YOU ARE NOT PHYSICALLY THERE. IN ORDER TO ACHIEVE WHAT YOU WANT, YOU MUST DEVELOP YOUR NAME INTO A BRAND THAT CONJURES UP AN IMMEDIATE GUT REACTION IN THE MINDS AND HEARTS OF YOUR CUSTOMERS, ASSOCIATES AND THOSE YOU DO BUSINESS WITH.

"One thing I got is a solid brand. People would kill to have my brand."

–Rick Ross

TRUE STORY

On this particular night in L.A., Rick had an interview scheduled at a local radio station. This was the last obligation of the day before driving back down to Long Beach. Nothing really stood out about Rick being scheduled for an interview, as he was generally doing an interview of some type almost daily. True to form, Rick made it a point to allow me to have some time to speak during *his* interview. I always say "his interview", because the hosts of the show usually didn't know who I was and because the purpose of the interview was to interview Rick Ross—not Kolie Crutcher. And so, I was always grateful for the opportunity to come in at the end and get a bit of airtime, even if it was only five minutes or so.

Because of the arrangement of the booth, I sat with Rick from the beginning of the interview. Of course, the host introduced Rick. Then he said, "I see you brought someone with you…" The host gestured to me and said, "Let the people know who you are." I pulled the mic close and said, "What's up everybody. I'm Kolie Crutcher, publisher of *GET MONEY Magazine* and author of *Electric Living: The Science behind the Law of Attraction…*" I was barely able to get the word "attraction" out, when Rick—as if he simply couldn't help it—breaks in with a big smile on his face and shouts, "Yea, and that's his *real name* too!"

Everyone there laughed uncontrollably as they immediately "got it". In one quick (and unplanned) comedic jab, Rick had managed the address the topic of "how do you feel about the rapper who stole your name?" before the interview even got started.

KEY TO SUCCESS

For those of you who may not be aware, there is a rapper from Miami who goes by the name "Rick Ross". The rapper is a physically big guy who often wears dark shades. He is covered in tattoos, and raps about selling a lot of cocaine. But the *real* Rick Ross isn't a big guy at all. The *real* Rick Ross rarely wears shades. The *real* Rick Ross doesn't have tattoos. But most importantly, the *real* Rick Ross doesn't *rap* about selling cocaine… because the *real* Rick Ross is not a rapper.

This news comes as a huge shock to many people. But unbeknownst to the casual fan of rap music, what has actually taken place is perhaps the music industry's most elaborate case of identity theft: The theft of the name RICK ROSS. But why take the name? Why take another man's name and use it—when you *already* have a name? The reason is simple. And it's the same fundamental reason that *all* identity theft occurs: *An identity is stolen (or "used") because the name has already built up great credit.* And that great credit can be used to get the thief certain things they want—things that they wouldn't qualify for (or don't believe they would qualify for) if they used their own name. In all honesty, people with FICO scores of 350 aren't worried about anyone "stealing their identity". It's the people who have sacrificed and built up high credit scores who must be concerned about identity theft.

Such was the case with Freeway Rick. Because of everything he went through, everything he lost and the sacrifices he made for all that cocaine he *really* sold, the name "Rick Ross" had built up great credit in the streets. The name was "qualified" and certified in the annals of cocaine lore. The name *meant something* to those who heard it and it guaranteed a certain ability and authenticity. And so, for an individual rapping about selling cocaine in an industry where reputations hinge on the ability to "keep it real", the "street cred" accompanying the identity of Rick Ross was analogous to having a FICO score of 850. In other words, that name—Rick Ross—carried weight!

If you are reading this book with some familiarity about Rick's story, it's easy to have a certain feeling when you hear the name "Rick Ross". In your mind it already holds weight. But aside from your personal experience and what you know—or think you know—simply focus on the *phonetics* of the name for a moment. In other words, what would it be like if you could say the name from the perspective of a person who was either very old or very young, who knew nothing about "rap music" or "cocaine" or even the "CIA's involvement in drug dealing"? Simply say the name: "Rick". "Ross". These two names are actually very common. Neither the first name—"Rick", nor the last name—"Ross", stands out in any particular way when you hear them separately. In your lifetime, you have probably run across several people named "Rick" or "Ricky". Likewise, you have probably encountered several people with the last name—or even the first name—"Ross". And so from that perspective, the phonetics of hearing the name "Rick Ross" is just as common and unremarkable as hearing the name "John Brown", "Jane Smith" or "Paul Jones"—all very common names. However, the *brand* "Rick Ross" is anything but common. "Rick Ross" is not just a name; it's a brand—a brand that carries weight. *But that wasn't always the case.* As ironic as it sounds, as young kid, "There was a time when I wanted to be anyone *but* 'Rick Ross'", the former kingpin once admitted.

On the other hand, if you are reading this book and are not familiar with Rick's story, you may have seen the name on the cover and mistakenly thought it was about the rapper. But as detailed earlier, this book is not about the rapper, it's about the real Freeway Rick Ross. Ironically, the rapper who goes by the name "Rick Ross" may actually somewhat be attempting to take advantage of this principle, KEY 10, but just not in the right way. The Key is "Make *Your* Name Carry Weight". But the rapper who goes by the name "Rick Ross" when he performs and sells music is actually named *William Roberts*. And so when he chose to take on the name "Rick Ross", he was not making *his* name carry weight, but rather taking advantage of the already established weight that the real Rick Ross' name carried.

Now, by no means is any rapper, performer or entertainer expected or obligated to build their career and perform under their government name. Many rappers and performers use names that are more catchy and clever-sounding than their government name. Chris Bridges changed his name to "Ludacris". Andre Young became "Dr. Dre". Clifford Harris changed his name to "T.I.". Marshall Mathers is better known as "Eminem". Mario Mims became "Yo Gotti". Percy Miller became "Master P". Tauheed Epps actually changed twice—from "Tity Boi" and later to "2 Chainz". In all these cases, we can see entertainers with basic and common names change their "stage name" or "performing name" into something that sounds catchier in order to stand out in the minds of fans that buy their music, or just because they like the new name better. But those new performing names—as catchy as they sound—were not the real name of another real person who had already built up real weight for that name.

The name "William Roberts" is just as common sounding (I'm sure you know several people with the names "William" and "Roberts") as the name "Rick Ross" when you don't factor in the brand appeal. This indicates that the only advantage to using the name is the *weight* it has already built up. And the mere fact that William Roberts uses the name "Rick Ross" proves the underlying point in this chapter. And that is this: Freeway Rick Ross—the real Rick Ross—made *his name* carry weight.

But how does one make his name carry weight? That's the question. As you sit here reading these words—wanting to "become relevant"—you already know that Rick Ross has a solid brand in *his* name. Ok, great. But how do *you* get to that point? It's quite possible that no one has a clue about who you are right now. And in all honesty, the fact that your name presently carries little or no weight may leave you feeling a bit uninspired or discouraged. But keep this in mind: Rick Ross himself admitted there was a time when nobody—including *himself*—wanted to be "Rick Ross". So how does an unwanted common name rise from obscurity to become the most wanted brand name in the world of cocaine—idolized by rappers who boast about selling it? Let's take a look.

In many ways the cocaine business is no different than any other "legal" business. In the streets, it may be more common to say that a person's name "carries weight". In the legal business world, this attribute may be referred to as "having a strong brand". But it's the same thing: In your business, your customers know that you're the real thing and you have the quality they want.

If I'm in the computer software business (or want computer software), and I hear the name "Bill Gates", I expect a certain quality of product, way of business and credibility that exists because of the Bill Gates brand (or Microsoft brand, which is an extension of Bill Gates). If I'm in the athletic shoe business, and I hear the name "Nike" or "Phil Knight", I have great trust and expectations for the performance of my athletic shoes. If I want coffee, and I hear the name "Starbucks", I'm supremely confident of the type of service I will receive when my coffee is prepared. If I want a package delivered overnight, and I hear the name "FedEx", I can sleep peacefully knowing that FedEx is making sure it arrives where I need it by morning.

And if I was in the cocaine business in the 1980s (or wanted cocaine), and I heard the name "Rick Ross", I got a certain image in mind. Why? The reason is because in the cocaine business, the name "Rick Ross" was a strong brand that carried weight.

In business and life, your brand is extremely important, because it is how your customers quickly identify YOU as the one who provides the product or service that they want, the way they want it. Your brand is what they depend on and your credibility depends on your living up to the expectations of what they have come to expect from you. Your brand is your signal to the world that YOU do whatever you "do" better than others who also do it. Therefore, the underlying message to customers is that they should come to YOU to get what they need.

Of course, becoming known as the leader in your field is not an overnight process. This is perhaps the most important thing to understand when attempting to make your name carry weight. *It takes time.* Although your brand—once established—can instantly signify you as being the "go to" for a specific product or service, *building that brand* to the point of evoking that feeling in customers often takes years of dedication, effort and sacrifice. Although you instantly know you are getting a quality running shoe when you see the "swoosh", Nike was not built instantly and it was not built overnight. So don't expect your name to become a "brand" in a few short months or a couple of years. As a matter of fact, in looking at the origins of the Rick Ross brand, we have to go all the way back to the 1970s.

In the late 1970s, what would eventually become two of America's best known brands were still in their infancy. Today, when you say the names "FedEx" and "Rick Ross", you might not think these two have much in common. However, when it comes to having a strong brand in their respective markets, both rank near the top. And the two also have more in common than many people think. Both were founded on ideas that outsiders said, "Would never work". Fred Smith's idea of a new way to deliver time-sensitive products seemed totally impractical. "*A worldwide overnight package delivery service...?* It'll never work! The logistics are impossible." For Rick Ross, the idea of his drug enterprise was deemed equally unrealistic to the doubters. "*Selling the expensive and glamorous drug cocaine in poor black communities...?* It'll never work. It's too expensive."

But by the 1980s both Federal Express and Rick Ross had proved the naysayers wrong. In fiscal year 1983, FedEx reported $1 billion in revenues, making it the first American company to reach that mark inside ten years of startup without merger or acquisition. And around the same time in the mid-'80s, Rick Ross was routinely generating (although not reporting) $1 million *per day* in revenue. Often, Rick's revenue was $2 and even $3 million per day! Both FedEx and Rick Ross had "arrived". The difference: FedEx founder Fred Smith was a Yale grad, and Rick Ross was illiterate.

Aside from both starting their business enterprise in the 1970s, the comparison between Rick Ross and FedEx is also pertinent due to the critical nature of the service provided. When you absolutely, positively must have a package delivered overnight, you don't just hand it over to any package delivery service. You go to FedEx. This became evident during the 1980s. Also, in the 1980s, it became clearly evident, if you needed keys of cocaine, you didn't just go to any drug dealer. You went to Freeway Rick.

The development of the "Rick Ross" brand was different mainly in the fact that the service Rick provided—as great as it was—was illegal. Furthermore, the product began causing a great deal of harm to those who consumed it, and to the communities in which it was prevalent. Because of these—along with several other factors—law enforcement targeted Rick to arrest him. And so Rick staying unseen and unidentifiable was a huge benefit to him in terms of not being arrested. At the same time, his anonymity did not diminish his brand. If you were in the cocaine business or smoked cocaine, you may not have been able to pick Rick Ross out of a lineup, but you still wanted to get your product the way he delivered it. In the same fashion, nearly all of us know a FedEx box when we see it. And we all want our important documents and overnight packages "FedExed". But how many of us could identify Fred Smith (FedEx Chairman and founder) out of a lineup? Not many.

Again, in numerous ways, the cocaine business is not dissimilar to other "legal" business enterprises. We already mentioned how a name that "carries weight" on the corner can be thought of as a name that is a "strong brand" in the corner office. It's the same thing, just different terminology. But beyond that, Rick Ross was not your typical drug dealer. Once, during an interview in Detroit, the interviewer referred to him as a "gangster". "I never considered myself to be a gangster," Rick politely interrupted. "I always considered myself to be more of a businessman." And so it only made sense that Rick Ross was able to develop into such a successful brand because branding is such a big part of successful business. In order to make your name carry weight, you must think of your name as your brand. In other words, stop thinking of your name as just an identifier that was stuck on you at birth and over which you had no input. Instead, take some time to think about one of your favorite brands and how you immediately feel when you see your favorite brand's logo. With this in mind, your mission is now to cause that same immediate feeling in others when they see or hear *your* name. The sight of "Your Name" should cause everyone else to feel like they feel when they see the "LV" on the Louis Vuitton bag. The sound of "Your Name" should cause everyone else to feel like they feel when they hear the name "Warren Buffett". Impossible? Hardly. But it takes time! And the time is going to pass anyway. So thinking of your name from this point of view will help steer you in the direction that ensures that the time is not wasted.

We hear the words "branding", "marketing", "brand name", etc., often. But when a person or company is "building a brand", they want to develop (in the consumer's mind) the relationship between the unique qualities of their product or service (which will benefit the consumer) and that "brand name" or picture representation of that brand name, also known as a logo. If this is done properly over time, when—for example—a purchaser of athletic shoes sees that Nike "swoosh" or Jordan "Jumpman" logo, he will automatically desire those shoes. This is because the Jordan Jumpman—in the mind of customers—is now highly associated with everything those who play basketball (or the "game of life" for that matter) want to be. What basketball player, alive today, doesn't want to be "like Mike"?: 6-Time world champion, undefeated in the NBA Finals, unmatched mental toughness, the greatest ever, billionaire, and the list goes on. Even if one didn't know who Michael Jordan was, the aforementioned qualities are qualities that people admire and want for themselves. And for the price of *only* $300+, you can get two steps closer to that dream, because all those qualities are wrapped up in that little Jumpman logo on those Air Jordan sneakers. This desire, because of the power of branding over time, happens instantaneously in the mind of the consumer.

Now, in certain instances, a brand becomes so strong and dominant that it causes confusion in the mind of the consumer. For example, have you heard someone say—when they want a razor—"get me a Gillette"? In this case, they mistake that certain particular *brand* of product—Gillette—with the actual product itself—razor. In their mind, razor = Gillette, as if Gillette were the only company that makes razors. To them, razor means Gillette and Gillette means razor. Of course, this is not true, but for the Gillette Company, it is great branding, because those consumers, who call a "razor" a "Gillette", may not even consider buying their razors from any other company.

Likewise, have you ever heard someone say "FedEx me that package"? What they often mean is "Send me that package overnight." But again, this is an instance of the particular *company that provides the service* being mistaken with the actual service itself. The fact is that other companies *do* provide overnight package delivery service (the United States Postal Service being one), but because of quality brand development (starting in the 1970s and '80s), today's consumer often believes "overnight package delivery service" to be synonymous with "FedEx".

In order to really grasp how to make your name carry weight, it is important to understand the difference between your reputation and your character. Your reputation is who people *think* you are. Your character is who you *really* are. The mistake that many people make is they believe branding is all about who or what people think they are. This manufactured image might last for a while, but as you move further along, it becomes increasingly difficult to maintain your reputation if it is not in line with your character. Therefore, as you are starting out, don't worry so much about the fame and what other people think of you. Invest slowly in your character so that you can genuinely be who you say you are.

Today—perhaps more than at any other time in history—people are very impatient when it comes to building character. Instead of slowly building character, most people are in a rush to quickly portray a reputation. We live in a social media-driven world, where any pretty girl on Instagram can be a "model", and the right clip on social media can get someone that much coveted "Internet fame"… for a short time anyway. But the fact that so many people are seeking to quickly get "famous" online is actually great news for the man or woman of character. Although there is now a much greater quantity of content out there and available to be seen, there is much less *quality* of content. Content that used to cost millions of dollars to produce and distribute can now be put out for free by anyone with a smartphone. As a result, the "gatekeepers" of our mass attention have been removed. The technology can make everyone visible, but the technology (by itself) cannot make anyone great. Always remember, your success is built on a foundation of quality. Once you produce quality and focus on your character, you've laid the strong foundation that will last, even though others may have seemed to pass you by as they focus on "clicks", "views", "likes" and "friends". All those things will come, but their arrival based on your character is more important than their arrival based on your reputation.

The rapper who used the name "Rick Ross" has suffered in the brand department because his character and his reputation have diverged. In other words, people are starting to see that who he *appears* to be (Rick Ross the drug dealer) isn't who he really *is*. This was bound to happen, because the real character of Rick Ross belongs to the *real* Rick Ross—Ricky Donnell Ross. And this really has nothing to do with the quality of the rapper's music. The rapper could have easily been great as "William Roberts". There was nothing wrong with him being who he was. There was nothing wrong with him making the name "William Roberts" carry weight. By all accounts the music he puts out is great. His lyrics flow and his beats drive hard and get people moving. It is obvious that he has spent many years perfecting his unique voice, his flow, his style, his lyrics, his beats, and the intricacies of music that make his songs extremely popular. The rapper has taken his talent and developed it into a refined skill. That is a reality that cannot be denied.

However, the problem is that he has built his reputation based on a character that belongs to someone else. And when the rightful owner of that character steps forward and says, "You're misrepresenting Rick Ross", that reputation crumbles in the presence of the real.

KEY 11
BE A CRITICAL THINKER

THE POWER IN YOUR THINKING IS NOT THAT YOUR THOUGHTS ARE "RIGHT" OR "WRONG" ACCORDING TO OTHER PEOPLE'S STANDARDS. THE POWER IN YOUR THINKING RESIDES IN THE FACT THAT YOUR THOUGHTS ARE UNIQUE TO YOU. THE MENTAL CHEMISTRY THAT OCCURS WHEN YOU USE YOUR MIND TO THINK HAS NEVER AND WILL NEVER BE DUPLICATED IN THE HISTORY OF MANKIND. INSTEAD OF THINKING LIKE EVERYONE ELSE, USE YOUR UNIQUE MENTAL FINGERPRINT TO PROACTIVELY THINK DIFFERENT AND STAND APART IN A WORLD WHERE MOST PEOPLE ARE BLINDLY FOLLOWING EVERYONE ELSE.

"I don't believe in God. God wouldn't have let what happen to me happen to me."

–Rick Ross

TRUE STORY

I'll never forget that day we were ridin' on the 605 Freeway with a young lady who had a small, self-run blog. There were many such occasions, because the size or notoriety of your enterprise didn't matter to Rick. Whether you were with a well-established media corporation—such as *Esquire* Magazine—or a start-up, one-person blogger, Rick would talk to you. And on this day, as this young lady was in the car with us, somehow, the topic of *God* came up. She casually asked, "So Rick, do you believe in God?"

Rick's answer: "Nope. I don't believe in God. God wouldn't have let what happened to me, happen to me." Needless to say, that was *not* the answer she expected.

That's right; Rick Ross openly stated that he did *not* believe in God. His answer shocked everyone in the car. Personally, I had never witnessed an individual voice his express *dis*belief in God. I had seen so-called "atheists" on television, and people in movies talk about how "there is no God", but this was the first time I heard it with my own ears. Of course, most of the conversations I was privy to never really got on the topic of God, but in those rare instances where the topic did arise, the subject matter was never a question of God's *existence*. From what I've seen, the overwhelming majority of people—even those who never attend church—claim some type of belief in a God, if they are asked. Even if this "belief" is just a selfish desire to not be held accountable for wrongdoing, the idea that "God forgives us for our sins, whether we deserve it or not" is comforting.

And when disaster strikes, or when situations get wildly beyond the control of man, "praying to God" is the first thing we tend to do. So even though most of us just want God to make a bad situation go away or "make things right" so that we can go back to our normal "ungodly" lifestyle, the habit of seeking God only in times of crisis still signifies our belief that He at least *is* out there.

But to hear someone—especially a *black* person—say, "Nope. I don't believe in God", really was unexpected. The church has traditionally been a staple and backbone of the black community in America. Even during the worst times of slavery—when blacks had zero hope of being treated decently in America—they still had hope that God would somehow hear their cries. And still in today's most crime-ridden neighborhoods, rampant with homicides, robberies, drugs, prostitution, violence and struggles of all sorts, the underlying hope is that "God still loves his children", no matter how far removed they are from a life that reflects "holiness".

But Rick stated that he didn't believe in God. I may not have thought much about it, if I hadn't heard him *say* it, so bluntly and matter-of-factly—"Nope. I don't believe in God." As odd and politically incorrect as it sounded in the moment, it was a bit refreshing to hear someone speak along the track of their actual belief (or disbelief), instead of speaking along the track of popular opinion or social normalcy.

Consider why you don't give much consideration to what a parrot "says". The bird is simply mimicking the sounds it heard from somewhere else. So when a parrot "talks", those sounds are no reflection of the bird or what it "thinks". In reality, the parrot isn't thinking at all. In a similar way, most of the things most people say throughout the day aren't worthy of giving serious consideration to. It is much easier and socially "safe" to mimic the popular opinions of the day, than to step out, think critically and voice your thoughts from your unique perspective. But if you ask the real Rick Ross a question—whether he's "right" or "wrong"—you get his *real* answer. And this got me thinking to myself, "If one simply goes along with what everyone else is already saying or thinking, one doesn't have to give much—if any—effort into forming his own unique 'belief'. However, if one believes (and voices) the opposite of the popular opinion, he has likely given more critical thought towards his 'unpopular' belief." And so, my next question was, **"Why didn't Rick believe in God? More specifically, what was his *thought process* that led him to his conclusion?"**

KEY TO SUCCESS

Ironically, I've seen Rick speak at several churches, and he has no problem going to church or speaking with "church folk". Rick's lack of interest in church tradition, singing holy praises, getting baptized and joining a church have never shied him away from speaking to a church crowd about his story. Now, some people will naturally say, "Of course *he* doesn't care about joining a church. He's a drug dealer!" And many will scratch their head and ask, "How can someone who *didn't believe in God* talk about 'God putting him here on earth to be the dope man' (as detailed in KEY 3)?" To answer this question, we get to the underlying spirit of James 2:17. This passage of the Bible states, "Even so faith, if it hath not works, is dead, being alone." What this means is that faith, by itself, if it is not complemented by *action*, is dead.

Though Rick openly stated that he didn't believe in God, when one looks more closely, what is seen is that Rick's *actions* show that he has more faith—*in something*—than most people who claim to believe so much in God. So why is there this seeming contradiction? Well, in order to understand, we must take a closer look at what's going on in society as a whole.

In our society, the concept of "God" is taught in such a way that the vast majority of people think of God as being akin to a powerful *genie* in a lamp. This genie "blesses" us if we worship Him and do His will. He oversees everything and has ultimate control over the universe. And so, if you want "good things" to happen in your life, you must "be good in God's eyes" and He (like Santa Claus) will bless you… *hopefully**.

This "*hopefully**" reflects the reality that we live in a world where so many things seem "unfair", according to our own interpretation of them. "Being good" does not always guarantee the avoidance of bad things coming our way. We all know that sometimes "bad things happen to good people". And just as unpredictably, sometimes "good things happen to bad people". And so it is; "Life is not fair." However, because this "unfairness" and unpredictability is so uncomforting to us, we find some solace if we can attribute it something. Therefore, the world's perplexing inequalities and unpredictable tragedies (that mankind simply can't "make right") are often attributed to the reasoning that "man can never know the ultimate plan God has" or "God allows man to suffer for his ultimate benefit" or "even though those bad people got rich on earth they will ultimately spend eternity burning in hell".

The bottom line is this: Man's limited knowledge—when compared to an all-knowing God—subjects man's interpretation of situations to the default position of "incorrect". Since man's limited consciousness does not allow him to see the totality of EVERYTHING, there is *always* part of the puzzle of life that man is simply not aware of. On the other hand, because God's perspective encompasses the totality of the universe, God can never be in the wrong, irrespective of how man feels based on the tiny sliver he can see. This brings us to a very important point: *Man's belief in God is often rooted in the acknowledgement and displeasure he feels towards his own limitations*. In other words, once a man admits that "something" outside of himself can cause things to happen that he doesn't want to happen—and there's nothing he or anyone else can really do about it—his only option is to somehow *persuade* (through worship) that "something" to be *for* him as opposed to being *against* him.

But whether you believe in God or not, one thing is certain: You can never know what Life (or God) has in store for you or what a situation actually means in the moment. The passage of time often changes the narrative on a situation as "being good" or "being bad".

But in reality, very few people have ever spoken on the *true* nature of God. In fact, this "outside God" that we are taught to pray to "up in heaven" and *hope* he hears our prayers is not the true God, but a false God (another control mechanism) that is put forth largely to keep society in check. The true nature of God is evident in the Bible itself. But man is generally not familiar with the Bible, because man generally depends on others—preachers and priests in a church—to lead him to God.

I understand that this is not a popular opinion, because with all the so-called "bad things" going on in the world, the church is supposed to be our refuge of truth and goodness, where we can come near God and find peace. But unfortunately, the problem with most people who "go to church" is that's all they do. They go and rely on some preacher or "ordained" individual to bring them to God. They are getting their religion retail when they should be getting it wholesale. If you want to "know God", go straight to the source—read and study the Bible. Self-reliance

(KEY 7) is not only key to finding riches or freedom, but key to finding God as well.

Most people who claim to "believe in God", don't believe in God because *they* believe in God. They believe in God because *everyone else* "believes" in God. In light of this recognition, Rick's "*dis*belief" in God could not be discredited, because at least he came to his conclusion via his own thinking. The *habit* of using your own mind to think critically to form your own opinion is long-term substantially more beneficial than simply using already-established opinions as a pre-fabricated mold for what your opinion "should" be.

When you go through the process of seriously thinking critically and meditating on the nature of God, it becomes harder and harder to believe in God… *as He is generally presented to us by religious organizations.* Although I go into the science, details and explanation of this much deeper in my book *Mechanism of Success*, I'll just state the bottom line reality here: **God is not some or any entity *apart* from man. God is *a part* of man**. In fact, God is forever so much a part of man that man does not recognize God. Man is erroneously taught to look out into the heavenly sky for that which is already inside of him! Furthermore, even to say that God is "near" to man is inaccurate, because nearness implies *some* separation. There is no separation whatsoever between man and God. The apparent separation is simply the individual's lack of consciousness of this reality.

If—when someone says "God"—you think of some distant entity outside of, or in any way apart from yourself, *you have the wrong perception of God*. And you are worshiping a false god.

Now, most people find the above statement *extremely* difficult to swallow. This is largely because of how we are taught about God by churches and religious groups, and partly because we simply don't feel "the power of God" (again, as we are taught it to be) in us as we go about our daily activities. Most of us feel a lot of things during the course of a day, but "the power of God" *ain't* one of them. And so, if there is a God in control of everything (which makes sense on some level to most people because of the order and power existing in nature that man seems to have almost no control of) that God is definitely "out there" somewhere. There is no way The Almighty God could be contained within "little 'ol me"—*so man believes*. However, there is a reason that you do not *feel* what you believe to be "the power of God" inside you, and this reason is thoroughly explained in *Mechanism of Success*. But for now, the important thing is to allow yourself to think critically about the true nature of God.

Because God dwells *within* man (and not "out there in the heavens" as we are taught), *Faith is God is demonstrated by man's confidence in himself.* That's worth repeating: **Man's faith in God is demonstrated by his confidence in himself.** If you praise and worship an Almighty God, but don't think highly of yourself, you are worshiping a false god.

And so what I felt Rick was saying—by his actions—is that he doesn't believe in the *concept* of God the way that we are taught to think of God, as an entity apart from man. God is not an entity *apart* from man. God is *a part* of man.

Now, this is not a religious or spiritual book, per se. But it need not be, because again, if God is within man, He is *always* with man. This is true even if man is in a bar getting drunk or in a Nevada brothel getting laid. God is no more in the church house than he is the whorehouse.

The notion that one could understand more about the true nature of God by listening to a drug dealer than from any preacher is not so much an indictment on religion as much as it is an endorsement of critical thinking. If you feel that God gave you a mind, then you should also feel that He expects you to *use* that mind. And when you use that mind to think critically on the essence of God, you realize that **the only place God could fit the "eternity" of Himself *is* within the unbound mind of man**. Ironically, this can't be discovered as long as one "believes" in God as he is traditionally presented to us—as a being "out there" in heaven, who we are attempting to assuage for our benefit.

As you grow in years you learn that that there is no jolly fat man with a white beard flying eight reindeer "out there" to bring you presents on Christmas Eve. "Santa Claus" didn't fly all the way down from the North Pole to bring all the children of the world (well, the "nice" ones anyway) toys in one night. Yes, the gifts came, but not from where you originally thought. They came not from outside your house, but from *within* your house. "Santa Claus" has always been there with you, living under the same roof. You usually call them "Mom and Dad", and they're the ones who ate the milk and cookies you left for Santa. Similarly, as you grow in the spirit of critical thinking, you understand that "God" ain't "out there" somewhere, but already under the "same roof". The gift of God doesn't come from without; it comes from *within*.

Often, the problem with just coming out and asking a person who's mastered something "how they do it", is that they consciously don't really know, or at least they don't consciously know how to relay the information in a way that can help others. For many, Rick Ross' comment that he didn't believe in God, would have been an instant turn-off, or a seeming justification to "point the finger" in criticism. I've heard several people who know about Rick not believing in God, shake their head and say things to the effect of, "See, until Rick gets God in his life, he's always going to struggle." While this may be true in general, those people make the mistake of listening to Rick's conscious talk instead of watching his actions.

Again, the successful man is a success because the principles of success have been embedded deep within his subconscious mind. Therefore, if you depend on him to *consciously* explain the reason for his success, he won't be accurate. It's the same reason that a failure can't consciously flip a switch and suddenly become a success. He can't clearly see those principles embedded deep within his subconscious mind. Often, that deep embedment of success principles in the subconscious of a high achiever registers to the outside world as "crazy talk" or causes eyebrows to be raised. And so, when you hear Rick say, "I don't believe in God", what he's consciously saying in incomplete as it pertains to being understood by other people. His complete truth comes from his subconscious mind, and his subconscious mind—based on the way he moves and acts—indicates that *he doesn't believe in God as some outside genie up in heaven who grants wishes like everyone else does*. It cannot be overstated that God is alive deep within *us*, so close that He is not even near—as nearness implies some separation. Therefore, belief in self reflects belief in God.

Now, is Rick going to tell you that? No. He will tell you, "No. I don't believe in God." But if you look at his actions, you see that Rick believes in God more than most people who fervently claim they believe in God. Why? Because if—when someone says 'God'—your mind thinks of some *outside* being, apart from you and your own wonderful human Imagination, you have a false God. If you look at his actions, Rick's faith in himself is stronger than almost anyone else I've met. And if there is no separation between God and man, then faith in God is best displayed by faith in self.

The desire to "attain success" is a common desire shared by nearly all men. However, so few actually attain the "success" they are seeking. Although every individual's situation and circumstances are slightly different, one of the most widespread causes of underachievement and failure is people's overwhelmingly strong tendency of waiting on the "world's" stamp of success to be placed on them before they actually *feel* themselves to be a success. One of the main goals of this book and the purpose of detailing these 21 Keys is to get the reader to realize that success never operates from the *outside-in*. Success always operates from the *inside-out*.

In other words, the very first person that knows (and must know and feel) you to be a success is *You*. It is not the people who buy (or don't buy) your product. It is not the record label that signs (or doesn't sign) you. It is not the publisher who publishes (or doesn't publish) your work. But if you never learn to develop your own critical thoughts, independent of the prevailing thoughts of others, you will always be at the mercy of (and in essence, waiting for) the world to "stamp" you with the label of "success". In reality, that stamp will never come. It only comes from the world once you feel it inside of yourself *first.* It may take years, but it will come. Always later does the world follow suit with the nature of your inner thoughts of yourself.

And so we begin to see why the practice of, and habit of being a critical thinker is so key to your success in life. It prevents you from automatically and by default taking on the thoughts of others as your own. As simple as it sounds, *no one else has the right to make you feel a certain way about you.* Even if you sometimes think your own thoughts and they turn out "not to work" to get you where you want, that is preferable to automatically taking on the thoughts of others with no real consideration. If your ideas are not always "the right idea", yet of your choice, you are equipped to soon get "the right idea" with practice and better information.

If you wait until you are on television to feel like a success, you'll never be one. If you wait until you live in a big house to feel like a success, you'll never be one. If you wait until you drive a fast sports car to feel like success, you'll never be one. If you wait until you've got a million dollars in your bank account to feel like a success, you'll never be one. If you wait until you've got a beautiful model as a girlfriend to feel like a success, you'll never be one. Why? *These material things and outer conditions of your world are simply reflections of your inner thoughts of You.* And in order to formulate your own thoughts from within, you must be able to think critically and toss away the seeds of doubt, uncertainty and fear that are prevalent in the outside world. You must be able to keep them from taking root in your own mind.

Learn to think your own positive thoughts about yourself and your condition in life. The uniqueness of those thoughts (being that they are a product of your own mind) is the magic that give them power in your life. In your very own life, there is a unique power wrapped up in your own unique thoughts, simply because *there is no other mind that can produce your thoughts!* So use your own mind to think your own thoughts. Stop relying on the "experts" and the television and the nosey relatives to do your thinking for you. There will be no success in your life unless you develop the ability to use your own mind to think your own thoughts. The magic in being a critical thinker is this: Even a so-called "bad choice" that you make using your own mind to think critically, ends up working out for your good in due time. Believe in yourself and the world will conform to believe in you.

Being a critical thinker means that you will often do and say things that the other people around you find odd, not normal or flat-out wrong (e.g., "I don't believe in God"). And you must be okay—even relish—in being this type of non-conformist. Sadly, most talented people never become standouts because they fear standing out. If you go along with what everybody does, you will get what everybody has. We normally don't think about it in those terms, but if the reason that you decided to think a certain way was simply because that's the way everyone else was thinking (even if it is something as "right" as believing in God), what reason do you have to support that way of thinking as being right for *you*?

You've got to periodically ask yourself, "If most people are *un*successful and *un*happy with their position in life, but I say that I instead want to be a success, why am I doing what most people do?" This is the type of question that a critical thinker will ask himself. One of the most admirable qualities about Rick is that he places his own opinion above the acquired human tendency to go along with "the popular choice" or "the choice that makes sense to everyone else". Is he wrong sometimes? Yes, of course he is in certain moments. On several occasions, I've seen Rick make what can only be described as the "wrong" choice. But that's okay, because one can never *ultimately* go wrong when he habitually makes his own decisions. It is perfectly fine to get input from others when you are missing information or need facts. But in the long run the only way you can succeed is by making up your own mind through a process of deep critical thinking. If you get into the habit of using your own mind to think critically to make your own decisions, you only need *one* of those decisions to "be right" in order to achieve success beyond your wildest dreams.

KEY 12
FIND COUR CONNECT –
DISCOVER YOUR IMAGINATION

SOCIETY FUNCTIONS BY EMPLOYING A SORT OF "NECESSARY EVIL". BY CREATING THE ILLUSION THAT THE ULTIMATE POWER RESIDES WITH THE STATE, AND SIMULTANEOUSLY DOWNPLAYING THE IMAGINATIVE POWER OF EACH INDIVIDUAL, CITIZENS FEEL THAT THE POWER THAT GOVERNS THEIR LIVES IS AN OUTSIDE ENTITY. THIS NECESSARY EVIL HAS THE EFFECT OF MAINTAINING GENERAL LAW AND ORDER, BUT LEAVES THE INDIVIDUAL TO IGNORE HIS REAL SOURCE OF POWER. WHEN AN INDIVIDUAL DISCOVERS HIS IMAGINATION, HE REALIZES THAT EVEN IF THE STATE HAS THE "POWER" TO SENTENCE HIM TO PRISON, HE—BY CONNECTING TO HIS VERY OWN HUMAN IMAGINATION—HAS THE POWER TO FREE HIMSELF.

"Most dudes that go out there and sell dope... it's because they don't know how to expand their mind. So they just go out and do what they see everybody else doing."

–Rick Ross

TRUE STORY

When Jesse Katz—then a reporter for the *Texas Monthly*—visited Rick in Lompoc Federal Penitentiary back in 1998, Katz thought Rick was either crazy, delusional, or both because of how Rick was talking. Here he was, this *convicted drug kingpin* sentenced to "life in prison without the possibility of parole", openly prophesying to the seasoned reporter about all the things he was going to do when he got out, *as if he were already free.* This, despite all the "facts", all the "evidence", and all the "proof" saying that Freeway Rick Ross was going to be locked away for the remainder of his natural life. But *in Rick's mind*, he was already free. As he later recalled while we were speaking to a group of students at Los Angeles' Hamilton High School in 2014, "When I was in prison, I sat back in my cell and visualized standing here talking to groups like you."

But sixteen years earlier, as he talked to Katz from behind the thick glass that apparently separated the "free" from the "imprisoned", Rick's grandiose future plans certainly were not taken seriously by anyone—*except him.* Ironically, the truth of the matter was that even though Rick Ross was physically "behind bars" and Jesse Katz was physically "free", Rick was actually freer than Jesse. Why? Because Rick Ross had discovered something Jesse had not yet found. Freeway Rick had discovered his true connect. And this time, it wasn't Danilo Blandon... *It was his very own wonderful human Imagination.*

KEY TO SUCCESS

Of course, each of us has *heard of* the imagination, and each of us thinks we have *used* our imagination from time to time as we so-call daydream. But very few people have actually *discovered* their very own wonderful human Imagination. The discovery of the Imagination is this: **When you make the conscious connection between the actual events in your life (which *everyone* can see) and your preceding inner thoughts**

and feelings of those events (which *only you* can see and feel), you have discovered your Imagination.

Your Imagination is your true connect—the only real source of everything that eventually manifests in your life.

Your outer world is literally your inner Imagination pushed out. And once you discover your Imagination, you understand through *experience* exactly why YOU—and you alone—are ultimately responsible for the success or failure in your life. It becomes abundantly clear to you that all other outside situations and circumstances that may *appear* to be in control of your life are NOT. However, for most people, those outside situations actually *do* take control of their lives, for the simple reason that they *seem* so "real" and personal. And because they seem so real and personal, people submit to them as "the facts of life", their "lot in life" or "their reality".

But this false evidence appearing real is simply the world's oldest and slickest con game. And the overwhelmingly vast majority of people fall for it because they are totally unaware that inner Imagination is the real determining factor in the life of man—despite any other outside factor. The universal weakness of man is allowing himself to become that which is around him, instead of causing that which is around him to become him. In other words man ignorantly allows himself to become a product of his environment, instead of consciously making his environment become a product of him. He allows this because he is totally unaware that he (as man) is the only life form that is designed and equipped to make his environment conform to become a product of *his thinking*. And what "piece of equipment" in the design of man makes this possible? IMAGINATION!

Yet, for all its power, if this wonderful inner feature called Imagination (that all humans are born with) is never discovered, it is as if it didn't even exist! And at that point, your life drably plays out much the same as any other living *plant or animal*, as these life forms are not born with Imagination. The result…? A life of limits marked by dependency on a pre-existing environment and the conditions and circumstances already put upon you from the outside. You are born around poor people… You die poor. You are born around negative-minded people… You die thinking negatively. You are born around failures… You die a failure. Without Imagination, a child born into poverty MUST remain in poverty. In the absence of Imagination, a child born into poverty has the same chance of becoming a multi-millionaire as a weed has of growing into a rose. Zero.

The crown jewel of mankind is his ability to magically transform himself and his condition into "something" from "nothing". Man's unique ability to be born in the weeds and grow into a rose is the underlying motivation of the human soul to celebrate success. However, despite every individual *having* an Imagination, most of us never *connect* with it, and therefore, success is absent in the lives of most. It is rather sad that we are not taught how to discover and connect to our Imagination in school. Fortunately, there is still hope, because *you can learn a lot from a drug dealer.*

Think on this...

Why would George Jung (Boston George) fly all the way from Massachusetts to the country of Colombia in South America? Why would Frank Lucas fly from Harlem to Southeast Asia and tread days through the dangerous jungles? Why would Tony Montana fly to Bolivia—again, all the way down on the continent of South America? The answer to all these questions is the same: **To connect to the source.**

Although the United States is the world's leading *consumer* of cocaine, cocaine is not a *product* of the United States. Cocaine is not like peaches from Georgia, wheat from Kansas or potatoes from Idaho. The coca leaf (from which cocaine is made) grows only in a very specific region and altitude in certain South American counties such as Peru, Colombia and Bolivia. Those countries are where cocaine actually comes from. *Those countries are the source.* When cocaine leaves Peru—for example—it is at its highest purity and potency. And therefore, if you're in the cocaine business, you know that having a "connect" as close to the source of where the cocaine originates is crucial to increasing your profit margin.

As the product moves further away from the source, the more people have touched it and the purity goes down if it is being cut to sell more. Also, transportation costs drastically increase the further you get from the source. Efficiently moving an illegal product is expensive because losing it or getting caught with it is expensive. And for these reasons, by the time the cocaine hits the streets of the United States it is generally nowhere near the purity it was when it left Peru; yet it is much more expensive to purchase. The closer a dealer can get to the source, the cheaper and purer his product. This translates into eye-popping profits once he sells in areas far away from the source, on the streets on New York, Chicago, Los Angeles, Detroit, Houston, Miami and all the cities and towns across the United States that so love the white powder known as cocaine.

And where was Freeway Ricky Ross' connect—Danilo Blandon—from? When you get a moment, find the country of *Nicaragua* on a map, and see its physical proximity in relation to the cocaine-producing countries of Bolivia, Colombia and Peru in South America.

And so, what we learn from drug dealers such as Freeway Rick, is that *being connected at the source* is key to getting the purest quality of product. Translating this principle over into your life, **the product that you are pushing out to the world is your thoughts from your Imagination**. Understand that whatever you are selling that you can hold in your hand MUST start out in the form of a thought. In *your* life, what is purer than *your* deepest wishes, *your* most cherished thoughts and *your* idealized version of yourself, just as *you* desire to be? There is *nothing* more pure and powerful. *Someone betraying you or putting you in a bad circumstance certainly isn't. You momentarily not having enough money to live as comfortably as you'd like certainly isn't. The negative thoughts and comments that come from other people certainly aren't.* All of these negative things you encounter in life should be viewed as "stepped on" product that has been cut with all kinds of agents and handled by all kinds of different people far away from the source. Rather than accept them, accept only that 100% "pure uncut" thought product. And the only place you can get that pure uncut thought is from your very own wonderful human Imagination. So discover your Imagination and make *it* your "connect", because it is the only true source of the success you want in life.

****

It was November 19, 1996 in the U.S. District Court in San Diego. In the case of "The United States of America versus Ricky Donnell Ross", Judge Marilyn Huff sentenced Rick Ross to "life in prison without the possibility of parole". Judge Huff had the "power" to take away Rick's freedom based on the laws of the United States of America. Immediately after the sentence was handed down, this same "power" of the State—the United States of America—used United States marshals to lead the shackled Ross out of the courtroom in his prison jumpsuit and out to a van in the basement parking lot. Rick's next stop would be the San Diego Metropolitan Correctional Facility down the street. Ross would be held there until his transport to the Lompoc Federal Penitentiary, where he was ordered to serve out his sentence.

And so it was, the United States of America, the richest and most powerful State the world has ever known, flexed its muscle and made full display of its "power" against one individual citizen of the State—who also happened to be illiterate, unable to read his own sentencing form. With such an imbalance of "power", Rick Ross seemed to be at a decisive—almost insurmountable—disadvantage. The result of this huge imbalance of power was his freedom forever stripped from him.

But the United States of America did not have *all* the power. There was one freedom that they simply could not deny Ricky Donnell Ross. And that was his freedom to *think*. This *mental* freedom—as Rick later discovered—would be the key to his *physical* freedom. After a period of much study and honest self-reflection, Rick finally understood the truth: The real power was not held by Judge Huff, the United States of America or even his lawyer. In reality, it was Ross himself who held the *real* power—the power of his very own wonderful human Imagination.

"Basically, the same creative power in the man tonight behind bars serving life, is the same creative power of the one who sentenced him for life."
-Neville Goddard

The United States of America can physically hunt you down. The United States of America can physically arrest you. The United States of America can physically throw your ass into a cold prison cell. All of these things can be done to you because you broke one of the laws of the United States. You didn't play by the rules *it* established, and so, you must feel its power. Once these rules (laws) are established, the citizens must adhere to the rules, or face the penalties of "breaking the law".

However, for all the apparent power and might of the United States of America when it comes to arresting and imprisoning its citizens based on *man-made* laws, the United States' power is not absolute. As a matter of fact, its power is far from absolute. Why? For the simple fact that the laws by which the United States flexes its power are laws that came about as a result of a man (or group of men) deciding what the "rules" should be for the citizens. In other words, the laws of the United States of America are *man-made laws*.

Unlike the laws of nature, such as the laws of gravity and electricity (which do not change and which affect all men the same), man-made laws can be changed, altered, revised, created, eliminated, etc.—all at the discretion of those men who come up with the laws. And so it stands, in the process of "law-making" by men, there will always be inherent "baked-in" biases, simply because *people are inherently biased.* Even under the best attempts to be "fair", people are naturally biased towards that which benefits them. This doesn't *necessarily* mean a person is racist, sexist or possesses a malicious tendency to discriminate against certain groups of people. It is simply a reflection of our survival instinct, and occurs for the same reason we don't voluntarily jump off cliffs. Self-preservation is part of our human DNA, and every person naturally leans towards that which benefits him and his affairs. And as all men do not share the same position or affairs, this natural lean *for* one man and his affairs may be a lean *against* another man and his affairs. Such is always in play regarding the decisions men make, and it is no different when it comes to the process of making "man-made laws". In other words, the laws of man simply do not affect all men the same—although the goal is to give the impression of "fairness" (justice is blind).

The problem with the "justice is blind" misconception is that those who are a level up and have the authority to make the laws connected to the justice *can* still see. As a matter of fact, their eyes are wide open. And so, the scales of justice are weighted even before anything is placed on them. This is not being cynical. It is just a reality of the human condition. If a group of people has the opportunity and privilege to make up the rules by which “everybody” must follow, **that group of people is not going to make rules that they see themselves (and people most like them) breaking.** Again, it’s just a simple matter of self-preservation and self-interest. And so, although the State does not like to admit it, the laws of the State are naturally subtly written in a way such that the ones who make the laws (generally older white men) have much more freedom of expression to do those things they would like to do or are of benefit to them. *It would be self-defeating for them not to do so.* As a result, they enjoy a much wider freedom to act, without so-called “breaking the law”. But those things that they simply would not be doing anyway—those are the things that could be deemed “illegal”. What’s the likelihood of finding a 70-year old white man pushing crack cocaine on the corner of 87th & Figueroa in South L.A.? It’s simply not happening.

Here’s an example of this naturally biased behavior that has nothing to do with drugs or crime. Let’s say I found a start-up company, and I make a rule that everyone must arrive to work every morning at 7 AM, or face some type of penalty for being late. If I say that this rule applies to everyone—including me—I seem “fair” on the surface. I’m not exempting myself or giving myself special treatment just because I’m the founder. I have to follow the rules just like everyone else.

However, as the founder of the company, what is the likelihood that *I’m* going to be late? I’m probably there all the time anyway. I probably eat, sleep, and breathe this start-up. I might sleep in the office, work 18-hour days, and rarely get away from the work. So the rule that I made is a rule to get everyone else to do what I’m already naturally doing anyway. So, the likelihood that *I'm* going to break that rule is slim to none. The likelihood that that rule is going to inconvenience *me* any is slim to none. But for regular employees, who may have families, kids, and honestly don't have the same level of commitment as the founder, it is likely not always convenient to arrive at 7 AM. And so, we can see that there is always bias baked into rules, because for any lawmaker or rule-maker to make a law or set up parameters that are going to inconvenience the rule-maker goes against human nature.

And this is just how the laws of man work. No man (or group of men) who has the freedom or privilege of making the rules is going to voluntarily place himself in a position where they lose that freedom or use this privilege against himself. And because of this inherent bias, man-made laws can also be tailored to unfairly target or "legally" cause harm to a certain group of people. Such was the case when the Anti-Drug Abuse Acts of 1986 and 1988 enacted a mandatory sentencing for possession of crack cocaine that was *100 times harsher* than possession of the same amount of powder cocaine. In other words, a person in possession of only five grams of crack would be sentenced the same as someone who was in possession of five hundred grams (½ kilo) of powder cocaine. A person with fifty grams of crack—slightly more than the size of a Hershey's Chocolate candy bar—would receive the mandatory minimum of ten years. Ten years was the same amount of time given to someone in possession of 5,000 grams (5 kilos) of powder cocaine. The effect of that law was the mass incarceration of a disproportionate number of black men to unjustly lengthy prison sentences for non-violent possession of very small amounts of crack cocaine. Despite the fact that crack cocaine and powder cocaine are nearly identical of a molecular level, most of those convicted of crack possession were black. And so this harsh penalty had virtually no chance of being felt by those who passed that law—whose skin happened to be white.

But as mentioned earlier, the laws of nature—because they were not conceived by any man—do not operate in such a way that any particular man or segment of the population is *more* at risk of "breaking the law" (and thus facing the consequence) than any other. And the laws of nature do not change to suit the pleasures of those who make the laws. For example, if the law of gravity operated like the laws of man, a person walking down the street with 50 grams of *powder* cocaine in his pocket would fall in slow motion—with enough time to regain his balance—if he happened to trip over something. A comparable person with 50 grams of *crack* cocaine in his pocket would fall immediately, with no chance to recover before he hit the ground. Fortunately, the law of gravity operates on all people the same. This ensures that a person carrying powder cocaine falls down just as fast as the person carrying crack cocaine—should either of them happen to trip and lose their balance.

Now that the difference between man-made laws and the laws of nature are clear, we can highlight the fact that there exists a subset of the laws of nature that have to do with the way humans think. These are known as *mental laws*. Mental laws are EXTREMELY important because, like the laws of nature, they are not the creation of any man (or group of men). Therefore mental laws *affect all men the same*. And here's the great news for those who are not in the position to be "lawmakers" for the United States of America: **A man-made law can never outrank a mental law**. When the two are in conflict, the mental law is infinitely more powerful. The reason is simple. The mental laws (which any and every person has access to equally use) work universally and are no respecter of person. This fact is the only way to ensure the biased laws of man—the laws of the State—are not the sole (and unfair) determiner of another man's future. Without the mental laws, certain groups of people (those born into the "wrong" social, economic, racial, etc. class) would essentially be born into generational slavery that they could never become free of!

Of course, we all know that slavery was once legal in the United States. But the following things were once illegal in the United States as well. In other words, doing the following would be considered "breaking the law":

- Before and during the Civil War, many states had anti-literacy laws that forbade slaves and often people of color in general from learning to read or write. Not only were slaves forbidden to read or write, but any person teaching a person of color to read or write was considered to be "breaking the law".
- In 1872, if you were a woman and you voted, you were "breaking the law". This is why we know the name Susan B. Anthony. In that year, Anthony voted in the presidential election. For this, she was arrested, put on trial and convicted. She was also fined $100 for her "illegal activity".
- In 1955, if you were black and did not give up your seat to a white person, you were "breaking the law". This is why we know the name Rosa Parks. Rosa Parks was arrested for civil disobedience when she refused to give up her seat to a white person as mandated by Alabama's segregation laws.

If mental laws did not hold more power than the laws of man, those groups of people who did not at first have the authority to make the laws would forever be—in the worst case scenario—slaves to those who look like and have common interests as those who make the laws. In the best-case scenario, they would never be on an equal playing field with those who make the laws, and could only hope that those in power might have enough compassion to not treat them *too* unfairly.

We see this in our current society, with the genesis of so many societal injustices originating from the fact that those who are systemically discriminated against are of a different class or appearance than those who built the systems and the "laws" which govern that system. If every man—regardless of his class or background—did not possess access to the real source of Imagination, there would simply be no hope for those not born of the "right class". The Imagination of man is often symbolized by a light bulb. This is because when you discover your inner Imagination, it has the effect of "turning on the light". The outside darkness cannot compete, and it must give way to what you want. But if you never discover your Imagination, you never turn on this light. The result is that the darkness from the outside invades your inner space. You feel helpless against that darkness.

A person who is sentenced to the darkness of "life without the possibility of parole" and fails to discover his Imagination experiences that darkness invading his inner mental space. That darkness seems all-powerful. But once he discovers his Imagination and flips that switch, the darkness—which seemed so powerful—must retreat. THIS IS A LAW. The State will try to scare you into doing this or not doing that because "it's the law" or "you're breaking the law". But the laws of man should not be your primary concern. Concern yourself with following the laws that govern the mind—the mental laws. In the end, the ultimate law is not any law brought forward by man. The ultimate law is the *mental law of attraction*, which you activate by discovering your Imagination. Your outer world becomes a reflection of your inner thinking. The State's job is to confuse you so that you use the law of attraction in reverse against yourself. They want to present you with a dreary outer world—poverty and prison—so that your inner thinking reflects what *they* present to you. And here's the kicker: Once you begin to take on those thoughts voluntarily, then you are now manifesting that outlook on your own.

What Rick discovered was that the law of attraction—activated by his Imagination—outranked the law of the State. Although his sentencing form read "life in prison without the possibility of parole", that condition was based on a man-made law that came from the outside. But *inside* the mind of Rick Ross, his inner Imagination form read, "freedom".

This is why the immense power of the Imagination and the law of attraction is NOT taught in school. If kids learned the hidden power within themselves at an early age and developed this power, the "power" of the State would be virtually non-existent. In reality, the State's power is virtually non-existent, but because the citizens don't use the power of their Imagination, the State has power by default. It's like a team winning a game by default because the other team didn't show up. Maybe the other team was actually better, and would have won—had they come to play. But they didn't. And so, this is what happens to us. The power of the State "wins" because we don't bring our power—our Imagination—into play. And we don't bring it into play because we don't know it exists. The other team—the State—knows you (and every other individual) possess the power. But they intentionally and systematically omit the key details that keep you from mentally "showing up". It would be akin to one team not telling the other team that the time or the venue had changed, so they don't show up. Then, they win by default.

From the moment we are born into this world, everything is designed and set up to make a show that the power in this world exists in the State, and *not* in us. By the State, we mean the government and authorities present where we live. Ever-present is the threat of fines, penalties, loss of freedom and even death for people who "step out of line" based on the law of the State. With this being said, it is important to note that we still need laws in our society. Many laws make society more safe and livable. For example, laws against speeding and driving drunk save people's lives. We need laws that protect children and the elderly. However, many laws are unnecessarily unjust. And when those unjust laws come into play—seeming to overtake us—it is crucially important that we focus our energy on being on the right side of the *mental* laws.

By the time we are three years old or so, and have a basic understanding of the concept of money, we want it! Even at this very young age, we glean the basic feeling that "money is power". Now, we may not desire to get money for the purpose of buying an apartment building or taking over a corporation, but we have probably been made aware that we can't just take candy out of the store. If not us, our mom or dad must have money to get that candy we so desire. At three years old, the ability to get candy signifies "power". And so, even before we begin kindergarten, the idea that "money is power" has been planted into our young minds. And of course, this idea is strengthened and grows as we continue through school and beyond.

Now, as this is simply the world into which we are born, there isn't anything we can do at such a young age to protect our mind from being molded in this fashion. However, after getting older and living with this belief for some time, we *may—if we are lucky*—get to the point of becoming disillusioned with the world, and begin questioning certain things in society. At this point as a young adult, now having the mental strength to question certain ideas and social norms, we can wake up and start to ***think!*** Along this line, the goal is to gain this ability to think while we are still young and energetic enough to take the necessary *actions* that coincide with our new way of thinking. Many people get older, and after having lived the majority of their life already, realize that the world does not really operate as was advertised in their early youth. But by then, they simply don't feel like putting forth the necessary effort that would put them in a position of personal power. Had they figured this out twenty-five years prior, when they were still full of youth and ambition, their story would be one of noteworthy personal success, instead of one of the masses of frustration, struggle and disappointment.

We are born into a world that promotes an illusion of power, and which *does not tell us*—as citizens—the true source of power that resides within each of us. *Each individual must discover the source of their true power in their own unique way.* The true power is not held by an individual due to being accidentally born into a certain family or in a certain nation or certain sex or certain skin color that aligns with the biases of man-made laws. The true source of power is found by connecting to your very own wonderful human Imagination. Once a man discovers this inner power—in his own unique way—no outer "power", be it judge, juror or country can imprison him. And that is why Freeway Rick Ross—although sentenced to "life in prison without the possibility of parole"—is a free man today.

KEY 13
BRICK BY BRICK – PERSISTENCE

ALL TOO OFTEN, PEOPLE LOOK TO OUTWARD SIGNS AND PEOPLE TO GUAGE THEIR "CHANCES" OF BECOMING A SUCCESS. HOWEVER, THE ONLY PERSON TO WHOM YOU SHOULD CONSULT AS TO WHETHER OR NOT YOU WILL SUCCEED IS YOURSELF. YOU ARE THE ONLY PERSON WHO CAN ANSWER THE QUESTION OF WHETHER YOU WILL WORK HOUR BY HOUR, DAY AFTER DAY, YEAR AFTER YEAR, TO DO THE BEST JOB WITH WHAT IS EXACTLY IN FRONT OF YOU IN THE MOMENT. YOUR GOAL IS NOT TO BUILD A HOUSE. YOUR GOAL IS TO LAY THE PERFECT BRICK. IF YOU DO NOT QUIT, YOU WILL SUCCEED, AND THE HOUSE WILL TAKE CARE OF ITSELF. IF YOU QUIT—FOR WHATEVER REASON—YOU WILL FAIL. IT'S JUST THAT SIMPLE.

"I mean... yea, I'm strugglin' right now. But you gotta just keep gettin' it in."

–Rick Ross

TRUE STORY

In the daylight hours, Rick and I generally spent most of the time in meetings, doing interviews, speaking at schools and attending community functions, etc. But when the sun went down, and after regular business hours, we hit the clubs! We weren't there to party or to drink. We were there to promote. And Rick—always having product to push—came to the clubs well stocked. During this particular time, the product that had most of Rick's focus was "The Real Rick Ross Is Not A Rapper" t-shirt. The t-shirt shop in Carson where the shirts were printed became Rick's makeshift office, and Rick thoroughly enjoyed the process of pressing up his own shirts.

But, when it came to *selling* these shirts, they didn't seem to move as fast as crack cocaine. People were buying a few shirts here and there, but it was generally a struggle. Many times, Rick would also front someone a 10-pack of shirts (10 shirts for $100 that could then be sold for $200), but it would often be hard to get the money back. However, Rick pressed on.

One night, after spending a large part of the day in the t-shirt shop pressing up product, we went to a club in Hollywood to promote and sell. The shirts were freshly packed in the nice cellophane wrapping, where the tilted crown that sat atop the head of the "Real" Rick Ross was highly visible. Like Santa on Christmas Eve, we fell into the club toting big bags stuffed with shirts. After settling in and mingling a bit, Rick even received a shout-out from the deejay. But for whatever reason, no one was buying shirts! It was rather disappointing, because it just seemed like all the effort to talk to people and ask them to buy a shirt was resulting in a huge waste of time. We may have sold three shirts in three hours. The night ended, and we drove back down to Long Beach as usual. Yet on the ride home, there was no hint of disappointment with Rick. To him, it was what it was. He was unfazed. By looking at Rick's demeanor, one could not tell whether he had sold three shirts or three hundred.

The next day, one of Rick's late afternoon interviews was the Joe Rogan show. Of course, Rick wore his "The Real Rick

Ross Is Not A Rapper" t-shirt, as he wore everywhere. During the interview, Rick and Joe mentioned the shirt and the interview went as interviews go. Joe Rogan had great questions for Rick, and Rick was very natural and open—like always. After the formal interview was done, everybody chatted for a bit, snapped some pictures, and we then went on our way… another interview completed.

The next morning, I went down to Rick's apartment to see if he was ready to leave. As I approached the door, I noticed it was already open. As I started to walk into the apartment, I saw that the whole living room was filled with mailing boxes, cellophane bags and "The Real Rick Ross Is Not A Rapper" t-shirts. On the computer were orders for t-shirts—seemingly thousands of them—from all around the world. "Wow", I thought. "Just two nights ago, there was a drought in sales. Now the orders are flooding in!" To witness firsthand the remarkable difference in sales—from one day to the next—was astounding. The ironic thing is that Rick hadn't suddenly done anything special or different from one day to the next. But he *did* keep the same level of commitment and enthusiasm from one day to the next—even when the results from one day made it seem that there would be little hope for the next day. And for some reason, at that moment, my mind flashed back to a certain speaking engagement from a few months prior. Rick was speaking to a group of high school students. And he mentioned to them something called "The Chinese Bamboo Tree".

KEY TO SUCCESS

The world is not set up for you to succeed. At first this sounds pessimistic or cynical. But when we say that the world is not "set up" for you to succeed, think about the "setup" of going out to eat at a nice restaurant or being invited over to a friend's house for dinner. Everything is already set up for you to eat with ease, just as you please. You don't have to buy the food, season it, cook it, or bring it out. The table is set and no effort is required on your part. All you have to do is sit down and enjoy.

Such is *not* the case as it pertains to noteworthy accomplishment in this world. If you don't *currently* have some form of wealth, status or power (as defined by the world), the world does not cater to your wishes of comfort and security. There is no outside entity whose responsibility it is to make sure you live the life you want and thoroughly enjoy your stay here on earth. You cannot simply *show up, and by virtue of being born onto this planet,* expect to have cash start rolling your way as if it were being served to you at Benihana's.

There is a *reason* that only about 1% of the American population makes over $420,000 per year, even though 100% would *like to*. If the world were "set up" for you to succeed, everybody would be in "the 1 %"; the "1 %" would then become "the 100%". But that huge discrepancy between the number of people who *wish* to attain that level of financial success and those who actually *do* attain that level of financial success indicates that the world is constantly providing a certain *resistance* to financial success—a certain resistance that only a small percentage of people can overcome. Although money is not the only measure of success, it is a measurable indicator of success that—because so many people can't figure out how to make more money—highlights the fact that the natural flow of the world's setup tends to move money *away* from you, not towards you. If that flow were opposite, there would be no resistance to financial success and all people would fulfill their wishes of becoming successful multi-millionaires doing what they want to do in life. But that's not the case. And it is for this reason that some form of "self-development" or "self-help" program is so valuable to people who aspire to great achievements. In a world *not* set up for you to succeed—whose flow tends to carry money away from you—you must set your*self* up to succeed. You must proactively and purposely change the direction of this flow for your*self*. And this requires a different state of mind.

Within the mind of the man who succeeds at something on a grand scale, there exists a rare quality that does not allow him to be "okay" doing "something else". It is this same rare quality that allows him to be "okay" with all adversity, struggles, setbacks and temporary failures he faces as he is engaged in his "something". For him, there simply is no "something else" in which he wishes to engage. *This rare quality is known as persistence.*

It is simply impossible to succeed without possessing the quality of persistence. The harsh reality is that unless you were fortunate enough to have parents who deeply understood the mechanism of success in the human mind, you likely spent your early childhood and formative years *unknowingly* taking on the negative flow of the world as your own mindset. Unfortunately, before you ever had the ability to choose your own thoughts, the thoughts of your pre-existing environment were literally forced onto you without your consent. And as a result, by the time you *were* able to think your own thoughts, you simply chose the negative flow that you grew up with—as it seemed to be the "right" choice.

However, because this negative flow carries you away from success, you later find yourself increasingly unhappy and frustrated with how your life is unfolding. Your only hope is to first recognize this flow, and then somehow change the direction. However, a river that has been flowing westward for twenty years isn't suddenly going to start flow eastwardly after just two weeks. Recognizing the misdirection of your own thinking is *only the first part*. You've now got to dedicate yourself to the process of changing the mental flow—understanding that repeated positive thinking (backed by the actions that show you have faith in your thoughts) is the only way to change the direction and get into the flow of money, success and happiness.

In speaking on the concept that the world is not "set up" for you to succeed, we emphasize "the flow" that generally resists a man's wish for success, and instead carries him towards failure and poverty. But is this really an accurate analogy? *Is there really some wind, current, river or flow that actually moves a man through life in a certain direction, to which he has little to no control?* Well, this subject is a bit tricky to explain, because if this flow is not properly understood, a man's success (or failure) can be seen as simply a matter of superstition or "dumb luck". And if such is the case, what's the point of even trying to succeed in this world? On the other hand, so much of the attainment of success pulls from the idea that those who succeed make **no excuses** regarding the circumstances around them. Those circumstances do not determine their ultimate lot in life. And this is true. So which is it? Well, *both are true*. Here, some deeper explanation is warranted.

Let's consider two men. There *does* exist a current (akin to a river) of life that takes one man towards failure and poverty, *against* his conscious wishes. Also, there *does* exist an oppositely flowing current that takes the other man towards riches and success, *as* he consciously wishes. The fact that *both men* wish riches and success, yet one man finds himself "caught up" in the current flowing in that direction, while the other man finds himself "caught up" in the opposite current flowing towards poverty and failure, gives the distinct impression that the reason each finds himself in his particular current is as arbitrary as a flip of the coin or a roll of the dice. Remember, all men *wish* for riches and success. No man wishes for poverty and failure. And men do everything within their conscious to avoid poverty and failure. And still, the majority of men cannot escape the flow that carries them exactly towards poverty and failure. No wonder most people feel that they really have no hope to succeed in this world unless they "get lucky". But the reason men cannot escape the flow of poverty and failure is because consciously wishing for success does not put you in the riches and success current.

Right here is a good place to be reminded of what this chapter is about: PERSISTENCE.

Because these currents exist deep in the subconscious mind, and because the subconscious mind can only be reached and influenced indirectly, persistence—many years of continuous effort—is the only way to "get to" your subconscious mind. Once you reach it, you can then lift yourself out of one current and place yourself into the other.

At this point, it may be difficult to fully grasp the significance of the above statement. So let's back up a bit and step through what's happening. First of all, let's picture a river flowing in a certain direction—say westward. On the banks of the river, there is a maple tree. In autumn, after the leaves change colors, those leaves fall from the tree, and into the river. Now, in which direction are those leaves going to move? The leaves are going to move west, because they are falling into a westward-flowing river. This is simple enough to understand, right? Now, you may say, "What does this have to do with people? People are not inanimate, unknowing leaves. If a person is in the river flowing westward, yet he desires to go eastwardly, he can choose to *get out* of the westward-flowing river and *get into* the eastwardly-flowing river. Or he can simply choose to move in the opposite direction of the river flow."

And this is certainly true. But let's examine *why* the leaf must always move in the direction with the river flow—why it cannot move in a direction other than the direction of the river flow. In the most basic sense, the leaf is unaware of itself, and so it cannot control itself. *Where there is a lack of consciousness, there is also a lack of control.* The leaf lacks consciousness. Therefore, the leaf is controlled by the flow into which it so happens to fall into. Now, man does *have* a consciousness. But here's a question... how does your heart continue to pump blood while you are asleep? Are you conscious of your breathing while you sleep at night? If something is approaching your face really fast, do you have to *think about* closing your eyelids to protect your eyes? If you cut your finger, do you have to *decide* to begin clotting your blood and forming a scab to prevent yourself from bleeding out? The point is this: Although man has consciousness, **there are aspects of himself of which he is totally unaware**. Although man identifies himself by those things about himself of which he is conscious, man is **much more** than the part of himself of which he is conscious. The deeper part of man—the part of him that keeps his blood pumping, breath going and heals his body—operates on a level below that of which he is conscious. This part of man—this ***sub***conscious part—is the part of himself of which he is totally unaware. And thus, because of this level of unawareness, a part of man is akin to the leaf. The leaf—unaware of itself—is automatically carried in the direction of the river into which it happens to fall. And there is nothing that it can do to move in the opposite direction.

For those not born into wealth, unless you can somehow conceptualize the presence of these two "streams of life", you will automatically fall into the stream of failure and poverty (the much bigger of the two streams). Again, the set up of the world is not for your success. And so it is, although no person *consciously* wishes to move in the direction of failure and poverty, that's exactly the direction in which most people move. This discrepancy between his actual movement and his desired movement causes the vast majority of men to be consciously frustrated throughout life. They find themselves moving towards failure, when they wish to be moving towards success. Why? The reason is because *the true steering mechanism of your life does not operate on the surface conscious level of your wishes*. It operates on the level of your deep subconscious. Like an underground (subterranean) river that flows out of the view of the inhabitants on the surface, every man has deep below his surface level of awareness, a subterranean subconscious river that automatically steers him through life. In other words, man moves through life in the direction of the current that exists in his subconscious mind. *You aren't what you think you are... you are what you Think you are.*

The good news for man is this: Man does also possess a consciousness. The leaf—not having a consciousness on any level—can't be frustrated by being moved against its wishes, simply because it has no will by which a wish can be formulated. Man—as indicated by his *frustration* of being moved against his wishes—has a will on the level of his consciousness. And it is only through the consciousness of man does he have the power to lift himself out of the river that flows towards failure and poverty and into the river that flows toward success and riches. Although man does not have *direct control* of his subconscious mind, he can *indirectly influence* his subconscious mind via his conscious mind. In essence, this continuous process of reaching and influencing the subconscious mind is the key to all genuine success.

Hopefully, it is becoming more evident why no success can occur without *persistence*. In the most elemental sense, the process of "becoming a success" is the process of taking that part of yourself that you are not consciously aware of, and putting it into the flow towards success and riches. This is no easy task. You must persist. You must keep going despite what you "see" on the surface of your conscious mind as indicators to quit.

First of all, you must understand that your own frustration is a personal indicator that you are moving in a direction that is not of your wanting. More importantly, you have no direct control of this unwanted movement. To further illustrate this point, let's say you are a passenger on a subway train. If you miss your stop, there is absolutely nothing you can do to stop that train from moving you further away from where you want to be. And this is how most of us live. When things happen, we just hope that we get off on the next stop. Contrast this with being on a bus, and missing your stop. Now, you still can't directly stop the bus. You are not driving in your own car. However, you may be able to *indirectly influence* the bus driver to stop the bus. Most often, you can get the attention of the bus driver because you can see him and communicate with him. On the other hand, once you are on the subway train, you cannot see the conductor or communicate with him. And this is why the *recognition* of the subconscious is SO important. If you are totally unaware of the operator—as you are on the subway train—you have no hope of influencing the movement. In both cases, you don't directly control the movement, but on the bus, you can recognize the one who *does* directly control the movement, and therefore you can indirectly influence him.

The key to success is using your conscious mind to indirectly influence your subconscious mind. This takes *time* because—by nature—you are simply not aware of your subconscious mind. And the only way to know whether or not you have been effective in influencing your subconscious mind is by looking at the results in your conscious waking life. Are you moving in the direction you really want to move? If not, you've got work to do.

The world is confusing because the things that are of real significance do not occur on the conscious "stage" of life in which we all seem to exist. You cannot really trust what people say or appear to do, not because they are "liars" or "intently dishonest", but because they (as are the rest of us) are being controlled by a deep running current—the presence of which they aren't even aware of.

The existence of a subconscious mind, that very few people ever recognize—much less understand how to influence—is the reason that so few people become successful and prosperous, despite the fact that everyone *wishes* to become successful and prosperous.

Concerning "the stream of life", there are only two directions—one flowing "up" towards success and riches, and the other flowing "down" towards failure and poverty. If you (even if by no fault of your own) happen to mentally "fall into" the current flowing down towards failure and poverty, you have absolutely no hope of moving in the opposite direction of success and riches in your real life... unless you (1) consciously recognize the presence of these two oppositely flowing currents that exist on the level of your subconscious, and (2) lift yourself out of the "down" flow and into the "up" flow. It cannot be overstated that **because this flow exists on the *sub*conscious level, you cannot lift yourself and switch currents directly.** If you *could* switch currents directly through your consciousness, success could take place as soon as you recognize the presence of the currents. You could say, "Oh, I'd like to go in *that* direction instead" and make the change, similar to how you could if you were physically in a stream and decided to get out or swim in the direction opposite of the flow. But because the streams exist below the level of your direct consciousness, the process of changing directions is much more challenging. You can only use your conscious abilities to indirectly influence the activity in the subconscious slowly over a period of time.

The process of "becoming a success" is basically the art of using your conscious mind to indirectly reach and influence your *sub*conscious mind. By its very nature, the subconscious mind can only be reached indirectly. And the indirect nature of this process means that going from "failure" to true "success" is generally a long, painstaking process that often requires years of continuous sacrifice and effort. Hence, it is simply not possible to go from failure to success without PERSISTENCE.

Your success is 100% within your control, because you have the ability to decide to keep going... or to quit.

As Winston Churchill once said, "It is the mood of man that determines his fortunes, rather than the fortunes which determine his mood." In this world, people give up because it "gets hard". But if it were easy, everybody would be a success. This warrants repeating: *If it were easy, everybody would be a success.* The form of your hardship may be different than someone else's, but every person who reaches the mountaintop must endure a tough climb.

Do not allow the grandeur of your dreams to backfire and prevent you from taking action. It is common for a person to desire to have a huge mansion of a dream to fulfill. But they never get started, because they look at all the bricks at the same time—the entire house—and think, "Wow, it's going to take me forever to build that house!" Or, "I just don't see how I'm going to lay all those bricks." So while they are initially excited by the "dream house", they never get started on actually building. They never start laying bricks. Or they quit soon after because they feel overwhelmed. This is a very common mistake.

But what the successful man understands is this: He's not attempting to build a dream house. *He's attempting to lay the perfect brick*—day in and day out. Now, he feels confident in getting started. And once he starts, it is simply plain 'ol persistence that keeps him going. There is nothing fancy or exciting, just the quiet agreement between you and yourself, that you will keep on keeping on, no matter what. Your goal is simply to lay the next brick and do the best job you can to lay that brick. You are not a failure because the job takes a long time. Nor are you a failure because you get off to a bad start laying bricks. You are a failure because you quit. If you keep going—if you persist—you will eventually win out. The "time it will take" to complete is not a reason to quit, because the time will pass anyway. And so you may as well be using it constructively.

Furthermore, once you begin using your time in this manner, you will see that time will begin working in your favor, giving you more time on the backend and in ways you couldn't foresee when you initially began working. Time always works *for* the benefit of the man who uses it constructively. And so, again, don't worry about "how long it will take". Time will see to it that you have all the time you need if you are using it constructively. And to be clear, "constructive" use of time means that based on your daily time account of twenty-four hours, you are habitually spending a large part of those hours focused and engaged in improving your skill as it pertains to developing "that thing" you do. "That thing" is what you choose it to be. We must all spend some time sleeping, eating, and maintaining ourselves. But outside of that, the bulk of our time should go towards "that thing" to be considered constructive. Time used constructively will always compound itself for your benefit, no matter how long you may think it takes to "get there".

And remember, you are not "building a house" anyway. You are simply "laying bricks". So, when you want to say that "it" will take too long, the only "it" that you can be referring to is the laying of that brick. Maybe it takes 3 minutes to lay? And once you lay that brick, you reset the clock again, with another 3 minutes. The key is to focus on the time in terms of the 3 minutes it will take to lay one brick, not the months or years it may take you to lay 10,000 bricks.

Inside the man who refuses to quit, there is a mental toughness that develops. This is what you are *really* after in life. It's not the money. It's not the cars. It's not the houses. It's not the fame. What you want in life—your most valuable asset—is the inner strength to persist and keep going through any and all circumstances. That is the most precious and rare thing on earth. New money is printed up every day. New homes are being built right now. New cars are being manufactured as we speak. New "toys" of all kinds are being developed and built all the time. But the ability to get deep within yourself, and favorably influence that part of you that determines your fortune in life—your subconscious mind—is a rare feat that can only be accomplished through persistence.

If you haven't Googled or YouTubed "The Story of The Chinese Bamboo Tree" yet, simply know this: The Chinese bamboo takes five years to grow. During the process of growth, the ground where the seed is buried must be watered and fertilized *every day*. But the tree does not break through the ground until the fifth year. *Up until that time there is no sign of growth*. However, once it breaks through the ground, the Chinese bamboo tree grows ninety feet tall in only five weeks!

The act of watering and fertilizing the seed of the Chinese Bamboo tree is simple. But how many people would actually do this simple act every day for five years? If—at any time—the watering and fertilization stops, the Chinese bamboo tree will never break ground. The seed will simply die in the ground.

All too often, when someone picks up a book such as this—a "success" or "self-help" book—they are looking for a way to get to that thing they call "success" faster. Many "gurus" claim they can show you how to succeed faster or with less effort or sacrifice. However in my experience, there is no "shortcut" or "easy path" to success. And so, at the end of the day, the purpose of a book like this is to help inspire you to keep going and keep giving your best effort, no matter the difficulties you face. Because if you persist in doing what you love to do, there is no way you cannot succeed.

Although the Chinese bamboo tree appears to grow ninety feet in five weeks, the reality is that it grows ninety feet in five years. And so, as you strive to grow, succeed and achieve, do not be discouraged when things aren't going your way or when you see people who appear to be overnight successes. Understand that the most important part of your growth occurs when you are least aware of it. However, unless you persist, like Rick Ross and like the Chinese bamboo tree he spoke of—you will never "break through" and reach you full potential.

KEY 14
PERSONAL INTEGRITY

IN ORDER TO SUCCEED, ONE MUST BE 100% WHOLE AND COMPLETELY HONEST WITH THEMSELVES REGARDING WHO THEY ARE AND WHAT THEY WANT. DO NOT SET YOUR GOALS BASED ON SOMEONE ELSE'S OPINION OF WHAT YOU "SHOULD" BECOME. TAKE PERSONAL INVENTORY OF YOURSELF TO UNDERSTAND THE UNIQUE QUALITIES YOU POSSESS, YOUR PERSONAL LIKES AND DISLIKES AND YOUR STRENGTHS AND WEAKNESSES. EVERYONE IS GREAT AT SOMETHING, BUT AS LONG AS YOU ARE LYING TO YOURSELF ABOUT WHAT YOU REALLY LIKE AND WHO YOU ARE, YOU WILL NEVER FIND THAT SOMETHING. HONESTY IN DEALING WITH OTHERS WILL NOT TAKE PLACE UNTIL ONE IS FIRST HONEST WITH SELF.

"The little boy looked up at me like 'Man, you comin' over here taking all the money again?' And I realized I was being a hypocrite. I was selling to everybody else's mothers, daughters and loved ones. But I didn't want anybody selling to my mother, daughters or loved ones."

–Rick Ross

TRUE STORY

One Saturday afternoon, Rick was invited to an informal gathering on the campus of UCLA. It was held in a small classroom and the host group served a very nice brunch. I don't recall the name of the organization, but it was a group of young college men. As happened on a few occasions, Rick's youngest son was along for the ride. Bricen—maybe three or four at the time—was always grinning and always wanting to play with his dad. As we walked into the classroom, the setting was very comfortable and inviting. Basically there was food, and a group of college guys choppin' it up on a Saturday afternoon. After eating and engaging in some small talk, everyone of course wanted to hear Rick tell his story and ask him questions.

After going to many of these types of events and social gatherings with Rick, I had heard most of the typical questions: "How much money did you make?" "How do you feel about the rapper stealing your name?" "How long were you in prison?" "Did you use cocaine too?" However, there was one question that I hadn't yet heard. And maybe no one asked it because they thought the answer was already obvious.

But one young man asked Rick, "Why did you stop selling drugs?" Rick's answer came in story form. He recalled the time he went to the house of a lady who regularly bought drugs from him. The lady was a regular crack smoker, and she had a small child. Every time Rick would go to her house to bring her drugs, he noticed the little boy. He also noticed that the lady never had any food in the refrigerator. However, *she always had money to give to Rick for cocaine.* On this particular visit, what stuck with Rick was the little boy's demeanor towards him. Rick recalled how the little boy simply looked up at him like, "Man, you comin' over here takin' all the money *again*?"

Ironically, because Bricen wanted to play, Rick recalled the story of the little boy with no food in the refrigerator as he held Bricen in his lap and bounced him around.

"After that," Rick said, "I decided to stop. I realized I was being a hypocrite. I was selling to everybody else's mothers, daughters and loved ones. But I didn't want anybody selling to my mother, daughters or loved ones."

KEY TO SUCCESS

For all the brilliance displayed by the mind of Freeway Rick to mass distribute crack cocaine across the nation, it is incredulous to believe that it never occurred to this same brilliant mind one important fact: *"This crack cocaine stuff is killing my people."* And so it stands, at some point, the man using powerful principles to push a poisonous product, had to take a deep look at himself in the mirror and ask, "What am I doing?"

No success can be complete without the fulfillment of the "Golden Rule". In the world of business and finance—and especially the world of illegal drug dealing, you sooner or later get back what you give out. Rick's success as a drug dealer was in large part to the "good will" he habitually showed to those who worked under him. Rick actually wanted to see his guys get money and he put them in positions to get very rich by selling cocaine. Furthermore, the Nicaraguans from whom Rick got his cocaine all wanted to connect with Rick because he—by applying the principles in this book—was the one who could most effectively and efficiently unload their product. So no one above or below Rick—from the coca farms in Colombia to the streets of South Central Los Angeles—wanted to cause harm to

Rick. As Rick was applying these keys of success in his business, Rick was all around seen as "good for business". The principles work—period. And it didn't matter whether the business was cocaine or Coca-Cola.

However, as with any business, someone has to eventually use the product. And unfortunately, all the "good will" that Rick showed his dealers selling his product could not be transferred to those who actually used his product. And that's where the cocaine business is different. If you are in the business of manufacturing and supplying Coca-Cola, you can have a few Cokes without it interfering with your ability to keep meeting the demands of your customers. In other words, you can use the product you sell. But with cocaine, once you start using the product you are selling, you are doomed. Pretty soon, you will no longer be able to function in a way that effectively supplies others. You won't be able to apply the principles of success because all you want to do is apply the powder to your nose, or the pipe to your lips. Consequently, you will be out of the business soon. Although the keys of success are beneficial in selling cocaine, using cocaine causes adverse health and mental effects that make it all but impossible to consistently apply these keys of success. Those who get hooked on cocaine generally take a quick downward spiral in every aspect of their life.

And so, the best drug dealers—like Freeway Rick—do not use their own product. By its very nature, the cocaine business is a hypocritical business. There is simply no way to be a success if you use your own product. You will never get high off the money if you get high off the drug. Of course, Rick knew this all too well. When he was still young in the business, he used cocaine for about a week. Not only did it strip his throat, but it also stripped his wallet. He vowed to never use again.

But being young, Rick definitely cared more about the money and power he wielded as a drug dealer than the fact that he was being a hypocrite. And so, after his vow never to use again, he got his money back up, and never looked back—until that fateful day when he saw that empty refrigerator and the little boy staring up at him… "Man, you comin' over here takin' all the money *again*?"

Rick was able to duck the cops in large part because of his mastery of KEY 9 (Move Efficiently By Keeping A Low Profile). But, in order to get the maximum benefit of this philosophy, it is necessary to apply these Keys in a way that they work together for the entire philosophy. And no matter how masterful Rick was at dodging and staying away from the cops, there was one person he couldn't avoid or get away from—*himself*. Rick could no longer sell to everyone's loved ones, while knowing he didn't want his loved ones being sold to.

Rick made millions in the drug game because he sold cocaine according to certain principles. And as paradoxical as it sounds, one of the most crucial principles of selling cocaine is the decision to *stop* selling it. How this comes about is different from person to person. Selling drugs is a lot like being an athlete. Both are generally a young man's sport, where the majority of players have short careers. Furthermore, a single misstep can end a career in a flash. Therefore, those who choose to play the game must understand that their ultimate success or failure in life has a great deal to do with how they exit the game.

To call Rick a "success" simply because he made millions of dollars selling cocaine paints an incomplete picture. As mentioned in the above paragraph, it is much more accurate to describe Rick as a success not just based on the millions he made selling drugs, but based on the fact that he also made the decision to stop selling drugs. Rick is a success because he had the courage and personal integrity to look himself squarely in the mirror and stop being a hypocrite. *Rick didn't stop selling drugs because he got caught.* Many people aren't aware that Rick had actually stopped selling drugs for more than a year before getting caught in the government's reverse sting operation involving Danilo Blandon. By simply introducing Chico Brown to Danilo Blandon, Rick was now involved in the 100-kilo deal. This of course, was a set-up. And even though Rick was not doing the deal primarily for himself, his involvement (basically being the go-between for Chico and Danilo), was enough to get him caught up. Rick's "involvement" in that deal for 100 keys eventually got him "life without the possibility of parole".

However, it is important to note that although Rick was legally involved (because he introduced Chico to Danilo), at that time he was not actively selling cocaine as he had so fervently done in the past. "Freeway Rick" had basically retired—no longer selling cocaine because he had firmly aligned himself with the principle of personal integrity. Rick traded in those keys of cocaine once he truly found the Key of personal integrity.

KEY 15
COMPARTMENATLIZED FOCUS

SUCCESS IS LARGELY A MATTER OF YOUR ABILITY TO FOCUS ON THE IMPORTANT THING WHILE SHUTTING OUT EVERYTHING ELSE. THE SUCCESSFUL MAN CAN MENTALLY COMPARTMENTALIZE, SO THAT THE MANY NON-RELEVANT ISSUES THAT PULL AT HIM DO NOT HAVE ACCESS TO DISTRACT HIM FROM HIS MISSION.

"I made no time for schoolwork, homework, parties, or even girls. Tennis was the focus of all my energies, consuming my free time. It became my life."

—Rick Ross

KEY TO SUCCESS

Many people think the story of Rick Ross begins with cocaine. But before Rick got into selling drugs, he was an up-and-coming tennis player at L.A.'s Dorsey High. Although it is a fact unknown to many, Rick was dedicated and extremely focused as a young tennis player. As Rick put it, "I made no time for schoolwork, homework, parties, or even girls. Tennis was the focus of all my energies, consuming my free time. It became my life." And so, this principle of compartmentalized focus—focusing on "the one thing" to such an extent that other aspects of life become neglected—was a principle that Rick practiced and applied as early as his high school years.

The problem with most people is that they are too "well rounded" to stand out and succeed. They are "okay" at a bunch of things, but they are not *great* at any one of those things. Success is largely a matter of working at one thing with your blinders on to everything else that doesn't pertain to that one thing. You figuratively "lock yourself away" for a time, while you focus on developing your skill. Do not be misled by the lure of overnight success. In whatever field or business that you are attempting to succeed, it will take many many many many hours of practice—focused practice. So, you simply don't have time to concern yourself with all the world's cares and distractions that have nothing to do with what you are striving for. As Peter Lynch once said, "*Your ultimate success or failure will depend on your ability to ignore the worries of the world long enough to allow your investments to succeed.*" Your utmost investment is the time and effort you put into becoming great. And in order to ignore the worries of the world, you've got to stay focused—extremely focused—on what YOU do.

Rick carries with him a type of focus on the task at hand that borders on—what others might describe as—neglect or irresponsibility, when it comes to other aspects of life. Most people generally take the more acceptable well rounded approach to life. But being "well rounded"—when it comes to success—is not a good thing. The well rounded person moves through life much like a round balloon. Defined by its round edges, it bounces around, able to be anywhere, but not able to make any impact on its surroundings. On the other hand, the focused person is more like a sharp sword. Razor-sharp on the edges and focused at the point, the sword's only purpose is to penetrate and cut—and that's it! The sword, because it is not well rounded, is good for one thing, and one thing only—cutting. But it does this one thing better than anything else.

Think about a person that you see as a standout in some field. Chances are that that person is not well rounded in other aspects of life. I once heard Max Kellerman, from ESPN's *First Take* attempting to sum up why Michael Jordan was considered to be so great. Kellerman said something to the effect of: *Michael Jordan played the game of basketball better than anyone else has ever done anything.* Now, I may be paraphrasing Kellerman a bit, but the spirit of what Max said was that what made Michael Jordan so great (the G.O.A.T) was not the endorsements or the Air Jordan shoes. What put Jordan on another level in society is the simple fact that when it came down to one thing—that one thing being playing the game of basketball—no one did it better than Jordan. Not only that, but when you take into account all the people who are "doing things", whatever their "thing" may be, Jordan arguably did "his thing" (basketball) better than anyone else has ever done "their thing". This takes into consideration other sports, business, politics, and many other fields of human endeavor. Of course, with so many variations among all the fields of human endeavor, there is no way to objectively rank someone as *the best* at doing their thing compared to all the others who were also the best at doing their thing. But subjectively, the immense skill at what Jordan did on the basketball court was palpable to others—others who may not have even known anything about basketball. And therefore it was understood as "greatness".

Speaking of "Mike", who was the greatest performer ever? Mike (Michael) Jackson. Who is the greatest swimmer ever? Mike (Michael) Phelps. Of course, the "greatest" is always subject to opinion, but no discussion can be had without mentioning these names as it pertains to their respective fields. And so, if you look at how these ultra successful individuals spent their time, as measured by what took up the majority of their twenty-four hours every day, your conclusion would be simple: All Mike Jordan did was ball (play basketball). All Mike Jackson did was dance. All Mike Phelps did was swim. Do you see a pattern here? This pattern reveals a principle of success. And that principle is focus that is so locked in and compartmentalized on what you do, that nothing else gets time or attention. This compartmentalized focus is an absolute must during the future achiever's early stages.

As a practitioner of this principle, Rick may come across as a bit callous or unemotional. However, the reality is that Rick is just super-focused—locked in on the task at hand. In general, people are not willing to make sacrifices in their life. For the ultimate greatness at what you do, the price you pay is "everything else". And this simple truth, as harsh as it sounds, immediately eliminates 9 out of 10 people who "say" they want to "be great". Because they just aren't willing to focus on that ONE thing—at the sacrifice everything else—in order to attain success. These examples are given to shed light on the thought process of Rick Ross. People don't amass fortunes of $600 million without sacrifice in the name of locking in on their mission. But these principles are universal and aren't just principles used to sell cocaine. To this day, Rick is one who is willing to make tremendous sacrifice in order to stay focused.

Granted, not everyone wants to sacrifice everything else, but for those who do, through compartmentalized focused, this key opens the door to you becoming the greatest ever at what you do.

Jordan used it for basketball. Jackson used it for entertainment (dancing). Phelps used it for swimming. And yes, Rick Ross used it for cocaine—becoming the greatest crack cocaine dealer who ever did it. And so it is, this key—compartmentalized focus—is available for all to use. What will you use it for?

For the average person whose aim is to rise above the masses and live the "good life" on their own terms, the world seems that it could care less about those dreams. Nothing is made easy while you are occupying space and time here on earth. As soon as you are born, the metaphorical "treadmill of life" gets plugged in and starts idling. And although at that young age (and for a certain number of years to come) you are given a certain "grace period" where you can exist in relative comfort while you play around on this idling treadmill in whatever way you want, the sands in that youthful hourglass soon run out.

As a teenager or young adult (depending on your situation), you begin to feel that treadmill start moving under your feet, and you can no longer just "be here" enjoying yourself without falling off. You've got to start walking in ONE certain way and direction and keep up. And that way and direction in which you must walk is called *money*. The reason you are forced to walk continuously in the direction of the money is that you've got to keep up with food, because you must constantly eat. You've got to keep up with clothing, because clothes wear out. You've got to keep up with rent and utilities, because they are billed every month. And these are just the bare basics. In this world, you "walk" by having the money to pay for these expenses as they roll towards you each and every month. It's like the designers of the treadmill (the system) made it so that this money that you need is limited and what you must do to get it is not of your pleasure.

Your dilemma is that you really don't enjoy the direction or way that you must walk to get money, *but* if you move in another way or direction (like you moved as a child and the treadmill was just idling), you won't get the money. Very quickly, you are going to fall off. And once the treadmill starts moving, it will continuously run until you depart from this earth. You can do nothing to stop the treadmill of life, despite the fact that *you never asked to be put on it in the first place*. As you get older and get tired of walking (or running by this time), you feel stuck and trapped. You would much prefer to be spending your time doing something else, but you are forced to keep running in the direction of the immediate and continuous money because the treadmill never stops.

We are groomed and taught that the way to live is to use our time and energy to run as fast as we can as we speed up the treadmill of life. "Buy this" and "buy that" and you will be happy in life. Yet the more things you buy that don't provide you income, the less freedom you have, because you are forced to move in the direction of a job that provides money to maintain those things. But this is all a distraction that should be—but is often not—ignored.

So if you should be ignoring the worries of the world, what should you be focused on instead? *Your focus should be on building your money machine.* You should be investing all of your time, energy and money that isn't necessary for the basics of food and clothing (sometimes shelter) into the design and building of your money machine that is powered by what you genuinely enjoy doing. The world will present you with all kinds of imagery, suggestions and worries to convince you that you need a BMW because it is "The Ultimate Driving Machine". No. A BMW is not the ultimate driving machine. Instead of getting a high-paying job so that you can afford your BMW payments, your ultimate driving machine should be the money machine you are building while focused and locked away in the workshop of your mind. After you build this machine, you can get 10 BMWs, if you want.

In case you didn't know, Rick was making over $1 million per day during the height of his drug business. Rick's cocaine enterprise was a machine that spit out money at a mind-boggling rate. But this machine would have never been possible had Rick been concerning himself with the traditional worries of the world. *He was minding his own business.* In the same vein, the worries of the world are none of your business. This cannot be repeated enough. The only thing that is of real importance is designing and building your money making machine. The world and the worries it presents to you do not intend to help you build *your* machine. Their goal is to get you to react in a way that helps keep someone else's machine running and spitting out cash for *them*.

In general, the things that want access to your mind from the outside are not concerned with *your* financial independence. Mind your business and keep yourself focused and mentally locked away in the workshop of your mind, working on *your* machine. All that other outside stuff matters little. What you are building is something that will overcome and outrank the petty worries of the world anyway. But it takes time to design and build, and while you are frustrated at the time and energy you are putting in without it yet working, it is easy to get distracted and think that the worries of the world are important or have some concrete influence over you. But think about the Marvel character Ironman and how he works. What does Tony Stark spend the majority of his time doing? He's locked away working on his machines. What is your machine? Building it is your supreme responsibility in life. If you never build one, you'll never have one. If you never have one, you can only survive by allowing yourself to be controlled by someone else's.

Most people think they should be keeping up with the news and what the Kardashians are doing. But those things don't concern you. However, if you don't have anything that you're seriously focused on and developing in the workshop of your mind, you feel a connection with people you see on television who don't even know you exist. You feel like you have to "keep up with the Kardashians" or whoever you enjoy living vicariously through. But if you are focused on something you're working on in your real life, you will be connected to that. You won't be so drawn in to the "real lives" of those you see on television.

Instead of trying to keep up with everybody else, you've got to believe in YOURSELF. But you can never develop real belief in yourself and your abilities unless you focus on "that thing you do"—be it basketball, dancing, swimming, whatever—to such an extent that it literally becomes a part of you, and does not allow room for distractions. Once this type of compartmentalized focus is developed, your deep belief in yourself creates a mental atmosphere that turns adversity into opportunity. We mentioned the "Snowman" Effect earlier in KEY 4, and the way you create the requisite "Cold Mental Atmosphere" is by staying focused.

You must not allow distractions to float through the atmosphere of your mind. Control your mental atmosphere and keep it "cold" by keeping focused. It is through this practice that those "bad" things beyond your control can still be used for your ultimate benefit. It's the atmosphere—the cold atmosphere—that changes an inch of rain into a foot of snow. You want to be "cold with it", meaning that the mental atmosphere that you create around yourself, automatically changes the dreary rains of life into a beautiful snow. It is impossible to create this type of atmosphere without deep belief in yourself. And you cannot have deep belief in yourself unless you can develop the ability to focus intently.

Everything that hits the atmosphere of your mind from the outside should "freeze on contact", as you look at how it actually benefits you and your mission. A person who laughs in the face of things others see as "tragedy" and "misfortune" is supreme and unshakable. Instead of getting drowned out by the deluge of "bad news", drop the temperature in your mental atmosphere and make a snowman out of the accumulating snow that would have only been rainwater before.

Most people get caught up in all that's going on "out there", not understanding that the most interesting and unique things that exist, are found "in there". Those things "out there" will have meaning based only on what's going on inside you. And so, it's up to you to work on you, so that the temperature in your mind stays "cold".

Rick is the ultimate "Snowman". The reason is not just because of all the cocaine he sold in the 1980s. But speaking in terms of the present day, everything "bad" that hits Rick's mind instantly freezes. Rick—refusing to get "drowned out" by any type of "disappointment" or "bad news"—simply allows that precipitation to fall as beautiful snow. And one can feel this in the atmosphere in the presence of Rick. No problem or adversity is upsetting, unsettling or worthy of a negative "wet" attitude. But this is not because he doesn't care. It is because he deeply understands that circumstances are not inherently "good" or "bad". They take on meaning based solely on the atmosphere of the mind they enter. This is the height of inner power and mental toughness, because how can you rattle someone who takes everything that comes at him as a "good" thing?

Most people feel good when they get good news. They feel bad when they get bad news. But they fail to realize that the news itself has no meaning—regardless of the opinions of others. No one has the same inner consciousness as you, and so how can anyone say how you *should* feel about a particular situation? No one else can ever feel your sense of consciousness, and so no one else has the right to say whether you should feel "good" or "bad" about it.

Where you stand right now, think of concrete reasons why other people would want to be in YOUR shoes!!! Everyone is trying to be like everyone else, "wishing they were living like their favorite celebrity" or "had as much money as Warren Buffet or Jeff Bezos". And yet, who knows what that experience is *actually* like on a daily basis? Be grateful for your unique consciousness and express this gratitude by staying focused on becoming the best possible version of YOU.

The ability to focus is key to seeing life properly. If you can't focus, you'll tend to get swept up by the random wandering thoughts of others. And once that happens, you become a mere copy of others, who in turn, are living as a mere copy of others. In the end, you live life as a diluted knockoff version of... well, who knows? It is much more noble and long-term rewarding to live as the real you.

For certain, you must put effort towards developing the skill of not being rattled by circumstances. Practice taking your "problems" that are stressing you out, and finding something about the situation that could possibly get you excited. It seems completely irrational at first, but the act of feigning excitement when you initially feel bad, flips a switch and drops the temperature in your mind (electricity flows better in the cold). Suddenly, you feel power where you once felt fear. Opportunities can now be seen where only roadblocks existed.

You have neither the time, nor the energy to spend on trivialities not related to your life's mission. The people who succeed choose what they love to do and go to work at that one thing. They focus on that one thing until they get so great at it that the imaginary "balance beam" of life suddenly tips in their favor. Although the balance changes suddenly, the work that is put on the scale over time is almost akin to individual grains of sand being placed on the scale. Although the last grain may be seen as the tipping point, it was the many grains that came before that played an equally important role.

Arguably the toughest part of the journey of self-development leading to success is that "life gets in the way". While you are developing your mind to attract success, fame and money, you can't just hit pause on life so that you are no longer in need of income for food, housing, bills, etc. And so, you find yourself taking on work that is unrelated to your dreams in life. And you do this type of work to eat and meet your "obligations" to life. While you are living here, everything costs money.

For most, this feeling of being pulled in two totally opposite directions is too much to maintain, and ultimately the dream is aborted in order to take care of your "worldly obligations". People have SO many obligations and cares. Even in the best situations and circumstances, everyone has a basic obligation for food, clothing and shelter. This just is what it is.

But at some point you must make a decision about what you allow to have contact with your mind. Successful people are not hard to get in contact with because they are successful. *They are successful because they are (or at one point were) hard to get in contact with.* If you constantly allow "the world" to pull at you from all directions, you'll never be a success. Again, the world is NOT concerned with, nor does it care, whether you "make it" or not. And so, what the world stresses to you as "important" really isn't. The way of the world is to put "urgency" on unimportant things, which diverts you from what's truly important in your life... YOUR SUCCESS. Do not allow YOUR SUCCESS to be diverted because you lack an essential key—*compartmentalized focus.*

KEY 16
DISDAIN INSTANT GRATIFICATION

IF SUCCESS CAME FAST AND EASY, THEN EVERYONE WOULD BE SUCCESSFUL. HOWEVER, ONLY A VERY SMALL PERCENTAGE OF PEOPLE ACTUALLY ATTAIN THEIR DREAMS. IN ORDER TO NOT BECOME LURED IN BY THE "SHORTCUTS" TO SUCCESS, ONE MUST DEVELOP A HEALTHY DISDAIN FOR INSTANT GRATIFICATION AND MEANS AND METHODS WHICH PROMISE TO ELIMINATE THE LONG HOURS OF HARD WORK AND SACRIFICE THAT MUST BE PAID IN FULL AS THE COST OF SUCCESS.

"Would you work for two years for $300,000, or would you rather work for $30,000 a year?"

–Rick Ross

TRUE STORY

A lot of people wonder how Rick and I met. Well, the story goes like this: I wrote Rick back in 2009, while he was still in prison. In my letter to him, I told him that I was a writer and that I found his story very interesting. I also asked him if he would be willing to do an interview and appear on the cover of my new magazine.

Several weeks later I noticed that had missed a call from a 310 area code. At the time, I only knew two or three people in California, but this number was unfamiliar. I called the number back, and it was Freeway Ricky Ross!

I was shocked, because at the time I wrote Rick, I didn't know that he was about to be released from prison. I figured that if he replied, he would just write me back. During that first conversation we didn't speak long, but Rick liked the concept of my magazine and we set up a later date to have a phone interview. But before the conversation ended, he told me to read three books: *Think And Grow Rich* by Napoleon Hill, *As A Man Thinketh* by James Allen and *The Richest Man in Babylon* by George S. Clason. I had already read *Think And Grow Rich* many times, and *As A Man Thinketh* once, but I had not yet read *The Richest Man In Babylon*. So I immediately ordered the book.

I'll be honest; the first time I read *The Richest Man In Babylon*, the book really didn't catch my attention or get me excited. I was a much bigger fan of *Think And Grow Rich*. And so although I did read *The Richest Man In Babylon*, I didn't give it too much thought. This was back in 2009.

It wasn't until 2013 that I became re-intrigued with *The Richest Man In Babylon*. As I was ridin' with Rick I noticed something that had previously slipped my attention: Every time Rick was around young people—especially kids in high school or young adults in their early twenties, he religiously had a copy of that little canary yellow book—*The Richest Man In Babylon*. He always urged them to read it and would give away copies if he had extras. One day, while he was doing an interview, he even sent me on a mission to get a copy for a young football prospect he was meeting with later that day. He just gave me the keys to the Kia Rio and said, "Go get that book... *The Richest Man In Babylon*." I drove 45 minutes through L.A. traffic to a Barnes & Noble just to pick up that book.

But why was that little canary yellow book SO important to Rick—especially when he was in the presence of young people? When I re-read it again, this time with a more open mindset, I understood why. For young people, time is THE greatest potential asset. BUT time can only be converted into an advantage by those who resist the strong temptation to be lured in by the delight of *instant gratification. The Richest Man In Babylon* is one of the best resources to develop that healthy disdain for instant gratification, in order to reap long-term riches.

KEY TO SUCCESS

As you read—or flip—through this book, you will notice something… There are no images within this text, except the following:

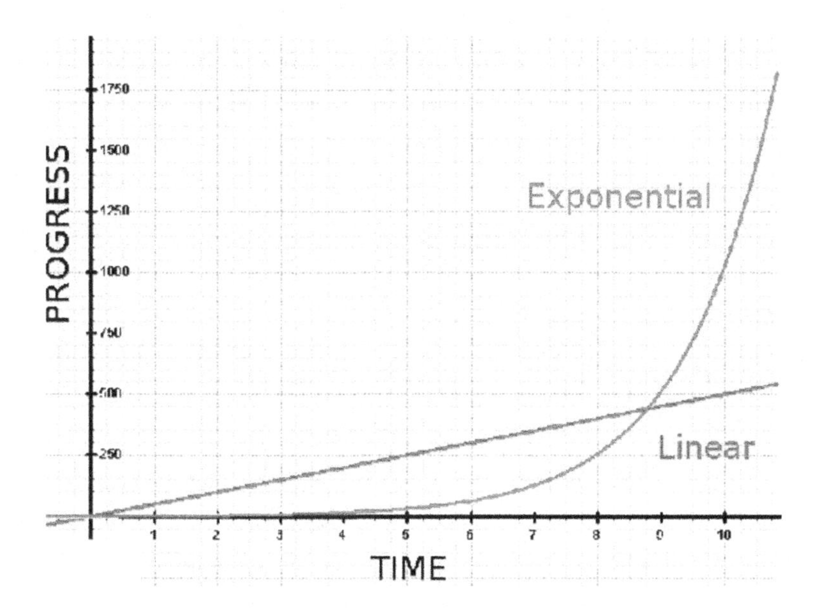

This graph represents the concept of something called *exponential growth.* The relative lack of images, graphs and charts in the book is intentional, and for the purpose of underscoring the consequence of this lone graph. "Why is this one graph so consequential?" you might ask. The answer is simple and straightforward: In order to become the uncommon "success" that you fantasize about becoming—that "1 %'er"—you must understand the concept of exponential growth, and... *adopt it as your mindset.* With that being said, exponential growth is characterized by improvement (or progress) that comes very slowly in the beginning, but increases very rapidly over time. The purpose of this chapter is to quell the reader's acquired taste and desire for shortcuts, fast tracks and easy-to-apply "secrets" to success.

Contrary to what millions of people have been sold by the "self-help" industry, the "secret to success" is actually the opposite of what most people think a secret to be. Most people think of a secret as some knowledge that—once discovered—provides an easy path and quick gratification for the one who discovers it. Yet ironically, it is the *disdain* of ease and instant gratification (not the *desire* for a secret promising quick and easy gratification) that is the real "secret" to success. KEY 16—the disdain of instant gratification—is the key that unlocks the door to the virtually unknown power of *exponential growth.*

It is worth noting the following distinction as it pertains to the word "secret". KEY 16 is not considered a secret for the reason that it smoothes the path to success, making it easier or faster. Rather, it is considered a secret because *so very few people recognize and apply it.* I'm often reminded of Thomas Edison's "Opportunity is missed by most people because it is dressed in overalls and looks like hard work" quote. The man who consistently comes prepared and eager to work is sprinkled with that coveted magic onlookers call "luck". And once this man attains outward "success", others want to know what the "secret to his success" was. But once that question is asked, people are already on the wrong track. Why? Because if we dig deep into the psyche of the person seeking a secret, they are very often searching for a secret because they don't want to put in those long years of hard work! In reality, if you want true success, there is just no way around insane amounts of effort over a prolonged period of time. Therefore, it is the man who turns up his nose in the presence of shortcuts, easy fixes, quick riches and instant gratification that is prepared to put in the work necessary to become successful. And that's all there is to the "secret" to success.

As true principles remain relevant regardless of the time period, it is no coincidence that Rick Ross built a fortune of $600 million dressed in blue jeans and tennis shoes. Even before Rick began selling cocaine, he was never known to be lazy or unwilling to work. And as a drug dealer, Rick actually sold cocaine without making any profit for a period of time. He was more interested in learning the game and studying the cocaine business than getting fast cocaine money for the purpose of being flashy and showing how rich he was. Coming into the drug business, Rick Ross didn't just desire that instant fame. As time passed, Rick doubled-down and mastered the principle of disdaining instant gratification, turning it into an art. Rick walked around South L.A. looking like the average person who lived in the community—poor, black and unimpressive. But it wasn't what Rick *looked like* that was the key to his success; *it was what he thought.*

Unlike most people selling cocaine, Rick Ross figuratively turned his nose up at the instant gratification of flashy cars and expensive jewelry. Although Rick could have easily afforded to enjoy the luxurious lifestyle of a "dope boy", he had a different mindset, and that's why he succeeded long-term. By its very nature, what it—success—looks like in the short-term present is often *opposite* of what it looks like in the long-term future. That being the case, simply professing the healthy disdain of instant gratification to be a "key to success" often rings hollow to people because the outward "payoff" from applying this principle is so far off into the future that there seems to be no connection. Even for those who *do* value a more long-term approach to attaining success in life, the long years that pass make any relationship between KEY 16 and success appear to be merely coincidental, rather than causal. As a result, KEY 16 can be—and often is—easily dismissed when it comes to its application by those seeking fame and riches.

However, *seeing* what exponential growth actually looks like over time (as represented by the graph) shows us *why* it is absolutely necessary to apply KEY 16 as we navigate through life—*if* we want long-term success. Hopefully, after studying this chapter, you will better understand the immense value in having a healthy disdain for the path of overnight success and fast fame. Because what is very likely holding you back right now—from your perspective as someone in a rush to "make it"—is your belief that delaying your gratification just doesn't seem "worth it". You desperately want to be rich, famous, admired and celebrated *now* (or in the next couple of years at the latest). The mere idea of having to put in ten or fifteen years of consistent hard work before anyone so much as looks twice when they see your name is unbearable. You feel that it is your *right* to be outwardly compensated, celebrated and acknowledged by the world the moment you try something or put in some time and effort. If you are twenty-five years old, the thought of not "making it"—not having your success celebrated by the world—until the age of forty *or forty-five* just "ain't worth it" in your estimation. *You want to ball out now!* And although you may think your motivation is money or fame, there are three deeper reasons why you really aren't willing to exercise patience in your pursuit of success; reasons why delaying gratification just doesn't seem "worth it". More aptly stated, there are three deeper *mindsets* that cause people to choose the instant gratification of having "the good now" instead of delaying their gratification so they can have "the much greater" later:

1. "TGIF"
2. "Successful people are lucky"
3. "Best foot forward"

Although these three mindsets may be hard to recognize in oneself, they can all but destroy the chances of long-term and lasting success. Referring back to the graph, the presence of any one of these mindsets causes one to habitually make decisions that put him on the *linear* path of growth, as opposed to the exponential path. And as we will show later, the danger of living on the linear path is that one gets the false impression of being on the path of success, when they are actually on the path to failure. Furthermore, the false impression is heavily reinforced by friends and by family members, who are also lost. The false impression is also heavily reinforced by mass media, as large commercial entities profit from the fact that the masses are lost. And once one figures out—*if* he ever does figure out—that the linear path is *not* the path of uncommon success, he often lacks the ambition and drive of his youth to do anything about it. The chances of a forty-five-year-old man—now saddled with a mortgage, two car payments, a marriage and three kids—deciding to now grind it out and work *without financial compensation* until he's fifty-five or sixty… are very slim. Of course, twenty years earlier, he sincerely wanted to become a massive success. But, not understanding the concept of exponential growth and what the beginning stages of exponential growth looked like, he set out on the wrong path to find success. And having the wrong mindset, he *stayed* on that wrong path (the linear path).

So, as you read about these mindsets, honestly ask yourself, "Is this my mindset?" If so, and if massive success is what you truly want, make the decision to change your mindset now. Because it is your mindset—not luck or some secret—that is the determining factor to where you end up in life.

TGIF

"TGIF" stands for "Thank God (or Goodness) It's Friday", and it is an acronym that is corrosive to success. This TGIF mindset is prevalent in most office environments and places of employment. The reason people are so happy for the arrival of Friday is because they don't really enjoy their jobs. Friday is the last day of the work week. And so people have two whole weekend days that they don't have to go in to the place they'd rather not be and do what they'd rather not be doing. As you progress through this chapter (and this book), you will better understand exactly why no man can be successful doing work he does not enjoy. So many people are unhappy with life on a day-in-day-out working basis. People hate their jobs, but they need to work in order to eat, pay bills, pay rent, have transportation, etc.

The opposite feeling of TGIF is felt on Monday morning. People who work jobs generally hate Monday mornings, as Monday morning signifies the beginning of the work week—five straight days of having to go in to the place they'd rather not be and do what they'd rather not be doing.

Successful People Are Lucky

When a person believes—even subtly—that their ultimate success has something to do with some factor outside of themselves, they have already failed. As described in KEY 13 on persistence, what people believe to be luck—is actually attributed to a great unseen force that is out of the conscious view. However, the fact that it is unseen by your eye or unable to be grasped by your reasoning mind does not mean that it is beyond your indirect influence. The successful make their own "luck" by rolling out definite plans with purpose. Failures wish for luck by rolling indiscriminant dice.

Best Foot Forward

Literally—just like Michael Jackson did with the word "bad"—you must change your relationship with the definition of the word "bad". I once heard someone once say, "Anything worth doing is worth doing right." This is a recipe for mediocrity and failure. When it comes to abnormal success, "Anything worth doing is worth doing *bad—really bad.*" Let me tell you something that should make you pumped. If you make it a habit to give your best effort at something you genuinely love to do, yet you are getting poor results and making negligible tangible progress… you should be extremely excited! Why? The reason is because you are likely on the path of exponential growth. Now, the problem—and the reason most people ultimately fail—is that they jump *off* the path of exponential growth in favor of the path of linear growth. Understand: It is not enough to simply be on the right path. In order to win in the end, you must *stay* on the right path. And the only way to stay on the right path is to really know you're on the right path. People start out on the right path, but they don't know it. And so most people who "give success a try", jump off because in general **the first ten to fifteen years (sometimes more) of the exponential growth path—the success path—*looks like* the path of miserable failure**. Your effort is within your control. Most people get down if they try hard at something, but don't get the result they hoped for. If you are going to succeed in life, you must eliminate the immediate desire to "look good", "be admired" and "have status" as defined by society and other people.

Here's what everyone has to contend with. The reason that so few people are massively successful is because the mere existence on this planet requires a person to meet a certain minimal level of "being good". For example, the basic necessities of food, clothing, shelter, etc. require money. Well, if you don't have a trust fund or an inheritance, you are going to have to work for someone in order to get money to eat, pay your rent, pay your bills, etc. Now, your employer is going to pay you immediately (or within the short time frame of a couple of weeks), and so he's going to want you to do a "good job". And from an early age, we are trained to do a good job immediately in order to get money immediately. This is another reason why you cannot work for someone else and become rich. If you want to become rich, you have to be your own boss. If someone else is your boss, they are not interested in letting you *suck* at what you do for ten years while you are on the path of exponential growth.

If—from reading this book—you only make *one* change, let it be that of changing your mental relationship with being bad. Right now, you are likely so concerned and worried about "being bad", "doing a bad job", "sucking", "looking silly", "being laughed at", "not looking successful" and because you know that you aren't presently good, you are straddling the shallow end of life (the linear path) where you can maintain some dignity. This is done to keep some status and not have people laugh at your incompetence. This is the path you choose instead of doing what you really want to do in life. You don't do what you really want to do in life because that choice will likely disrupt your income, lower your credit score, and cost you all sorts of "points" in society's measure of status. Why? Because for an extended period of years you simply will not be good enough at doing what you really like to do to make enough money from it to support yourself financially. As a broke entrepreneur or struggling artist, you will not be looked upon as a valuable member of society. Your social status will be in the toilet and you will be treated badly by banks, lenders, landlords, mortgage companies, insurance companies, the DMV, credit card companies, etc., because you are unreliable when it comes to paying them money. And why are you unreliable when it comes to paying them money? You are unreliable because you have chosen to give up the reliability of a steady paycheck from an employer. Sure, you might make a bit of money here and there, but the off-and-on nature of your income is incompatible with the *continuous* monthly expenses that simply won't wait.

And so, that is the dilemma. Most people just aren't willing to be treated like society treats people with little or no money. Financial struggle is embarrassing and can become downright humiliating. But, if your financial woes are due to the fact that you are working towards something exponentially more rewarding for you than a nine-to-five and the shallow approval of friends, family and society, then you must start to take great pleasure in "being bad". You make struggle your best friend instead of trying to be friends with people who judge you based on your income, the type of car you drive or the zip code you live in. Look at the first years on the exponential growth graph. That explosive growth in the later years cannot happen without those lean, unimpressive years of struggle in the beginning. That's the formula for success. It's a mathematical function!

With that being said, your newfound friend "bad" can only be welcomed if you are at the same time working your ass off and giving all out effort. If you are broke, with no friends, no job, no skill, and are doing "bad" in life because you lazily sit around playing video games all day, then this message does not apply to you! People find success from all walks of life and from all circumstances and situations, but here's the commonality to all those successful people you admire: Years of hustling… without receiving outward immediate reward for their effort. But you've got to put in the work; more work even than if you worked a job! As a matter of fact, if you don't want to spend 40 hours per week working for someone else, you need to spend 80 to 100 hours per week working for yourself. Again, this type of work ethic reflects a disdain for instant gratification. Think about how much fun, leisure time, and yes—sleep, you are going to miss by working 80 to 100 hours during the week. Are you willing to give up the instant gratification of sleep? Are you willing to give up the instant gratification of hanging out and partying on the weekends? Are you willing to give up the instant gratification of social events with friends and family members? Are you willing to work twice as much for less than a tenth of the financial compensation… *for years*? Most people aren't. And that's why there's the 99%.

How you feel about what you must give up in order to be a massive success depends on your mindset. Waking up at 5 AM every morning, working 18 hours per day, giving up "social life" and dealing with the everyday struggles of those first lean years on the exponential path is not a big deal for the man whose mindset carries a disdain for instant gratification. In a strange way, it's not that he experiences *no* pleasure during this journey, but rather that his pleasure comes from the love of what he does, the struggle and hustle and knowing he is in the minority. This is in contrast to the pleasure that comes from outwardly-directed gratifications, such as money, fame, awards, etc. And so because he works because of something that comes from within, he doesn't quit because compensation or recognition is not showered on him from the outside. But this is a 1% mindset. Having the above three mindsets of "TGIF", "Successful People Are Lucky" and "Best Foot Forward" will keep you in the ranks of the 99%, because you simply won't buy in to the concept of exponential growth. Instead, you will maintain on the path of linear growth because the linear path provides that instant gratification from the outside world that you seek.

Absent of a complete visual explanation of *what actually happens* over a period of many years when a person can work and live without instant gratification, the practice of getting compensated for your efforts as soon as possible seems to "make much more sense". Yet in the long run, delaying your compensation is the smart move, because in doing so, what actually happens—what you are setting yourself up for—is the explosion known as exponential growth.

To be clear, applying KEY 16 is not an *easy* thing to do. Yes, the mathematical formula is simple. But simple and easy are not the same things. In this “dog eat dog” world, where people are trained to get paid up front or at the latest a couple of weeks after the work is performed, living in a way that *delays* compensation seems totally backwards to most people. Yet, in reality, *most people* still struggle financially and do not achieve the success they hope for. So, as it pertains to *you* (a person presumably attempting to join the ranks of the tiny minority of truly successful people), what other people think is really none of your business.

If you are new to the idea of thinking exponentially, you may see it as “risky” to not get yours ASAP. You may feel that if you don’t get yours now, you may never get it. Well, with that mindset, you can certainly guarantee yourself to “get yours”. The problem is, “yours” will also be guaranteed to be a relatively small amount, compared to what you *could* have. You’ll live your life constantly worrying about money and struggling to get by, which is a much worse risk to take because it lasts a lifetime and it is a risk that offers no reward. Always remember, there is a difference between taking a risk and taking a *calculated* risk. Again, the beautiful thing about exponential growth is that it is based on a mathematical formula. Therefore, it is a calculated risk, rather than just a risk. The only “risky” thing about choosing to grow exponentially is that you must be prepared to work hard, sacrifice and hustle for a decade *or more*, and still not know exactly *when* that explosive growth will take off. *It will many times feel as if it will never happen*. However, because it is a calculated risk, the laws of mathematics and nature are working in your favor to pay huge dividends. Therefore, if you persist… you will eventually win. The time is going to pass anyway, so why quit? Besides, knowing in advance every detail of when the experiences in your life will take place, defeats the entire purpose of living. Once the element of unpredictability is totally eliminated, the most basic essence of "life" is suddenly gone. Realizing this, setting yourself up to grow exponentially is no more risky than the life you currently live, where you are set up to grow linearly. Although exponential growth *feels* risky and unnatural at first, the truth is that it is just as natural as any other type of growth that occurs in nature. But people struggle with accepting it as natural, because most other types of growth that they have witnessed or experienced are not exponential. But we truly marvel at the things that display exponential growth—such as the Chinese bamboo tree.

In closing this chapter, understand that it is never too late to choose the right path of growth. However, the sooner you choose the path of exponential growth and figuratively turn up your nose at the lure of instant gratification, the more bountiful your fortune will be. Although *The Richest Man In Babylon* teaches about the power of exponential growth in terms of gold, many other things that you wish to develop can be grown exponentially… IF you can resist the world's overwhelming temptations of "easy money" and "overnight success" by instead developing a healthy disdain for instant gratification.

KEY 17
MY BALLS AND MY WORD

LIFE WILL HIT YOU IN THE MOUTH AND ATTEMPT TO BEAT YOU DOWN. THIS, YOU CANNOT AVOID—ESPECIALLY IF YOU SEEK SUCCESS. IF YOU ARE NOT TOUGH, YOU WILL QUIT AND YOU WILL NOT SUCCEED. MAKE IT A HABIT TO DO WHAT YOU SAY YOU WILL DO AND BE WHERE YOU SAY YOU WILL BE, EVEN IF YOU FIND THAT STANDING BY THE COMMITMENT IS NOT IMMEDIATELY FRUITFUL. HAVING THE COURAGE TO KEEP YOUR WORD—TO YOURSELF AS WELL AS TO OTHERS—IS THE BASIC ELEMENT THAT FORMS THE MENTAL TOUGHNESS NECESSARY TO WITHSTAND LIFE'S UNEXPECTED BLOWS AND UNFORESEEN TRAGEDIES.

"You know, when I sit in prison and I look back at my life as a drug dealer, I noticed that I was willing to put it all on the line. And I look at these other people who do business, and then I wonder, 'Can they compete with me?' Because, all they're willing to put up is their money. And some of them are so afraid of losing their money that they don't make the investment. But with me, I was willing to put all my money on the line, and then my life on the line, then the life of my brothers, and in some circumstances—you know, when I sit in prison and look back—I was like 'Wow, you was even putting your mother and your children's life on the line.'"

–Rick Ross

TRUE STORY

One day, as Rick and I were driving north on the 710 Freeway, he asked me what I thought about a speakerphone meeting he had just finished. The meeting was with a tech guy who supposedly had the access and ability to blast out any message Rick wanted sent to X number of phones. At this time, I had just started ridin' with Rick in California, and had not yet formulated the concrete idea to "write a book" about my experiences. So although I was listening to the meeting, I wasn't taking detailed notes regarding the ins and outs of the deal. But looking back, what I remember—what stuck with me—about the meeting during that ride was the fact that Rick had absolutely no fear about the possibility of losing $5,000. And to me, losing the money seemed to be a very real possibility because I didn't think the guy could do what he was promising or deliver the results Rick was expecting. That feeling, I distinctly remember.

Most people won't spend $5,000 on something that has already been proven to work. But here was Rick, seriously considering spending five grand on something that *might* work—but probably wouldn't. On top of that, this wasn't the "1980s Rick", when $5,000 was just pocket change. This was a Rick who no longer had coke money; a Rick struggling to rebuild his financial means after years in prison. Therefore, a $5,000 loss would be a bigger "L" than when Rick was moving cocaine across the nation. The deal was a risk.

And this got me thinking. I had always known Rick to be a risk taker. If it *might* work, Rick was with it. It was almost as if the odds of failure—no matter how great—were never enough to dissuade him from seeing the possibility of success—no matter how small. Rick seemed to possess the classic "shooter's mentality" that is heard of so often in sports. Like a Russell Westbrook in the NBA, no matter how many times he shoots and misses, he is never afraid to jack up that next shot—believing he'll make *that* one.

And just like Russell Westbrook, Rick was always under harsh criticism from many people for "only having one gear" and "throwing caution to the wind". Several people close to Rick became very critical and frustrated with him in this regard. Their thinking was along the line of, "Damn Rick, do you have to take *every* shot? Do you have to take *every* meeting? Do you have to do *every* drop? Do you have to do *every* interview?" But Rick's mentality was "You just never know... So you take the 'big' meetings *and* the 'small' ones. You take everybody's phone call." This belief was one that Rick simply would not deviate from. It was so pronounced, that when people began to see me ridin' with Rick every day, they even tried to get me to "talk to him" about being more selective and more cautious; and to *stop giving out his number to everybody*.

But I never said anything to Rick about changing. First of all, I realized that *that was just who Rick was*. And it takes courage to simply be who you are—especially in the face of criticism. Furthermore, I figured that a man who made $600 million *even though he couldn't read*, probably knew something about success that other people just didn't understand. Someone like that could never be successful by following the conventional thinking of "everyone else", even if "everyone else" was so-called "right". Someone like that *had* to succeed in his very own way. More than that, someone like that *defined and measured* success by the degree to which they were doing things *their* own way. Someone like that had to succeed—and fail—by taking huge risks. I figured that someone who routinely made more money in a single day than most people will ever make in their lifetime probably had a different baseline in terms of the amount of money that it takes to motivate or excite them. Someone like that must be wired different: *The thrill of risk in the game itself was more important than the money made from the game.* Someone like that had to know that he always had the courage to bet on himself and *be* himself.

And yet, for all the criticism he got for "throwing caution to the wind", Rick always kept his word. I've seen Rick hop a flight across the country for an interview with a virtually "unknown" media outlet—just because Rick said he would. We've driven east of L.A.—through the desert—for a couple of hours, to have a brief meeting with someone—just because Rick said he would. I've seen Rick show up at people's events when hardly anyone else showed up—just because he said he would. During the months I was ridin' around Southern California with Rick, I wasn't always the only one in the car. And if Rick *said* he was coming to get you or going to drop you off, you could bank on that little gray Kia Rio showing up—just because he said he would. Rick's willingness to do what he said he would do and be where he said he will be was one of his most admirable traits. So while Rick was the ultimate risk-taker—often losing money, time and other resources—the one thing he wasn't willing to risk was *his word.*

That's when it hit me: Could it be that the ones most likely to keep their word (including saying what they mean and meaning what they say) are the same ones who have the absolute courage to always take the big risk—to always shoot? I began to think so. The reason: a man cannot keep his word to another man if he cannot keep his word to himself. And he cannot keep his word to himself, if—once he tells himself that he will succeed—he then quits or looks for an excuse to justify his lack of success. The man who never quits on himself and doesn't make excuses is never afraid of losing because he understands that persistence is the only insurance against permanent failure. Therefore, the man who keeps his word is also likely to be the man who takes big risks—risks others are too afraid to take. Taking a temporary "L" on a risk doesn't shake him, because he knows that the only way he can *permanently* lose is by quitting. And quitting is something he has already promised himself he would never do.

KEY TO SUCCESS

Life operates in such a way that even if you do everything "perfect", "play by the rules" and act as a "good person", you will inevitably be met with *some* sort of adversity or difficult obstacle that will cause you to scratch your head and wonder, "Why the hell is this happening to me?" If you are attempting to live a life where you completely isolate yourself from the possibility of "bad things" happening to you, then you will soon become sadly disillusioned.

Because life does operate in this manner, one cannot simply "play along" and feel that everything will work out comfortably in their favor. If you passively "play by the rules", or even follow the laws of society too closely, you will never succeed. To succeed, you must break some rules and take risks. This mentality has nothing to do with trying to be a "badass", but everything to do with simple common sense. Do you think rules and laws are put in place to aid *you in particular* to rise above the status quo and get ahead of everyone else in society? Of course they're not. A law that aids a general purpose often hinders another's specific purpose. And if you purpose to be a success, that purpose is specific to you. In the same way that the speed limit is put in place to keep everyone safe, it is also *not* put in place to help any *one* traveler get to his destination ahead of everyone else.

So, should you speed? Should you do 90 in a 65? Well, that truly depends on your reason. Does your reason warrant the risk you take? In most cases it doesn't, because not only are you putting yourself at risk, but you are also putting the other people on the road at risk. However, you may be in a special "life or death" situation where you absolutely must get somewhere fast—way before everyone else on the road. Are you going to go the speed limit just because "that's the law"? If you do, you will get there when everyone else gets there. But that may be too late for *you*.

The point here is not that you should speed simply because you are impatient. The point is that in special situations, you need to *not* follow the rules. And what is the ultimate special situation? Success!

Here's what must be understood: The moment you say you want "success" you are admitting that you want to get ahead of everyone else—that you have a special situation. You may not see it like that because you genuinely care for other people. You don't want to hold anyone else back, nor do you like to see people struggle through life. But looking at the figurative race to "make it" on this earth—based on the nearly eight billion people alive—the overwhelming majority of people struggle and never even get close to success. Consequently, if you are one of the very few whom "makes it", you are going to leave a LOT of people behind. This is not your *fault*. Billions of people are born into situations where there is so little hope of living a better life that the thought of "success" is something that will never even cross their mind. And for the rest of the people who do have some ambition for a better life, the sacrifices that success demands are sacrifices that most people simply aren't willing to make. As such, the truly successful in society are the extremely small minority.

But back to the original point: Declaring yourself to become a "success" means declaring your situation as "special". And the rules of becoming a success do not line up with the rules of society. Therefore, as you follow the rules of success, you will often find yourself in conflict with the rules of society. You must have the balls to break the rules of society in order to keep your word to yourself that you will indeed become a success.

A man's willingness to take risks is a measure of his eagerness to succeed. I'm not talking about the type of risk you take when you play the slot machines in Vegas or Atlantic City. No, this type of bet is a bet *by* you *on* you to ultimately win the game of life. This requires courage because the odds are that you will lose *in the short term*. But having the "balls" to take risks is what—over time—separates the winners from the watchers.

There are no "guarantees" in life. Even within the context of following the principles in this book—by following The 21 Keys—it is critically important that you realize that one of the principles is based on the fact that Life is full of surprises and unexpected situations, and so there is no way of knowing (*"You just never know"*, as Rick says) in what form or from what direction your opportunity may presents itself. This being the case, you must be willing to take the risk. A situation may present itself where you don't have all the information you would ideally like to have to make it easy to "apply the key" or "follow the principle". And when you take a risk, you are capitalizing on the fact that the prospect of *losing big* is the payment for the opportunity to *win bigger* than anyone else.

Contrast the calculated thought of "big risk, big reward" to the faint hope of a big reward from buying a lottery ticket. Sure you "might" win big. But it's virtually impossible because there is absolutely no risk in spending $1 for a Powerball ticket. You don't need courage to go to the corner store and give the clerk a set of "lucky" numbers that lines up with the birthdays of your first-born child and your mother.

In life, there always exists a certain element of the unknown. For example, no one knows the day they will die. The very nature of the "unknown" is that it is unknown. Therefore, there can be no principle or key to apply to solve a situation that is yet undefined. If you try to "hide" from the unknown by living a life that is so safe that nothing bad, unexpected or out of your control happens, then the unexpected will still find you. Instead, learn to deal with Life's unexpected and unknown by forcing yourself to take calculated risks in life. In this way, you are actually going *with* the natural flow of the unexpected and unknown that ultimately makes life worth living.

A huge part of success is not about a principle, but rather whether or not you have the balls to take a risk when you are just not sure what to do. At a certain point, everyone chasing a dream in life is going to encounter situations that "ain't in the book".

And when those unexpected, unknown situations occur, you've got to have the balls to say, "Fuck it! I'm going to bet on me! And no matter what happens, I'm gonna keep betting on me until I win!" That has more to do with your heart than your head. And that's something that you just can't get from a book.

When everything breaks down, all you've got is your balls (your courage) and your word (your ability to keep your promise of success to yourself). They work together because it takes tremendous courage to be 100% true to you. Master this, and you will have no problems "keepin' it real" with anyone else.

KEY 18
DON'T FRONT WHAT YOU CAN'T LOSE

IN YOUR DEALINGS WITH PEOPLE, YOU WILL SOMETIMES GET TAKEN ADVANTAGE OF OR STOLEN FROM. SOMETIMES YOU WILL LOSE SOMETHING YOU MEANT AS AN INVESTMENT. THIS IS JUST PART OF LIFE. DON'T FRONT ANYTHING THAT YOU ARE NOT ALSO WILLING TO LOSE. AS YOU EXERCISE THIS PRINCIPLE MORE OFTEN, YOU WILL BEGIN TO SEE THAT YOU REALLY DON'T HAVE ANYTHING TO LOSE. THE REALIZATION THAT YOU HAVE NOTHING TO LOSE OPENS YOU UP TO A GREAT RESERVOIR OF UNTAPPED POWER THAT ELUDES MOST PEOPLE.

"If I could afford to give a guy some drugs, I could afford to lose them."

–Rick Ross

KEY TO SUCCESS

Of course, we've all heard the sayings "You gotta give to get" and "It takes money to make money". On the surface most people can rationalize the concept of "giving before trying to get", because the "giving" can take on a wide array of situations. For instance, the notion of "If you don't work, you don't eat" is not prescribed out of a sense of charitable giving, but rather that one who works for an employer does not reasonably expect to *get* his paycheck before he *gives* his labor for the week. So even the most selfish person—if they work a job—believes that he must give (his time and effort) before he gets (his paycheck). He is paid after he has given his labor, not before.

Unfortunately, most people don't practice the principle of giving before trying to get on a *macro* scale. Why? Because everyone has had experiences in the *micro* that have shown that giving is not a **guarantee** of getting back what you want or when you expect it. Much frustration in life can be traced to micro (or short-term) giving that does not result in the desired micro getting back. For example, at some point in junior high or high school, every guy (or girl) has liked a girl (or guy), who didn't like them back. As an adult, every person has applied to a company that didn't hire them. What about applying to a school and not getting accepted? Or what about when you auditioned for that role and the casting director didn't pick you. The list goes on… The point is that Life puts us in what seems to be a bit of a quandary: We know that we cannot rightfully expect to get unless we give. However, just because we give, there is no guarantee that we will get what we want—or even what we *deserve*.

Most people have at some point worked for someone, and not gotten paid for their work. Everyone in business has—or will—at some point sell to a customer on credit and not receive payment. You fronted someone something and you lost. So how do you deal with these situations—when you give, but don't get back what you expect or deserve? The answer to this question is found in this chapter and exists as a key way of thinking.

Because giving before getting is a proven life principle, it *does* pay off, but often the payoff is in the macro—in the big picture—of your life. Therefore, in the micro—your day-to-day-dealings—you may very well give and not get anything back. Does that mean that the life principle of "giving before getting" doesn't work? No. It simply means that *your expectations* of what you get back and when you get it back may be unrealistic. And they may be unrealistic because you are attempting to apply a long-term success principle to a short-term situation. Day-to-day life is unpredictable. We all know this. In order to deal with the reality that you will sometimes give and not get back (in the short term) what you *thought* you would, you must adjust your short-term expectations so that you are *okay* with giving (which is still a MUST DO to even be in contention of get something back). But in the event that you don't get anything back "today" (which happens because day-to-day life is unpredictable and uncertain), you are still good. Being "good" means being okay emotionally and okay with your resources, and is signified by your willingness and ability to give again. Because you must give again, if you want to qualify to eventually get. You must still give to get, even though sometimes—in the short term—you will *not* get. If you lose, and that loss blocks you from future giving, don't give it. In other words, *don't front what you can't lose.*

Rick has definitely taken losses. When we hear that Rick lost $70,000 because a guy he was dealing with ran off on him, the message is clear: Winning long term entails handling loses short term. Was Rick Ross the first drug dealer to lose money or front someone cocaine and not get back the money or the coke? No, of course he wasn't. But the reason that Rick Ross reached such an elevated status long term is because he understood that giving to get is a sure bet *long term*. And therefore, in the short-term and day-to-day situations he was sometimes *not* going to get when he gave. So Rick didn't front what he wasn't willing to lose. If

$70,000 or $70,000 worth of cocaine left Rick's hand, he wasn't totally dependent on that deal going right to remain in business. And he knew this before he ever gave the guy the drugs or the money. The loss was a bump in the road, not a sign to pull over or stop.

The spirit of this principle is not to convince you to avoid taking chances because you *don't want* to lose. In contrast, the idea is to expand the types of losses you can take, yet still keep going. If you can get into the habit of taking calculated risks, you will fail more. By failing more, you will see that those temporary failures are not enough to prevent you from moving forward and trying again. Instead of wallowing in self-pity and doubt after you front something and lose, you go at it again with the same amount of enthusiasm because that's just one more "obstacle" that you have bypassed on your road to success. Soon, you get to the point of being able to front things and take chances on things nobody else is willing to front, because you believe in yourself and have the confidence that you can overcome any temporary loss. The principle is more about the mentality of the individual than the dollar amount of a loss. It's about changing the mentality from "Damn, I just lost $70,000… I'm ruined!" to "Damn, I just lost $70,000… and I'm still in the game!" Whether you realize it or not, the loss is not the real issue. The issue is your decision to quit because of the loss. Taking a loss and quitting destroys your self-confidence. Taking a loss and choosing to keep going builds supreme confidence.

The man who is a true success does not wait for outward signs that *other people* can see before he inwardly feels compensated from his work or craft. As strange as it may seem, it is the sustained feeling of immediate inner compensation (from your chosen craft) that results in the eventual outer gratification that other people can see and by which they call you a "success". *This outer gratification may lag behind the initial feeling of inner compensation by many years*. However, as the true success is fueled more by the inner compensation, the delay in outer gratification is not seen as a reason to quit. This is the difference between the winners and losers in life. *Winners never quit and quitters never win*. The man who is a failure in life quits because he is "in the game" more for the outer gratification than he is for the inner compensation. As a result, that long delay in experiencing outer gratification causes him to give up on waiting for "success". *After a while, it's just not worth it to him anymore.*

On the other hand, the winner never quits because he understands the true reality of success: *As soon as* one becomes fully engaged and committed to his craft, he is immediately compensated through a unique inner feeling, *even if the world does not yet acknowledge or compensate him for his work.* That labor of love *is* his success. In contrast to the failure, who quits because he gets tired of putting in the work and waiting on his success to arrive (as defined by other people), the winner keeps on keeping on because putting in the work and the accompanying feeling *is* his success. By way of the doing, success is *already* with him and will remain with him as long as he stays locked in and engaged with his labor of love. As a result, he has no reason to quit.

Think of yourself as a star—a star like the sun. When you wake up before daybreak so that you can see the sunrise, you may note that the official "sunrise" occurs at a certain time. Suppose for your geographical location on a certain day, the "sunrise" will occur at 5:28 AM. So, if you are at a place like the ocean, where there is an unobstructed view of the horizon, at 5:27 AM, you can look out into the ocean and there will be no rays of sunlight coming forth yet. But at 5:28, the first rays of sunlight will come shining through. And so, we say that on this day, the sunrise occurred at 5:28. But those rays of sunlight that we initially see at 5:28 AM actually left the sun at 5:20 AM. Why?

Sunlight travels at the speed of light, which is 186,282 miles per second. The earth is about 93 million miles from the sun. And therefore it takes about 8 minutes and 20 seconds for the light from the sun to reach our eyes here on earth. So how is this scientific principle relevant to our personal success in life? It's simple: When the sun shines, it takes time for us here on earth to *see* the sunlight. In other words, because of the distance between the sun and earth, it takes time for that sunlight to traverse space and reach our eyes here on earth. Even though nothing travels faster than light, there is still a time delay. What a person on the sun would see immediately is delayed by 8 minutes and 20 seconds to a person on earth.

Likewise, when you shine, *it takes time* for other people to see your shine. In the physical world, objects like the sun and the earth are separated by physical space. It takes time to get from Point A to Point B. In the mental world (the place where success occurs) people are separated by their unique perspective (or point of view) that defines each of us as a unique conscious individual. But likewise, *it takes time* to get from "point of view John" to "point of view Joe". It takes time to get from "point of view Mary" to "point of view Sally". This is simply a principle. And it is crucial to understand, because it allows you to understand that the time it takes for "other people" to see your shine is as natural as the time that elapses as sunlight travels from the sun to earth. It will take 8 minutes and 20 seconds for people on earth to see that, which is seen immediately at the sun. But during that 8 minute and 20 second journey across space, the light is no less bright or hot. It may take 8 years and 2 months for people in society to see your shine that you currently see. *So don't stop shining during the time that your light is traveling from your consciousness to their consciousness.*

What if the sun shone like most of us think? In other words, not understanding the role of time, and because here on Earth we didn't see its shine *immediately*, the sun said, "You people on earth aren't recognizing my shine, so I'm going to quit shining." What if, 8 minutes after those rays of light left the sun, no one on Earth said, "Wow, look at that beautiful sunrise!" After waiting 8 minutes, the sun said, "Forget this. Nobody is seeing my shine. I quit." And the sun stopped shining? Now, eight minutes may not seem like long to wait, but the sun is very close (relatively speaking) to the Earth. It's our star. However, the next closet star to Earth is called Proxima Centauri. Proxima Centauri is 4.24 light years away. How far is a light year? Well, it is the distance that light travels in a whole year. So considering the fact that light travels 186,282 miles in a second, a light year is about 5.88 trillion miles! In other words, the sun is at a distance from earth (93 million miles) such that light from the sun takes 8 minutes and 20 seconds to reach the earth. Proxima Centauri is at a distance from earth (about 24.9 trillion miles), such that light from Alpha Centauri takes 4.24 years to reach earth. Now, this question becomes a bit more in context with the timeframes in which we live life. What if stars shone like most of us think? If they did, there would never be any light in the universe.

Understand: You can't expect the world to see your shine after only a short period of time. True, *your mother* may see your shine after 8 minutes. She's close, she's familiar, and she's yours. *But what about everyone else?* It may take those not familiar with you 4 years to see your shine. It may take 8 years. It may take 20 years. Are you going to stop shining because of the time that passes before your shine hits other people's eyes and they say, "Wow, that's a beautiful sunrise?" *If so, you aren't a star.*

Stars shine because they are stars—not because they are waiting for someone else to experience their shine as a "sunrise".

If the sun waited for *us* to see it shine and say, "Wow, what a beautiful sunrise!", before it started shining, then it would always be dark! It cannot be overstated that *stars shine because they are stars*. If you are a star, then shine! If you are a star, then be hot. Your "shine" and your "heat" are not based on the eyes of everybody else. Nobody will see your shine or feel your heat at first. Your shine and heat is something only you feel.

And so, as an entrepreneur—a real entrepreneur—you've got to be willing, day in and day out to front your hours. You've got to be willing to work and give effort for twelve, fourteen, sixteen and even eighteen hours every day, and be prepared to *lose* them. By lose them, what is meant is that you are not entitled to a "paycheck" after two weeks like on a job. Hell, you are not even entitled to a paycheck after two years. You are never entitled to receive financial compensation "just because" you showed up. You are not working for your boss. You are working for yourself. What this means is that you will be compensated beyond your wildest dreams, *but only once you meet the demands of the market that you are serving.* And there is no specific timetable on when this will happen.

The problem with so many "wantrepreneurs", is that they have the mentality of employees. An employee is always looking for something from the boss or the company. Whether it's the $11.56 for that hour they just worked, or those benefits, or that severance pay, or that bonus, etc., an employee is never willing to front his time with the possibility that he may lose it for a few years. Again, by "lose it", we mean that he is not immediately compensated. As a matter of fact, before he even takes the job, he knows the hourly wage (or salary), his benefits, and all the things he is entitled to receive. And so, there is no fronting for the employee. He even knows that if he works more than a certain number of hours, he is entitled to 1.5 to 2x the normal hourly wage. This is the employee attitude. But here's the kicker: *You can "work for yourself" or be an "entrepreneur", yet still have an employee attitude.* Not everyone is cut out to be in business for themselves. Don't front what you can't lose. In this game, you must be willing to give everything you've got, with the understanding that you can very well lose because you simply are not *entitled* to anything. But once you create true value in the market you won't have to worry about a paycheck from a boss.

Drug dealing isn't for everyone. If you aren't willing to lose your freedom then don't front your time. If you can't do the time, don't do the crime. Once Rick was asked how prison was for him. His reply, "Prison was great for me." Why? Because again, Rick didn't front time he wasn't willing to lose. Rick knew of the real possibility of losing his freedom because of the freedom that selling drugs gave him—money, women, power. Rick knew of the real possibility that by fronting his time in an effort to gain insane amounts of time (in the form of money), that he could still lose a lot of time. All together, he lost nearly 20 years. The problem with most people who do crime is that once they get caught—once they lose—and go to prison, they find that they weren't willing to lose. They can't deal with the loss. In response, they snitch. They turn to using drugs and alcohol. They become depressed, and become a worse version of themselves from the prison experience, because they can't cope. They were never willing to lose, but they fronted their time and freedom anyway.

Many people don't understand why Rick is so respected. Critics lament, "He should not be respected or admired because he sold drugs." The respect and admiration for Rick has less to do with being a drug dealer, and more to do with the fact that Rick eventually became a better version of himself after he "lost" (and went to prison) than before he "won" (when he was making millions of dollars daily). And the key to maintaining this steadfast sense of mental bedrock is in understanding a simple principle of success: *Don't front what you can't lose.*

KEY 19
JUSTIFIED ANGER

THE NATURAL STATE OF MOST PEOPLE IS COMPLACENCY—A SORT OF WALKING DEATH. THEREFORE, IN CERTAIN SITUATIONS, WHEN YOU NEED TO GET A POINT ACROSS, YOU MUST FLASH A CONTROLLED ANGER TO SHOCK PEOPLE INTO ACTION. YOU ARE NOT TRYING TO KILL THEM, BUT CAUSE THEM A CERTAIN PAIN TO GET THEM TO WAKE UP AND START MOVING IN THE RIGHT DIRECTION. LIKE THE SURGEON WHO SHOCKS THE FLATLINED PATIENT TO BRING HIM BACK TO LIFE, YOU ADMINISTER THE SHOCK FOR A DEFINITE PURPOSE, AND YOU ARE NOT NEGATIVELY AFFECTED BY THE SHOCK YOU GIVE.

"None of ya'll read the books. I don't have anything to say."
–Rick Ross

TRUE STORY

Over the years, I have spoken at many schools to many kids. Likewise, Rick has also spoken at many schools to many kids. There is something special about speaking to junior high and high school students who can see you as a success, but can still relate to you. You know you have a chance to truly impact lives while young people are still impressionable. So anytime Rick and I were able to speak at schools together, it was always a great opportunity that we looked forward to. Such was the case in 2014, when Rick and I went to speak at one of the high schools in the Los Angeles Unified School District.

As a book author, getting speaking time in front of an audience was always a golden opportunity. At the same time, in this particular situation, I wasn't the main speaker. I was invited by Rick, and because Rick was invited by the school, Rick was the main speaker, the main focal point. I—as someone invited to come along after everything had already been set up—expected to have maybe around three to five minutes to speak. Maybe I'd give some brief quotes from my book, *Electric Living: The Science behind the Law Attraction*, and that would be about it. Rick Ross and his story was the headliner and I completely understood that. I was grateful for the opportunity to be invited. Little did I know that I would get more time—way more time—to speak than I expected.

The thing about this speaking engagement was that it was actually our *second* time coming to this particular school. The first visit took place a couple of months earlier and it went great. During that first visit, Rick spoke the majority of the time. Everyone was fascinated by his story, the connection to the CIA and how he couldn't read until he was twenty-eight years old. And when the kids finally figured out that the real Rick Ross was not a big tattooed rapper from Miami, they were even more intrigued. Towards the latter part of that first visit to the school, I spoke for maybe five minutes about my book, but really the focus of the engagement was about Rick. At the end of the talk, the administration and students said that they would love to have us back. Rick said that he would come back. But, he *did* say that he was giving the class an assignment: **Get these three books:**

1) *The Richest Man In Babylon*
2) *Think And Grow Rich*
3) *As A Man Thinketh*

Rick told the students, "When I come back, I want you guys to have gotten these books. I'm going to ask ya'll about them. And you can't say that you don't have the money. There's about 75 or so of you here in this group. These books are inexpensive. You can put your money together and get these books. You guys are a corporation. You have so much power if you put your minds together to achieve."

Rick even brought his own copy of *The Richest Man In Babylon* and had referred to it several times during his talk to the students. So it was evident what the canary yellow cover of the book looked like.

Now, two months later, we had returned to speak to the same group.

As the students filed in—most of their faces familiar from our last visit—the administrators went through the normalcy of re-introducing us and asking the students to be respectful and pay attention. As the students settled into their seats, Rick got up to speak: "Who got the books? ..."

The group went silent. Not "paying attention" silent, but "Uh-oh" silent. The uncomfortable silence of 75 normally energetic and talkative students—now unable to utter a word—so amplified the ticking second hand on the wall behind Rick, that it sounded as rhythmically pronounced as a snare drum. And that uncomfortable silence distinctly underscored the uncomfortable truth:

No one had bothered to get any of the books.

The students were now desperately wishing that someone—*anyone*—had got at least *one* of those books. But no one had bothered. And it was obvious that the students *knew* they were dealing with someone who was serious. So any answer that sounded like an excuse or an attempt to spin the situation using slick talk would only make the situation worse. Consequently, all they could do was sit there in their awkward silence, kinda glancing at one another, yet knowing they could not speak unless someone magically produced a copy of one those assigned books. I actually felt bad for them. Rick is by no means a large person in stature. But the class could *feel* his anger taking on a physical presence that made him seem to grow a foot taller with each second of silence that passed. By the time Rick spoke again, his anger resonated to the students so strongly; it was as if King Kong himself were staring them in the face:

"*Nobody?* Nobody bothered to at least get *one* of the books? What's the point of me coming here if ya'll don't even care to do something so simple that is going to benefit you. I *told* ya'll that I was going to ask you about these books. If ya'll don't care, why should I? I'm done. None of ya'll read the books. I don't have anything to say."

And he sat down.

"Ok? ..." I thought to myself, as I picked my copy of *Electric Living* and stepped up to the podium. "I guess now I'll have more than five minutes to speak today."

KEY TO SUCCESS

If you've ever spent any time around him, you know that Rick Ross is not an angry person. As Rick moves, he does not "carry" anger around with him. He is calm, even-tempered and in control of his emotions. The successful person always is. So what flashed that day at the school? What must be understood is that even though Rick's anger was intense, he remained in control of that anger because *he was not angry for a self-centered reason*. In other words, Rick's anger was not rooted in the fact that the students had not done something *he* told them to do. Rick's anger was rooted in the fact that the students had not taken the time or effort to invest into themselves for something that was so important for *their* long-term benefit. Rick's anger was not a selfish, ego-driven rage; therefore he remained in control. This is the good, productive anger, also known as "justified anger".

Getting those books was not a "do it 'cause I said so" assignment. Getting those books was a "do it 'cause it's going to benefit *you*" assignment. And when the students blatantly brushed off the books by putting zero effort into getting them, Rick wanted to hit them hard and fast. He saw them unknowingly brushing off an important opportunity to start thinking as a successful person thinks. Maybe he even saw shades of himself as a high school student—dismissive of opportunities to grasp education. Remember, Rick didn't learn to read until he was twenty-eight years old. Throughout his school years, he didn't consider reading a priority, and at no point did teachers or administrators hold him accountable for his illiteracy or his attitude towards reading. Rick was simply passed through school, and there were no apparent consequences for not being able to read. However, when Rick was being considered for a scholarship to play tennis at Long Beach State, his opportunity evaporated when it was discovered that he couldn't read.

Now, I never asked Rick if his own personal experience of being passed through school even though he was illiterate was his conscious motivation to "light a fire under those kids' ass". But I do believe his intent was to make them FEEL some temporary pain as a way to possibly keep them from having to endure a lifetime of pain that results from living unsuccessfully. It is no exaggeration to say that *reading saved Rick's life*. When he was sentenced to life in prison without the possibly of parole, he was still illiterate. But Rick *read* himself to freedom, and he found his true power in books such as *As A Man Thinketh*, *Think And Grow Rich* and *The Richest Man In Babylon*. What if Rick had the same attitude towards reading as an inmate that he had in school? Well, it's safe to say that he'd still be locked away in federal prison, and he knows it!

The key to using justified anger is using it sparingly, to hit people quick and hard, to "wake them up" to something that is extremely important. Most people are walking around in a habitual fog. Nothing has any urgency to them, and so they never get anything done. They slowly drift off into the masses of the unaccomplished. And so, occasionally it is necessary to "shock" people into waking up. This is not dissimilar to the method paramedics or surgeons use to get a person's heart back beating once they have flatlined. When a person's heart stops beating, you can't kindly tap them on the shoulder and say, "Hey, can you please wake up?" You've literally got to charge up the paddles and hit them with that strong electric current. "Clear!" Hopefully, the shock will get the heart back to beating and their life is saved. Of course, once the heart starts beating again, there's no need to shock them. But if someone has flatlined, the only option to bring them back may be to hit them hard and fast with a zap of electricity!

Now, I'm sure that you know a person or people whose general personality comes across as loud and angry. They walk around "zapping" people with their mouth all the time. They seem to always be yelling and they carry themselves in a loud and blustery way. But this type of person generally has deep-rooted insecurities (often unknown to them) that they don't know how to deal with. All of that yelling only makes them seem out of control. And how can someone who has no control over his or herself effectively lead or give advice to others? They can't. And so, after a while, people simply begin tuning them out. Their overall effect on other people—while possibly effective in the short term—is extremely limited. Because they always seem to be yelling, other people tend to stop paying attention to them. In the minds of others, nothing they say has real importance because they are always yelling. They are always "at 10" and so when they talk, it just begins to sound like "Blah blah blah, blah blah, blah blah blah blah…"

But when you habitually carry yourself in a calm and controlled manner—handling your business low key—when the time comes that you *do* need to "flash", "get mad", "go off" or "go to 10", your words, actions and demeanor carries weight and significance. People will naturally and intently pay attention because you are using your electrical "zapping power" as the skillful surgeon saving lives instead of the village idiot angrily walking around sticking forks in power outlets.

It should be noted that these 21 Keys work together to form a complete philosophy—or way of thinking—of success. And so, some of these Keys will seem to overlap, because they build on each other to facilitate proper thinking and action in the *real-life* situations you will encounter, which are often complicated. A single Key by itself is somewhat helpful, but it's like a single step. What is most helpful is multiple steps, which work together to form a complete set of stairs to elevate you. A single string is helpful, but the more of the strings you have braided together, the stronger the rope becomes, and the heavier loads it can handle. If you only use a single step, you won't climb very high. Your goal is the staircase. If you use a single string, you won't be able to lift much. Your goal is the rope. And if you only use a single Key or two, you won't reach the full potential of your ability to achieve. Your goal is the entire philosophy. The more of these Keys you master, the more you will find yourself able to successfully handle the real-life situations you encounter.

For instance, even though you are reading this Key 19 today, you probably won't be able to habitually resist the temptation to get angry and "go off" tomorrow when a person does something to you (in real time) that would normally get you upset. This type of restraint generally takes time develop, and may not occur until you get an understanding of KEY 4, KEY 11, KEY 16 and KEY 19. If you only understand one of these Keys or a couple of them, when it comes down to "crunch time", and you find yourself in a position where it is easy to get angry or you feel that getting upset is the right thing to do, you may still automatically "go off" on the person who made you angry.

One thing I learned about Rick is that it is extremely difficult to *make* him mad. I've never seen him lose his temper or "go off". When you refrain from angrily reacting in the heat of the moment to someone yelling at you, "disrespecting" you, or something petty long term, it doesn't make you soft. I'll admit, I never thought this way before. But I noticed that Rick never yelled or got upset, even when he was in a situation when no one could really blame him if he had.

So, what was it that he knew? I figured whatever it was he knew, it must have been something better than the immediate benefit of getting angry and "going off".

What I began to understand was this: When you don't allow others to get you upset, you are not allowing others to control your thinking. It is proof that you believe the statement that so many only give lip service to. And that is this: *Ultimately, your thoughts control your life.* And who is in control of your thoughts and emotions? *You. Control your thoughts—control your emotions—and... control your life!*

KEY 20
ADDICTED TO THE GAME

HOW YOU MOVE IS A REFLECTION OF WHO YOU ARE. A PERSON ADDICTED TO DRUGS OFTEN MOVES IN A CERTAIN WAY. IN THE SAME VEIN, A PERSON CAN BECOME ADDICTED TO SOMETHING POSITIVE AS WELL. IF SO, THEIR MOVEMENTS WILL REFLECT SUCH. THE MORE YOU TASTE THE PRINCIPLES OF SUCCESS, THE MORE OF THE PRINCIPLES OF SUCCESS YOU DESIRE. YOU BEGIN TO LOSE THE TASTE AND DESIRE TO DO THE THINGS UNSUCCESSFUL PEOPLE DO. WHEN YOU BECOME ADDICTED TO THE GAME—YOUR GAME—YOU ARE GUARANTEED TO SUCCEED, NOT BECAUSE YOU "WANT TO BE A SUCCESS", BUT BECAUSE YOU SIMPLY CAN'T STOP DOING THE THINGS SUCCESSFUL PEOPLE DO. YOU MOVE LIKE AN ADDICT HOOKED ON THE ULTIMATE DRUG.

"Because one thing about cocaine... The more you use it, the more you're going to need to use it."

–Rick Ross

KEY TO SUCCESS

It is often easy to spot someone addicted to drugs—especially hard core drugs like heroin or crack cocaine—by *how they move*. For the addict, their drug of choice causes a mental and physical dependency. And this dependency all but ensures the ultimate aim of most of their actions is getting the next high.

People who are *not* addicted to drugs move in a way of seeking different, more "natural and basic" needs. These needs include the need for food, shelter, clothing, sex, financial stability, freedom of expression, love, respect of peers, etc. In contrast, the addict's need for drugs pushes aside the "natural and basic" human needs to such an extent that their life becomes dominated by the need to use the drug. Over time, the consequences of drug addiction are not just the physical and mental effects of putting poison into the body. Additionally, the strong desire for drugs takes away the desire for pretty much everything else that may have been important to them at one time. And the way an addict moves in life (loss of income, jobs, friends, homes, loved ones and sense of self) begins to demonstrate this fact.

Ironically, the *user* of the drug is not the only one in danger of becoming an addict. The cocaine business—although not legal—generates staggering sums of cash that will spend just as well as any money generated from "legal" enterprise. And the fact that cocaine is not a revenue source that dealers pay taxes on, means that those in the cocaine business keep significantly more of their income than if their business were a legal (and subject to taxation) business entity.

Keep in mind that Rick was getting his cocaine from Danilo Blandon, a Nicaraguan trafficker. But the origin of cocaine is the coca leaf. And the geographic origin of the coca leaf is an area further south of Nicaragua, in the Andean Mountains of Colombia, Peru and Bolivia. Due to the specific temperature, altitude and soil type found in this region, coca leaves originate and flourish here. Once the leaves are cultivated here at the source, the process of making cocaine begins; the drug becoming increasingly more expensive as it is eventually trafficked north towards the United States (and Europe). As we discussed in KEY 12, the closer a dealer can get to the source, the better is his position to profit. And so, although Rick was getting his keys from the Nicaraguan Danilo Blandon, and able to make huge profits, what about the people that Blandon was getting *his* keys from? What about the Colombians? One can only imagine the type of revenue the Colombians cartels were generating from cocaine.

Well in 1987, *Forbes* Magazine published its first international billionaires issue. The magazine listed 96 of the world's richest people, and making this list was none other than Pablo Escobar, the boss of Colombia's notorious Medellin Cartel. In 1987 *Forbes* estimated that Escobar had a cash flow of $3 billion and a net worth of over $2 billion. Escobar made *Forbes'* list seven years in a row (from 1987 to 1993), and in the 1989 issue was ranked as the 7th richest person in the world. By the early 1990s Pablo Escobar had an estimated personal net worth of $25-30 billion USD ($48.5-$56 billion in 2017 USD). Even after his death in 1993, Pablo Escobar is generally known as the richest criminal in history.

And so, when there is *that* type of money to be made from a particular industry, the danger of addiction becomes the dependency on the huge sums of tax-free cash that one becomes accustomed to. We note the immense wealth of Pablo Escobar to paint a broader picture of the cocaine business, and show how the incredible American demand for a drug that comes from a naturally growing leaf in the mountains of Colombia creates staggering profits—the likes of which most people will never experience. Of course, Escobar was at the top of the world cocaine trade, but there was *so* much money in the international cocaine business overall that addiction to the money and lifestyle could easily become a problem for the average unknown "no-name" trafficker. Many were content with a few hundred thousand dollars a year—especially when that money was tax-free. Earlier we stated that the user is not the only one in danger of becoming addicted to cocaine. This type of "high"—the high of the money… the high of the deal—is a very real phenomenon, and one that dealers often get hooked on.

While Escobar reigned as the undisputed "King of Cocaine" on the global stage, Rick Ross wore the crown as the "King of Crack" in the United States. During the mid-1980s, Rick was routinely generating $1 million per day from selling cocaine. Often he was generating $2-3 million per day in cocaine revenue. Think about that for a second, and you can see how that amount of *daily, tax-free* cash flow can lead to an addiction that is incredibly hard to break. Furthermore, Rick often spoke of how—at a certain point—it actually became more about the rush of making the next deal than it was about the money itself.

This makes sense, because at a certain point, having so much money "numbs" you to the initial pleasure you would experience from your first encounter—or first few encounters—with lots of money. Not dissimilar to a person who gets high for the first time, after being sober and natural their entire life. After living an entire lifetime where having money to provide the basics of life has been a struggle, to then suddenly be in a position where you've got all the money you want or need feels absolutely amazing. However, as time passes and you get accustomed to having lots of money, you need more and more money to experience the high you felt in the beginning. At a certain point, what else can you buy? Then getting money becomes more about power and influence over other people, as opposed to experiencing the pleasurable things in life.

But regardless of whether those in the cocaine business get hooked on the huge sums of cash they eventually generate, the power they possess, or the sheer thrill of the deal, those addicted to the business of selling drugs (the game) often move in a certain way. Knowing this to be the case, some dealers try to conceal their movements as much as possible, keen to the fact that law enforcement may be watching. Think of a drug user trying to conceal his addiction from those around them. The drug dealer attempts to conceal his addiction to cocaine money from the rest of the world through a series of "legitimate" businesses and the appearance of leading a normal life. The user conceals for fear of ridicule, stigma and embarrassment. The dealer conceals for fear of prison time. But in each case, the addiction carries with it a certain persistence, which always seems to push through into view of the lives of both the user and the dealer. And even before this breakthrough, the pressure to not be found out makes it difficult to find peace of mind.

However, one can also use the persistence of an addiction to their benefit as well, *if* they become addicted to the *right thing*. And this is a principle that Rick has grown to understand and master better than most. Having seen addicts of his product up close and personal, as well as having been an addict of the cash from his product, Rick deeply realizes the power of addiction. Having seen addiction work both ways, Rick has found that as a *principle*, addiction can work in other ways also. Not just two ways, but maybe three or four, or whatever way one chooses. That's right, a person can "get hooked" on anything they want. And although some things are much easier to get hooked on, once hooked, that addiction will take over their life, slowly… but surely.

The key—as Rick found—was to truly get hooked on the right thing. He learned that those who got hooked on using cocaine simply didn't fare well over time. Rick recalled many instances where he had to cut business ties with people because they simply couldn't function properly once the need to snort or smoke cocaine had taken over their life. He also learned (through his own experience) that those who got hooked on selling cocaine would likely end up in prison. But seeing how the principle of addiction universally operated in people's lives, why not try changing the *product*, knowing that the *principle* would still operate? In this manner, a change in the product could yield different (and better) long-term results. In other words, one could still be addicted to "the game", but "the game" didn't have to be (or remain) cocaine.

To this day, Rick still carries around duffel bags. But instead of carrying around duffel bags full of cash for keys of cocaine, those duffel bags are stuffed full of books for keys of success. Recently, after a move back to the East Coast, I met Rick in Philadelphia for the promotion and signing of his first book (*Freeway Rick Ross: The Untold Autobiography*). And right on cue, there was Rick—*addicted to the game*—toting a huge orange and black duffel bag stuffed to capacity. "Come on Kolie, put this in your truck!" he said. How ironic it is that the illiterate kid, who used to float all around L.A. with duffel bags full of cocaine cash, now moves all around the country with duffel bags full of books! It is the same principle of addiction, but a totally different product.

People believe money buys freedom. In certain ways, it does. But in many ways, Rick is freer today than he was back in the '80s when he was a hood millionaire many times over. Today, because his addiction to the book game is a "legal game", he can move freely and openly, without having to conceal those telltale signs that he is a big-time drug dealer. Truly, once addiction takes over, the signs of addiction are nearly impossible to hide forever. All addictions affect the addict the same, but a person can become hooked on something that does either long-term benefit or long-term harm. One who becomes addicted to things such as alcohol, cigarettes, drugs, drug money, gambling, sex, etc... these things tend to be much easier to become addicted to. One of the things that made crack cocaine so notorious was its ability to get users hooked after just one hit. On the other hand, beneficial addictions, such as reading, writing, working out, waking up early in the mornings, setting goals, investing part of your income, controlling your thinking, etc., take more time and effort to become "habit-forming". But once these beneficial addictions take over your life, you'll notice that the long-term benefits you experience are much more desirable than other short-term benefits you may have felt from those detrimental addictions.

Here's what most people never figure out regarding success: If you want to be a success, *you must become addicted to what you do*. You must "get high" from your work. How else are you going to do it for twelve, fourteen, sixteen or even eighteen hours per day, every day, for years? The thought of working these "extreme" hours terrifies most people. And that's why there are so many "self-help" and "success" books that make a fortune off of the legions of people wanting shortcuts to success. But there are no shortcuts to success. There are only *keys* to success. Ironically, the search for the shortcut to success wastes precious energy that should instead be used towards actually working to become successful. The key is to choose the right thing at which to fully commit your energy. If you choose the right thing, you'll know, because you will begin to move like an addict. *That Thing* becomes all you do and all you think about. *That Thing* will "talk to you" and influence you as you move through your day.

A person who becomes addicted to negative things, such as drugs and alcohol moves in a way that cuts them off from becoming a success. But a person who becomes addicted to positive things (such as working at what they love) cuts himself or herself off from becoming a failure. The greatest blessing in life is to find *That Thing* that you would *never* stop doing—even if you tried to give it up. It means that you are addicted to the game (your game), and it leads us into the final Key—the Master Key of this book…

Cocaine Love.

KEY 21
COCAINE LOVE

THE MASTER KEY. COCAINE LOVE IS THE APEX OF THIS PHILOSOPHY. ONCE THE OTHER 20 PRINCIPLES HAVE BEEN MASTERED, YOU WILL AUTOMATICALLY HOLD THIS MASTER KEY.

"I believe that we're supposed to work simply for the pleasure of working... and the joy of working."
–Rick Ross

KEY TO SUCCESS

This final Key is the culmination of all the other keys, and serves as the apex of the overall philosophy. It is the reason that Rick Ross became "Rick Ross". *A man will—without fail and often through the most unforeseeable means—attract and become that which he deeply loves.* Rick Ross—because of his love for the game of selling cocaine—became the most notorious crack cocaine dealer in the history of the United States. In short, Rick was the best at what he did because *he put his entire heart into selling cocaine.* Rick sold cocaine with such a single-mindedness and exclusive dedication of heart, that there was simply no room left for anything other than cocaine. One can judge whether this use of one's heart and emotional energy is "appropriate", however the universal nature of a principle means that it is neither more or less effective based on the mere opinions of others.

The 21st Key can only be fully understood after some time of practice at applying the other Keys into your life. Of course, being able to use any one of the Keys on a consistent basis will benefit you. But as you habitually incorporate more of these Keys, you will find that they are slowly guiding you towards understanding this Master Key. This Master Key can be thought of as the totality of your natural way of thinking and living. This master Key—The 21st Key—is known as "Cocaine Love".

The average person is looking to work only as much as they need or have to. Furthermore, they feel better when they are *not* at work. On the contrary, the successful man puts in much more work than what would be deemed as "acceptable", for the reason that *he feels his best while he is working.* In essence, his work provides him a "high" that he can find nowhere else. This high does not result from doing work for the sake of receiving a paycheck. This high is a function of working at something he *loves* doing. In our society, this mentality is generally foreign territory because we are almost exclusively trained to believe that the purpose of work is to generate a paycheck. But in reality, the purpose of work is to generate love and happiness.

And so, as you read this book, think not so much about the cocaine and the money, but rather the love—that feeling and that "high"—you experience from finding and indulging in a labor of love that is so gratifying and so delightful to you that when you are engaged in it, you feel as if you are in heaven. That is the ultimate key to success. For once you have found *That Thing*, you know it, and no one can stand in the way of your success.

Rick did it. But because this Key—Cocaine Love—is invisible to everyone else, the thing that other people could see was the many physical kilograms of cocaine he was moving. Those keys of cocaine were just the tip of the iceberg—the visible reason for his success. But the real key to Rick's success was not the cocaine itself (many people were trying to sell cocaine), but rather the principles Rick used to sell the cocaine, which became an unspoken philosophy… Cocaine Love.

And so, as you finish this book and contemplate the ways and means by which you will strike out on your own path of success, do not be led to believe that the key to your success is necessarily tied to cocaine or selling cocaine. However, *do* understand that your success IS tied to the love of whatever you choose to involve yourself with—be it cocaine, computers, cosmetics or cooking. Know that *you can change the product, but keep the same principles that lead to success.* If you are into beauty products, this Key for you would not be known as "Cocaine Love", but "Cosmetic Love" instead. If you are into computer engineering, this Key for you would not be known as "Cocaine Love", but "Computer Love" instead. If you are into being a chef and cooking, this Key for you would not be known as "Cocaine Love", but "Cooking Love" instead. And yes, IF you are into selling cocaine—as was Freeway Ricky Ross—the Key for you—this 21st Key—would be known as "Cocaine Love".

But keep in mind that this Key is a principle. And just as with any scientific principle of electricity or gravity, a principle is neither "good" nor "bad". But the *results* in the life of the individual who employs that principle will be *felt* as good or bad, based on how (through intelligence and intent) the individual chooses to use that principle. So choose wisely what you pursue as your labor of love, because all choices have consequences.

Understand: The most important thing you produce is not any physical product that you can touch and lay your hands on. It's not your cocaine, your clothing line, your music, your books, your food, your paintings, or whatever it is you happen to make. The most important thing you produce is the LOVE you have for whatever it is you happen to make. The love that pours from you as you are engaged—developing and involving yourself with it in every possible way—is the essence of success. *That* is what ultimately attracts riches to you! There can be no true success without this feeling pouring forth from you. Although you may think the product (cocaine) is the key to your success, it is not. This principle (Cocaine Love) behind the product is the real key to your success.

And there is a very good reason for this. People can rob you of the tangible things you make or sell. A person can rob you of your keys of cocaine. But no one can rob you of your understanding of keys of success. No one can steal your Cocaine Love, because Cocaine Love is *intangible*.

In essence, we read books such as these—"success" books—for one reason, and one reason only. And that is to alter our consciousness. We want to alter our consciousness from poverty consciousness to money consciousness. We want to alter our consciousness from failure consciousness to success consciousness. We want to feel better, do better, look better, live better, be better, and put ourselves in a "better state" than we currently feel or perceive ourselves to be. And all perceived states are perceived states of *consciousness*. Deep down, our reason for reading a "success" book is to go from feeling or perceiving "bad" to "good" or from "good" to "great" or from "great" to "outstanding". That's our true aim—to elevate our mood, our feeling, our perception and our esteem to a *high*er level.

In light of this truth, we go to the *"book man"* for the same reason we go to the *"dope man"*—to get something that will change our perceived consciousness from its *current* level to a *future* higher level. The "dope man" can help you get something that elevates your perceived consciousness immediately and drastically. *But it doesn't last.* That feeling—that high—comes fast and leaves fast. And after the high is over, you crash and fall lower than you were before you decided to elevate yourself. The "book man" can help you get something that elevates your perceived consciousness very slowly by comparison. However, this high is a high that you can build upon, because as long as you are "using" and "applying", you don't have to worry about crashing.

With that being said, there is perhaps no one better or more qualified to push keys of success than Rick. The former "dope man"—who made millions masterfully pushing keys of cocaine—has now reinvented himself into a "book man". And with this reinvention, it is only natural that he progress into pushing a drug that is long term more potent, more profitable and capable of providing a more intense high than even cocaine. Although cocaine is definitely "one hell of a drug" (for better or for worse), it isn't the ultimate drug. The ultimate drug—while *still* packaged in keys—is *not* snorted or smoked. Yet, the effects—*once they reach your mind*—provide a high like no other. And hopefully, it is here where you realize that the *ultimate* drug—more potent, more powerful and more profitable than cocaine—is something called *SUCCESS*. Success IS the ultimate drug. And who better to push the ultimate drug… than the ultimate drug dealer—Freeway Ricky Ross!

ABOUT THE AUTHORS

Rick Ross is best known for his role in the spread of crack cocaine in the 1980s. Despite being illiterate at the time, "Freeway Rick" masterminded and orchestrated a cocaine network that stretched from Los Angeles to all parts of the United States. Although initially sentenced to life in prison without the possibility of parole, Rick was released in 2009. Since then, Rick has involved himself with numerous legal business ventures, including books. He is the *Los Angeles Times* Bestselling author of *Freeway Rick Ross: The Untold Autobiography* (with Cathy Scott). Contact Rick at **www.freewayrickyross.com**, on FB **@FreewayRickyRoss** and IG/Twitter **@FreewayRicky**.

Kolie Crutcher is an internationally published, award-winning and best-selling author. He is also the publisher of *GET MONEY Magazine*. In addition to *The 21 Keys of Success*, Kolie's other books include *Electric Living: The Powerful Life!*, *Electric Living 2: The Science Behind The Law of Attraction* and *Mechanism of Success: Attracting The Life You Want*. Contact Kolie at **www.koliecrutcher.com**, and on social media **@KolieCrutcher**.

Appendix I
KEY SUMMARIES

IN THE 1980s, "FREEWAY" RICKY ROSS ROSE TO POWER AS THE MOST NOTORIOUS CRACK COCAINE DEALER IN UNITED STATES HISTORY. DURING THE HEIGHT OF HIS REIGN, ROSS WAS MAKING $2-3 MILLION PER DAY, AS HE TRAFFICKED UNTOLD KILOGRAMS—KEYS—OF COCAINE ALL ACROSS THE NATION. BUT AFTER BEING SET UP BY HIS NICARAGUAN CONNECT AND THE UNITED STATES CIA, ROSS WAS SENTENCED TO LIFE IN FEDERAL PRISON.

TODAY, ROSS IS A FREE MAN. AND ONCE AGAIN HE IS PUSHING KEYS—KEYS OF SUCCESS.

IN THE 21 KEYS OF SUCCESS, AWARD-WINNING WRITER KOLIE CRUTCHER DETAILS THE 21 SUCCESS PRINCIPLES—THE 21 KEYS—THAT HE WITNESSED THE FORMER KINGPIN USE DAILY WHILE "RIDIN' WITH RICK" AROUND LOS ANGELES OVER THE COURSE OF SEVERAL MONTHS. THESE KEYS NOT ONLY MADE RICK ROSS A FORTUNE OF OVER $600 MILLION, BUT THEY ULTIMATELY OVERTURNED HIS LIFE SENTENCE AND FREED HIM FROM PRISON. AND NOW, THESE 21 KEYS ARE AVAILABLE TO YOU, THE READER.

KEY 1 – HUMBLENESS

BEING HUMBLE DOES NOT MEAN BEING WEAK OR A PUSHOVER. RATHER, YOU DO NOT ELEVATE YOURSELF ABOVE ANOTHER "JUST BECAUSE". YOU UNDERSTAND THAT YOU ARE NOT FUNDAMENTALLY GREATER THAN ANOTHER MAN. CONVERSELY, YOU UNDERSTAND THAT NO OTHER MAN IS FUNDAMENTALLY GREATER THAN YOU. FROM THIS PERSPECTIVE, YOU LIVE IN A MODE OF CONTINUOUS IMPROVEMENT BECAUSE YOU UNDERSTAND THE REALITY: ALL MEN ARE CREATED EQUAL, BUT YOU CAN MAKE YOURSELF GREATER BY PURPOSEFULLY DEDICATING YOURSELF TO GREATNESS. YOU THINK LIKE THE BOSS, YET YOU WORK WITH THE EFFORT AND DETERMINATION OF THE UNPAID INTERN.

KEY 2 – HEALTH CONSCIOUSNESS

IN ORDER TO MAINTAIN THE EFFORT AND ENERGY TO WORK LONG HOURS, CONSTANTLY DEAL WITH ADVERSITY, TAKE ADVANTAGE OF OPPORTUNITIES AND BE PREPARED TO BEST APPLY THE PRINCIPLES OF SUCCESS, ONE MUST TAKE MEASURES TO ENSURE THAT HE IS NOT BETRAYED BY HIS OWN BODY. LITERALLY, YOUR BODY IS THE VEHICLE IN

WHICH YOU TRAVEL THE PATH OF SUCCESS. NO AMOUNT OF MONEY, STATUS OR POWER CAN BE ENJOYED IF ONE DOES NOT HAVE THE PHYSICAL HEALTH TO EXPRESS ONESELF.

KEY 3 – BE A MAN OF THE PEOPLE

THERE CAN BE NO SUCCESS OR CREATION OF WEALTH WITHOUT SERVING OTHER PEOPLE. HOWEVER, THE INITIAL GROUP OF PEOPLE TO WHOM YOU BEST SERVE IS NOT ARBITRARY. EVERY SUCCESSFUL MAN BEGINS BY SERVING A CERTAIN GROUP OF PEOPLE—"HIS PEOPLE"—WITH THE PRODUCT OR SERVICE THAT BEST EMBODIES WHO HE IS. IN THIS WAY, HIS SERVICE IS GENUINE, AND THE PEOPLE WHO PURCHASE FROM HIM DON'T FEEL LIKE SIMPLY DOLLAR SIGNS. RATHER, THEY FEEL AS THOUGH THEY ARE PART OF SOMETHING BIGGER. THE LEADER IS ONE OF THEM. SOON, "OTHER GROUPS" SEE THIS MOMENTUM AND JOIN THE MOVEMENT TOO.

KEY 4 – CREATE A COLD MENTAL ATMOSPHERE - THE "SNOWMAN" EFFECT

EVERYONE ENCOUNTERS ADVERSITY, OBSTACLES AND PROBLEMS THAT FALL UPON HIS LIFE. FOR MOST PEOPLE, THEIR ADVERSITY RAINS DOWN ON THEIR MIND LIKE A SUMMER DELUGE, WASHING AWAY THEIR HOPES AND

DREAMS AND DROWNING THEM IN MISERY. BUT A SELECT FEW HAVE LEARNED TO CREATE A MENTAL ATMOSPHERE WHERE THE TEMPERATURE IS MUCH “COLDER”. AS A RESULT, WHEN THE PRECIPITATION OF ADVERSITY FALLS, IT DOES NOT COME DOWN AS A RAIN THAT DROWNS THEM, BUT RATHER AS A BEAUTIFUL “SNOW”. FROM THIS SNOW, THEY BUILD A GREAT MONUMENT THAT REMAINS LONG AFTER THE STORM PASSES—A “SNOWMAN”.

KEY 5 – MISSION-MINDEDNESS

IT IS NOT ENOUGH TO DESIRE TO BE GREAT. IN ORDER TO SUCCEED, YOU MUST DEVELOP THE DESIRE TO BE THE GREATEST. THE AVERAGE MAN DOES WHAT HE DOES BECAUSE IT PAYS HIM ENOUGH TO GET BY AND LIVE COMFORTABLY. THE TRULY SUCCESSFUL MAN—THE MISSION-MINDED MAN—DOES WHAT HE DOES BECAUSE HE BELIEVES HE CAN BE THE BEST WHO EVER DID IT!

KEY 6 – GAIN INDEPENDENCE BY NOT WORKING FOR MONEY

MONEY IS A CONTROL MECHANISM. THEREFORE, IF YOU GET INTO THE HABIT OF WORKING FOR MONEY, YOU CAN EASILY BE CONTROLLED AND YOU WILL NEVER TRULY BE

FREE. YOU MUST GAIN YOUR INDEPENDENCE BY NOT WORKING FOR MONEY. INSTEAD, WORK FOR THE LOVE OF WHAT YOU DO, AND MAKE THE MONEY WORK FOR YOU.

KEY 7 – SELF-RELIANCE & PERSONAL INITIATIVE

REGARDLESS OF ANY WELL INTENTIONS, GOOD WILL OR FAVORS DONE ON YOUR BEHALF BY ANOTHER, YOUR SUCCESS IS YOUR RESPONSIBILITY, NO ONE ELSE'S. YOU WERE GIVEN AN INDEPENDENT MIND WITH THE ABILITY TO CONTROL YOUR OWN THOUGHTS FOR THE PURPOSE OF GUIDING YOURSELF TO SUCCESS. WHILE OTHERS MAY BE INFLUENCED TO HELP YOU SUCCEED, THE RESPONSIBILITY TO SUCCEED CANNOT BE PUT OFF ON ANOTHER. FURTHERMORE, NO ONE WILL FOR LONG HELP A MAN WHO THEY DEEM HAS NEITHER THE ABILITY NOR INITIATIVE TO FIRST HELP HIMSELF.

KEY 8 – THE RE-UP

AFTER HAVING A BIT OF INITIAL SUCCESS IN BUSINESS, MOST PEOPLE DO THE WRONG THING WITH THE MONEY. INSTEAD OF REINVESTING THEIR PROFITS BACK INTO THE BUSINESS TO BUY LARGER QUANTITIES OF PRODUCT AT BETTER PRICES, THEY WASTE

THEIR PROFITS ON LUXURY ITEMS. THESE LUXURY ITEMS—SUCH AS CARS, JEWELRY, EXPENSIVE CLOTHES—DO NOT GENERATE INCOME, YET THEY REQUIRE ADDITIONAL MONEY TO MAINTAIN. IN ORDER TO FULLY LEVERAGE YOUR BUSINESS, YOU MUST PUT THE SMALL DOLLARS BACK TO WORK SO THAT THEY ATTRACT AND GROW BIGGER DOLLARS.

KEY 9 – MOVE EFFICIENTLY BY KEEPING A LOW PROFILE

YOU'VE ONLY GOT 24 HOURS IN THE DAY. IN ORDER TO MAXIMIZE YOUR TIME, YOU MUST MOVE EFFICIENTLY. THE KEY TO THIS EFFICIENCY IS LEARNING TO KEEP A LOW PROFILE AND NOT GETTING SLOWED BY YOUR OWN DESIRE TO "APPEAR SUCCESSFUL". MOST PEOPLE ONLY HAVE THE INTENT OF APPEARING TO BE A SUCCESS. INSTEAD, MAKE YOUR MOVES WITH THE INTENT OF ACTUALLY BEING A SUCCESS. AT FIRST, OTHERS CAN'T TELL THE DIFFERENCE. BUT AS TIME PASSES, YOUR GROWTH INCREASES EXPONENTIALLY BECAUSE ALL OF YOUR EFFORT HAS BEEN PUT INTO ACTUALLY BECOMING THE SUCCESS THAT EVERYONE ELSE CAN ONLY APPEAR TO BE.

KEY 10 – MAKE YOUR NAME CARRY WEIGHT

YOUR NAME CAN BE IN PLACES WHILE YOU ARE NOT PHYSICALLY THERE. IN ORDER TO ACHIEVE WHAT YOU WANT, YOU MUST DEVELOP YOUR NAME INTO A BRAND THAT CONJURES UP AN IMMEDIATE GUT REACTION IN THE MINDS AND HEARTS OF YOUR CUSTOMERS, ASSOCIATES AND THOSE YOU DO BUSINESS WITH.

KEY 11 – BE A CRITICAL THINKER

THE POWER IN YOUR THINKING IS NOT THAT YOUR THOUGHTS ARE "RIGHT" OR "WRONG" ACCORDING TO OTHER PEOPLE'S STANDARDS. THE POWER IN YOUR THINKING RESIDES IN THE FACT THAT YOUR THOUGHTS ARE UNIQUE TO YOU. THE MENTAL CHEMISTRY THAT OCCURS WHEN YOU USE YOUR MIND TO THINK HAS NEVER AND WILL NEVER BE DUPLICATED IN THE HISTORY OF MANKIND. INSTEAD OF THINKING LIKE EVERYONE ELSE, USE YOUR UNIQUE MENTAL FINGERPRINT TO PROACTIVELY THINK DIFFERENT AND STAND APART IN A WORLD WHERE MOST PEOPLE ARE BLINDLY FOLLOWING EVERYONE ELSE.

KEY 12 – FIND YOUR CONNECT (DISCOVER YOUR IMAGINATION)

SOCIETY FUNCTIONS BY EMPLOYING A SORT OF “NECESSARY EVIL”. BY CREATING THE ILLUSION THAT THE ULTIMATE POWER RESIDES WITH THE STATE, AND SIMULTANEOUSLY DOWNPLAYING THE IMAGINATIVE POWER OF EACH INDIVIDUAL, CITIZENS FEEL THAT THE POWER THAT GOVERNS THEIR LIVES IS AN OUTSIDE ENTITY. THIS NECESSARY EVIL HAS THE EFFECT OF MAINTAINING GENERAL LAW AND ORDER, BUT LEAVES THE INDIVIDUAL TO IGNORE HIS REAL SOURCE OF POWER. WHEN AN INDIVIDUAL DISCOVERS HIS IMAGINATION, HE REALIZES THAT EVEN IF THE STATE HAS THE “POWER” TO SENTENCE HIM TO PRISON, HE—BY CONNECTING TO HIS VERY OWN HUMAN IMAGINATION—HAS THE POWER TO FREE HIMSELF.

KEY 13 – BRICK BY BRICK - PERSISTENCE

ALL TOO OFTEN, PEOPLE LOOK TO OUTWARD SIGNS AND PEOPLE TO GUAGE THEIR “CHANCES” OF BECOMING A SUCCESS. HOWEVER, THE ONLY PERSON TO WHOM YOU SHOULD CONSULT AS TO WHETHER OR NOT YOU WILL SUCCEED IS YOURSELF. YOU ARE THE ONLY PERSON WHO CAN ANSWER THE QUESTION OF WHETHER YOU WILL WORK HOUR

BY HOUR, DAY AFTER DAY, YEAR AFTER YEAR, TO DO THE BEST JOB WITH WHAT IS EXACTLY IN FRONT OF YOU IN THE MOMENT. YOUR GOAL IS NOT TO BUILD A HOUSE. YOUR GOAL IS TO LAY THE PERFECT BRICK. IF YOU DO NOT QUIT, YOU WILL SUCCEED, AND THE HOUSE WILL TAKE CARE OF ITSELF. IF YOU QUIT—FOR WHATEVER REASON—YOU WILL FAIL. IT'S JUST THAT SIMPLE.

KEY 14 – PERSONAL INTEGRITY

IN ORDER TO SUCCEED, ONE MUST BE 100% WHOLE AND COMPLETELY HONEST WITH THEMSELVES REGARDING WHO THEY ARE AND WHAT THEY WANT. DO NOT SET YOUR GOALS BASED ON SOMEONE ELSE'S OPINION OF WHAT YOU "SHOULD" BECOME. TAKE PERSONAL INVENTORY OF YOURSELF TO UNDERSTAND THE UNIQUE QUALITIES YOU POSSESS, YOUR PERSONAL LIKES AND DISLIKES AND YOUR STRENGTHS AND WEAKNESSES. EVERYONE IS GREAT AT SOMETHING, BUT AS LONG AS YOU ARE LYING TO YOURSELF ABOUT WHAT YOU REALLY LIKE AND WHO YOU ARE, YOU WILL NEVER FIND THAT SOMETHING. HONESTY IN DEALING WITH OTHERS WILL NOT TAKE PLACE UNTIL ONE IS HONEST WITH SELF.

KEY 15 – COMPARTMENTALIZED FOCUS

SUCCESS IS LARGELY A MATTER OF YOUR ABILITY TO FOCUS ON THE IMPORTANT THING WHILE SHUTTING OUT EVERYTHING ELSE. THE SUCCESSFUL MAN CAN MENTALLY COMPARTMENTALIZE, SO THAT THE MANY NON-RELEVANT ISSUES THAT PULL AT HIM DO NOT HAVE ACCESS TO DISTRACT HIM FROM HIS MISSION.

KEY 16 – DISDAIN INSTANT GRATIFICATION

IF SUCCESS CAME FAST AND EASY, THEN EVERYONE WOULD BE SUCCESSFUL. HOWEVER, ONLY A VERY SMALL PERCENTAGE OF PEOPLE ACTUALLY ATTAIN THEIR DREAMS. IN ORDER TO NOT BECOME LURED IN BY THE "SHORTCUTS" TO SUCCESS, ONE MUST DEVELOP A HEALTHY DISDAIN FOR INSTANT GRATIFICATION AND MEANS AND METHODS WHICH PROMISE TO ELIMINATE THE LONG HOURS OF HARD WORK AND SACRIFICE THAT MUST BE PAID IN FULL AS THE COST OF SUCCESS.

KEY 17 – MY BALLS AND MY WORD

LIFE WILL HIT YOU IN THE MOUTH AND ATTEMPT TO BEAT YOU DOWN. THIS, YOU CANNOT AVOID—ESPECIALLY IF YOU SEEK SUCCESS. IF YOU ARE NOT TOUGH, YOU WILL QUIT AND YOU

WILL NOT SUCCEED. MAKE IT A HABIT TO DO WHAT YOU SAY YOU WILL DO AND BE WHERE YOU SAY YOU WILL BE, EVEN IF YOU FIND THAT STANDING BY THE COMMITMENT IS NOT IMMEDIATELY FRUITFUL. HAVING THE COURAGE TO KEEP YOUR WORD—TO YOURSELF AS WELL AS TO OTHERS—IS THE BASIC ELEMENT THAT FORMS THE MENTAL TOUGHNESS NECESSARY TO WITHSTAND LIFE'S UNEXPECTED BLOWS AND UNFORESEEN TRAGEDIES.

KEY 18 – DON'T FRONT WHAT YOU CAN'T LOSE

IN YOUR DEALINGS WITH PEOPLE, YOU WILL SOMETIMES GET TAKEN ADVANTAGE OF OR STOLEN FROM. SOMETIMES YOU WILL LOSE SOMETHING YOU MEANT AS AN INVESTMENT. THIS IS JUST PART OF LIFE. DON'T FRONT ANYTHING THAT YOU ARE NOT ALSO WILLING TO LOSE. AS YOU EXERCISE THIS PRINCIPLE MORE OFTEN, YOU WILL BEGIN TO SEE THAT YOU REALLY DON'T HAVE ANYTHING TO LOSE. THE REALIZATION THAT YOU HAVE NOTHING TO LOSE OPENS YOU UP TO A GREAT RESERVOIR OF UNTAPPED POWER THAT ELUDES MOST PEOPLE.

KEY 19 – JUSTIFIED ANGER

THE NATURAL STATE OF MOST PEOPLE IS COMPLACENCY—A SORT OF WALKING DEATH. THEREFORE, IN CERTAIN SITUATIONS, WHEN YOU NEED TO GET A POINT ACROSS, YOU MUST FLASH A CONTROLLED ANGER TO SHOCK PEOPLE INTO ACTION. YOU ARE NOT TRYING TO KILL THEM, BUT CAUSE THEM A CERTAIN PAIN TO GET THEM TO WAKE UP AND START MOVING IN THE RIGHT DIRECTION. LIKE THE SURGEON WHO SHOCKS THE FLATLINED PATIENT TO BRING HIM BACK TO LIFE, YOU ADMINISTER THE SHOCK FOR A DEFINITE PURPOSE, AND YOU ARE NOT NEGATIVELY AFFECTED BY THE SHOCK YOU GIVE.

KEY 20 – ADDICTED TO THE GAME

HOW YOU MOVE IS A REFLECTION OF WHO YOU ARE. A PERSON ADDICTED TO DRUGS OFTEN MOVES IN A CERTAIN WAY. IN THE SAME VEIN, A PERSON CAN BECOME ADDICTED TO SOMETHING POSITIVE AS WELL. IF SO, THEIR MOVEMENTS WILL REFLECT SUCH. THE MORE YOU TASTE THE PRINCIPLES OF SUCCESS, THE MORE OF THE PRINCIPLES OF SUCCESS YOU DESIRE. YOU BEGIN TO LOSE THE TASTE AND DESIRE TO DO THE THINGS UNSUCCESSFUL PEOPLE DO. WHEN YOU BECOME ADDICTED TO THE GAME—YOUR GAME—YOU ARE

GUARANTEED TO SUCCEED, NOT BECAUSE YOU "WANT TO BE A SUCCESS", BUT BECAUSE YOU SIMPLY CAN'T STOP DOING THE THINGS SUCCESSFUL PEOPLE DO. YOU MOVE LIKE AN ADDICT HOOKED ON THE ULTIMATE DRUG.

KEY 21 – COCAINE LOVE

THE MASTER KEY. COCAINE LOVE IS THE APEX OF THIS PHILOSOPHY. ONCE THE OTHER 20 PRINCIPLES HAVE BEEN MASTERED, YOU WILL AUTOMATICALLY HOLD THIS MASTER KEY.

SO WHETHER YOU ARE A STREET HUSTLER ON THE CORNER OR A "LEGIT" BUSINESSPERSON IN THE CORNER OFFICE, THE 21 KEYS WORK UNIVERSALLY FOR ALL STRIVING TO OVERCOME LIFE'S ADVERSITIES AND LIVE THE LIFE YOU WANT. AFTER RIDIN' WITH RICK, YOU WILL UNDERSTAND HOW TO TURN FAILURE INTO FAME, POVERTY INTO PLENTY, AND SETBACKS INTO SUCCESS!

Made in the USA
Coppell, TX
24 April 2024

31625877R10174